Winning Sustainabili

M000282091

"At Familia Torres we believe that the more we care for our earth, the better our wine, and since 2008 we have reduced already by 25% our carbon footprint per bottle. In line with this viewpoint, Winning Sustainability Strategies is fast-tracking companies to deliver better products: helping to change towards a decarbonized economy should be paramount to 21st century companies. This book is highly recommended."
—Miguel A. Torres Riera, *Presidente Familia Torres*

"This book is a valuable compass for companies intending to capture opportunities inherent in a sustainable business strategy and operating model. It also educates investors who want to understand why companies embrace and actively manage financially material ESG topics."
—Daniel Wild, PhD, Co-CEO, *RobecoSAM*

"Clear sustainability strategies are more important than ever before for companies that are aiming at leading position in their industries. 'Winning Sustainability Strategies' gives a excellent insight on how the leaders embed sustainability in their business models—very inspiring reading!"
—Simo Honkanen, *SVP Sustainability and Public Affairs, Neste Corporation*

"In their new book, van der Kaaij and Leleux have found an apt metaphor and method when it comes to navigating the inevitable transformation to sustainability that lies ahead for business: Through "Vectoring" the authors provide clear guidance for first achieving the necessary direction and focus followed by practical approaches for selecting the fastest route to the destination."
—Stuart L. Hart, *Steven Grossman Endowed Chair in Sustainable Business, University of Vermont and author of Capitalism at the Crossroads*

"This book offers an intriguing vector approach and practical self-help tools for business leaders who want to lead the transformation towards a more sustainable business and who want to get up to speed. Take up the book, make it happen, and dispose of those old ways that hold us back."
—Susanne Stormer, *Vice President of Corporate Sustainability and Chief Sustainability Officer at Novo Nordisk*

"Generally, I regard sustainability as a source of opportunities that inspires to innovate. Winning Sustainability Strategies and its concept of Vectoring provides useful insights to C-suite practitioners how to focus on the right opportunities and make the most out of them."
—Léon Wijnands, *Global Head of Sustainability at ING*

"At Umicore we demonstrated that, whilst there may be short term trade-offs between sustainability and profitability, in the long term they reinforce each other. I hope this book may help to inspire others to take the long-term view."
—Thomas Leysen, *Chairman Umicore*

"This is book for everyone interested in sustainability innovation. The SDGs are a great framework for organisations to make sustainability part of their business, but there is a need to find strategies and methodologies that are truly helpful in making them actionable and successful. Vectoring offer just that. A way to improve and make it work."

—Christer Windeløv-Lidzélius, *CEO and Principal at Kaospilot*

"Integrating Purpose, Health and Sustainability into our daily business is key to engage new generations. Techniques such as vectoring as described in this book can help this integration process and accelerate positive business impact. Not only for Carlsberg, but also for its peers in the brewing industry and beyond."

—Cees 't Hart, *CEO Carlsberg A/S*

"Speed is of essence in terms of global sustainability, in particular regarding climate change but also from a simple human everyday survival perspective. The focus of this book on acceleration to achieve this, is a great feature that differentiates it from other books on sustainability. We need speed to deal with our global challenges."

—Morten Engelstoft, CEO, *APM Terminals and member of the Maersk Executive Board*

"At Lenzing we believe that innovation is key to developing a more sustainable future. 'Winning Sustainability Strategies' and the concept of vectoring encourages and supports companies from the fashion industry and beyond to do just that. The many case studies and tools present a high value resource for C-suite professionals from around the globe."

—Stefan Doboczky, *CEO of Lenzing AG*

"'Winning Sustainability Strategies' presents several cases of companies that are 'doing well by doing good'. The book also contains excellent tools and frameworks to help other companies to do the same. It's a must-read for C-suite executives all over the world."

—Sunny Verghese, Co-Founder and Group CEO, *Olam International*; Chairman, *World Business Council for Sustainable Development*

"For years Benoit Leleux and Jan van der Kaaij have been studying organisations that are doing well by doing good for the world. I am delighted that these years of research have now come together in the form of a powerful framework and a set of insightful and practical tools and techniques that any organisation can use. Doing well by doing good has just become a little bit more achievable!"

—Jean-François Manzoni, *President and Nestlé Chaired Professor, IMD Business School*

"Not only is 'Winning Sustainability Strategies' academically rigorous, in terms of data and research, but it also embodies a real-world guide for practitioners, that is packed with relevant tools and approaches for implementing successful sustainability programs."

—Roy Sharon, *Vice President Corporate Responsibility at Liberty Global*

"Lots of people all over the world are now dreaming about building a better working world. This reveals unprecedented opportunities for financial markets and institutions around the globe. 'Winning Sustainability Strategies' offers business high quality navigation for the sustainability journey and outlines the space for action for investors willing to make an impact."

—Ruben Vardanyan, Impact investor and social entrepreneur, *Founding Partner and Vice-Chairman of the International Advisory Board, Moscow School of Management SKOLKOVO*

Benoit Leleux • Jan van der Kaaij

Winning Sustainability Strategies

Finding Purpose, Driving Innovation and Executing Change

Benoit Leleux
International Institute for Management
Development
Lausanne, Switzerland

Jan van der Kaaij
Finch & Beak
Breda, The Netherlands

ISBN 978-3-319-97444-6   ISBN 978-3-319-97445-3   (eBook)
https://doi.org/10.1007/978-3-319-97445-3

Library of Congress Control Number: 2018954895

This Palgrave Macmillan imprint is published by the registered company Springer Nature Switzerland AG
The registered company address is: Gewerbestrasse 11, 6330 Cham, Switzerland

To my favorite global citizens, Josée, Bob and Anneroos. Many, many thanks for your love, inspiration and support.
(Jan van der Kaaij)

Putting a book together is always an exercise in both excitement and frustration. The excitement feeds on itself, but I am certainly much indebted to Dina for the unrelenting patience demonstrated in coping with my regular bouts of frustration. I also beg forgiveness from Egor and Sofiia for my hopefully not too frequent mental absences: sustainability does require focus and momentum! And to Julie and Marine of course.
(Benoit Leleux)

Preface

Over ten years ago, our paths intersected when Peter Bakker, the then CEO of TNT, came to present at IMD his company's famed corporate philanthropy program. Looking for a successor of this successful and edgy business example (documented in an IMD case study referenced as IMD-2-0125), we jointly embarked on a journey of discovery of the latest developments, trends and perspectives in the field of sustainability, culminating in a first joint case development, the Happy Shrimp Farm.

This book is very much the culmination of that ten-year+ journey of collaboration between practice and academia. And what a difference a decade makes for the field of sustainability! Back then, sustainability leader TNT managed to take the global number one position in the Dow Jones Sustainability Index *without* even communicating on a CO_2 reduction target. The topic as a whole was still in its infancy, and sustainability reports an exception rather than the rule. It is of course with amazement and great pleasure that we stood witness to the (r)evolution of sustainability in business through our classes, advisory business and presentations with companies and business schools around the globe.

That initial momentum and excitement of the first results achieved were clearly hard to maintain, so a few years ago we became acutely aware that acceleration was now required if society was to achieve the ambitious targets laid out by the Sustainable Development Goals (SDGs). Realistically, across industries, sustainability programs were still in their infancy in terms of impact and effectiveness. Many companies still openly struggled with making strong business cases for sustainability. So, in early 2017, after a remarkably short and concise phone call, we agreed to move the journey to a second stage, namely collating and synthesizing all our experiences and case studies into a book, a compendium of our thoughts, ideas, insights and tools and a call for action to reinject a sense of urgency and direction into sustainability programs worldwide.

This book is thus first and foremost meant to inspire business practitioners, that is, managers from a wide range of disciplines facing the challenges of developing and accelerating the execution of sustainability strategies. But clearly their mandates will never be ambitious enough without the strong buy-in and support from their Board members, so the book also had to be a call for action for these key governance bodies. It is only through the combined action of purposeful strategic intent, strong governance and operational effectiveness that impactful results can be achieved, and the book addresses all three dimensions. A second audience for the book is naturally also managers-in-the-making, that is, business students and MBAs in particular. If the objective is to improve the capabilities of future managers to develop effective sustainability programs, then vectoring and its key principles need to be imbedded in them at their formative stage.

The book capitalizes not only on the knowledge and experience of its authors but also on critical outside investigations. We grounded our initial propositions by researching the patterns from sustainability leaders using the Dow Jones Sustainability Index (DJSI) data, enriched by a selection of in-depth case studies. A total of 13 clinical case studies were used as well as more than 30 company examples as we attempted to cover a broad array of industries and company types, from small family businesses to some of the largest-listed firms, and many different functional perspectives.

To facilitate further the implementation of the various models and tools, four canvasses and a collection of exercises and tools are concurrently made available online for free, downloadable at will.

Lausanne, Switzerland   Benoit Leleux
Breda, The Netherlands   Jan van der Kaaij

Acknowledgments

We express our gratitude to all the people who contributed to this book, sometimes perhaps even unknowingly, with their ideas, suggestions and numerous comments, supportive and critical! In particular, we would like to sincerely thank:

André Nijhof, Andrey Shapenko, Annelies Poolman, Antoine de Saint-Affrique, Barbara Kux, Bart Brüggenwirth, Bas Huurman, Bérangère Magarinos-Ruchat, Betty Huber, Bruno van Parys, Cees Hoogendijk, Christian Rood, Claudio Mellace, Claus Stig Pedersen, Den Denison, Edoardo Gai, Eelco Kraefft, Emile Scheepers, Eric Mieras, Eskild Andersen, Etienne Zeller, Fons Maex, François van den Abeele, Frank van Ooijen, Gabriela Straka, Geanne van Arkel, Helga Vanthournout, Henk Jan Beltman, Ineke Rampart, Jacobine Das Gupta, Jan de Grave, Jan-Willem Vosmeer, Jasjit Singh, Jayanth Bhuvaraghan, Jeff Turner, Jeroen den Boer, Jim Pulcrano, Jochen Rother, José Lopez, Jvan Gaffuri, Laurent Gaye, Leif Sjöblom, Léon Wijnands, Luke Disney, Marie Mathiesen, Marjella Alma, Marleen Janssen Groesbeek, Marthijn Junggebürth, Melchior de Muralt, Michael Goebbels, Michel Bande, Miguel Torres, Miriam Subirana, Morten Pedersen, Natalia Zaitseva, Nick Haasnoot, Nicko Debenham, Noemi Rom, Paul-Peter Feld, Peer Swinkels, Peter Bartsch, Peter van Minderhout, René Boender, Rob Goyens, Robert Dornau, Rodney Irwin, Roy Sharon, Simon Gobert, Stefanie Holz, Stéphanie Engels and Yannick Foing.

The list is likely not exhaustive and we apologize in advance to those who may have been left out! Their contributions were probably equally material but our memory is playing tricks on us!

A special word of thanks is due to our great support team consisting of Beverley Lennox, Camille Simm, Lindsay McTeague, Nikkie Vinke, Susan Stehli and the whole case administration team at IMD. Without your grit and determination this book would not have been possible.

Contents

List of Figures

List of Tables

Part I

Vectoring: Of Direction and Speed

1

Introduction

Contrary to popular belief and the optimism generated by the ambitious global targets set by the Conference of the Parties 21[1] (COP 21) and the United Nations Sustainable Development Goals[2] (SDGs), the implementation of corporate sustainability programs has been slow at best, sloppy and ineffective at worst. Less than a third of global companies have developed clear business cases or supported value propositions for their approaches to sustainability [1]. With many initiatives stuck in storytelling (i.e. good stories but little action) or cherry-picking (i.e. some actions but with limited objectives) mode, the need for the executive level to start thinking about transformation toward a more sustainable business model is rising as rapidly as the levels of carbon dioxide in our atmosphere. As reference, according to the UN weather agency, CO_2 levels are at their highest in the last 650,000 years, and so are the average temperatures, with the world's nine warmest years all having occurred since 2005, and the five warmest since 2010 [2]. Companies and executives need to develop a new sense of urgency when it comes to

---

[1] The 2015 United Nations Climate Change Conference, COP 21 or CMP 11, was held in Paris, France, from November 30 to December 12, 2015. It was the 21st yearly session of the Conference of the Parties (COP) to the 1992 United Nations Framework Convention on Climate Change (UNFCCC) and the 11th session of the Conference of the Parties (CMP) to the 1997 Kyoto Protocol. The Conference negotiated the Paris Agreement, a global agreement on the reduction of climate change.

[2] The Sustainable Development Goals (SDG's) are a collection of 17 global goals set by the United Nations, with some 169 targets, covering a broad range of social and economic development issues such as poverty, hunger, health, education, climate change, gender equality, water, sanitation, energy, environment and social justice. The SDGs are also known as "Transforming our World: The 2030 Agenda for Sustainable Development" or the "2030 Agenda" in short.

© The Author(s) 2019
B. Leleux, J. van der Kaaij, *Winning Sustainability Strategies*,
https://doi.org/10.1007/978-3-319-97445-3_1

sustainability, moving it from the realm of compliance to that of a key driver of performance and innovation, which requires imbedding it deeply into their core strategies. And crossing the chasm [3] in this case, that is, getting wider acceptance and implementation of this new reality in the higher circles of management, requires education, new skills, competences and tools.

As managers look for guidance in this new quest for speed and efficiency in sustainability implementation, the authors realized there was a need for an easy-to-use, practical book that would take them by the hand in this novel, high-velocity field and equip them with the tools required to ensure the smoother definition and adoption of ambitious sustainability objectives in their firms. Capitalizing on the experience of a large collection of award-winning sustainability champions, such as Unilever, Umicore, Novozymes and Bodegas Torres, and years of experience consulting with executive teams and companies effecting similar changes, this book attempts to reveal the keys to designing and implementing a stronger sense of focus and momentum in sustainability efforts.

The effective combination of direction and speed, which generates impact in sustainability programs, is dubbed *Vectoring* in this book because it is analogous to the navigation service provided by an air traffic controller, whereby the controller decides on a particular path for the aircraft, composed of specific legs or vectors, which the pilot then follows. Sustainability programs, unfortunately, lack air traffic controllers or often pilots for that matter. First, they tend to have weak direction, that is, with respect to the specific sustainability issues (referred to as *materialities*) that will be most relevant and impactful. Second, we argue that the board of directors and CEO should assume the role of air traffic controller. The absence of directional bearings, or the selection of inadequate ones, lead to misguided, uncoordinated actions and usually unsatisfactory results from the sustainability initiatives. Simultaneously, we discovered that "vectoring" is also used as a term in telecommunications[3] to refer to a transmission method that employs the coordination of line signals for the reduction of crosstalk levels and overall improvement of performance, similar to the principles used in noise cancellation for headphones. The analogy is particularly poignant here, where, as will be shown later, an inappropriate sense of direction and the consequent lack of resources often conspire in many companies to generate limited results from their sustainability efforts.

---

[3] For example, in boosting VDSL2 bit rates with vectoring. Very-high-bit-rate digital subscriber line (VDSL) and very-high-bit-rate digital subscriber line 2 (VDSL2) are digital subscriber line (DSL) technologies providing data transmission faster than asymmetric digital subscriber line (ADSL). Source: Wikipedia.

How to Use This Book

Vectoring is presented here both as a diagnostic tool and a prescriptive method. As a diagnostic tool that has been developed based on clinical studies of actual business situations as well as data analytics from the Dow Jones Sustainability Index (DJSI), vectoring offers a practical framework for identifying the relative positioning of companies compared to their peers. The framework, and its associated four fundamental archetypes, delivers valuable insights for sustainability practitioners, such as how to identify and locate inhibitors and how to overcome them. It is in that latter prescriptive role that vectoring becomes a key strategic tool, with numerous applications, such as:

- Designing and executing new sustainability programs
- Embedding the SDGs into the company's core strategy
- Assessing the impact of sustainability programs on competitiveness and valuation.

The ultimate objective of vectoring is to provide a clear, potent framework that offers directions for executives to help shift their companies from integrated reporting to truly integrated sustainability thinking. To make the journey from compliance and reporting to integrated sustainability compelling and easy to understand, the book is organized in a very intuitive and logical manner, mimicking the natural cycle of adoption and acceleration of an effective sustainability strategy. The book's structure is schematically summarized in Fig. 1.1.

Developing winning sustainability strategies based on the vectoring approach can be visualized as a three-part process, corresponding to the three parts of the book. Part I introduces the concept of vectoring in general terms, identifying characteristics and themes from sustainability leaders and compiling the empirical evidence into a simple diagnostic framework with the four major archetypes unearthed during the research. The framework is then used to explore the key success drivers of winning sustainability programs, including the need to develop a clear business case for sustainability.

Part II proceeds to investigate in great detail the first pillar of effective sustainability programs, namely setting the direction or bearings right. More specifically, Chap. 3 focuses on the role a company purpose can play in successfully designing and implementing a sustainability strategy. Chapter 4 elaborates on the concept of sustainability issues, particularly how they can be mapped elegantly into a materiality matrix. The materiality matrix is a critical

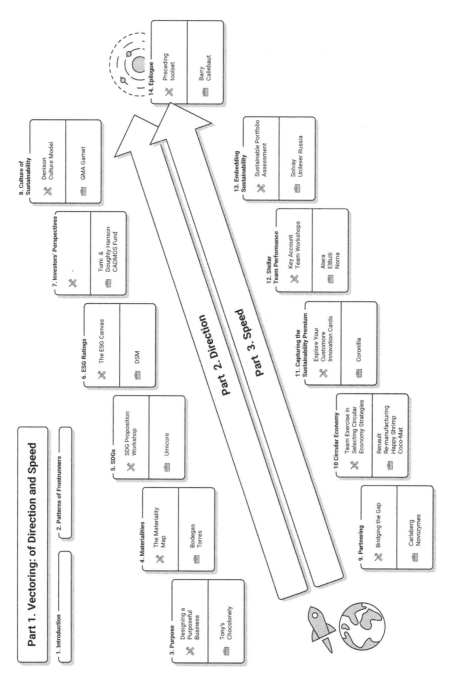

Fig. 1.1 A schematic view of the book structure encompassing the *vectoring* approach

tool for the development of an effective sustainability program, requiring insights from multiple stakeholders. The chapter will review possible business-induced complexities and various approaches for uncovering the most material of these issues and assessing their business impact in a constructive way by covering both risks and opportunities.

Chapter 5 investigates the role played by multi-governmental efforts, such as the SDGs, in putting sustainability front and center in business. With an estimated $5 to 7 trillion required to finance the SDGs on an annual basis [4], the private sector has been entrusted with providing the engine for innovation and technological development. Incorporating these SDGs into the company strategy is no easy task, but the alternative, not incorporating them properly, is probably even less palatable. The chapter is thus devoted to making the adoption of SDGs as painless as possible, offering tools to select the most relevant SDGs for a company, how to align them with existing sustainability programs and the overall business strategy and how to develop action plans.

To gain a better understanding and help navigate through the jungle of non-financial reporting challenges and environmental, social and governance (ESG)[4] ratings, Chap. 6 looks at the increased shareholder demands for transparency and the role of ratings agencies. To help calibrate the size of the new burden, the Reporting Exchange initiative by the World Business Council for Sustainable Development (WBCSD) [5] identified some 1750 reporting requirements and resources across 60 countries and 70 sectors in its 2017 report. An approach is also presented to reduce the burden of non-financial reporting while improving its effectiveness. Chapter 7 investigates how professional investors, such as venture capitalists, growth and buyout specialists, hedge funds and mutual fund managers have responded to the higher callings of sustainability, either for themselves or their portfolio companies, or by adopting sustainability as an investment theme. If, as hypothesized earlier, sustainability is ultimately about value creation, then it should not be surprising that the most astute minds in the financial world have already incorporated sustainability into their decision making.

Finally, the importance of leadership and culture in both discovering and maintaining the directional bearing is covered in Chap. 8. Very pragmatically, the chapter investigates what we can learn from sustainability champions and

---

[4] ESG criteria is a set of standards for a company's operations that socially conscious investors use to screen potential investments for their environmental, social and governance practices. Source: Investopedia.

their executive leaders, the role played by culture and how to measure it, and the growing importance of multi-company, ecosystem-like sustainability movements.

A vector is defined not only by its direction but also by its magnitude. For example, a velocity vector might have a direction of 27° from the horizontal and a magnitude of 5 meters/second. Part III of the book investigates the latter component, that is, magnitude or speed. The primary objective here is to identify how companies can accelerate their sustainability programs and effectively progress from initial target setting to measuring the progress of well-executed action plans.

Chapter 9 addresses the critical role played by partnerships in modern sustainability efforts, not only to share the costs of ever-more complex product and service developments but also to capitalize on immense opportunities. Partnerships are vital for execution. A recent research paper by MIT Sloan revealed that, while more than 90% of respondents saw partnerships as critical enablers of sustainability innovation, only 47% engaged in them with varying degrees of success [6]. The chapter introduces a number of tools to support the establishment of effective sustainability collaborations along the value chain.

Looking beyond the current *take, make and dispose* industrial model based on extraction, Chap. 10 introduces the concept of the circular economy, which is restorative and regenerative by design [7]. The circular economy is both a source of challenges and opportunities for companies, highlighting the emergence of entirely new ecosystems, eliminating waste and minimizing negative impacts. Again, supporting instruments for the creation of circular value propositions and business models are presented.

With the reality of climate change starting to bite and more extreme weather conditions no longer a distant prediction, much action is needed, and needed quickly, to prevent the global situation from turning worse [8]. It is in this context that Chap. 11 concentrates on developing sustainability-based value propositions, looking at emerging business models and technologies that accelerate the crucial transition.

The last two chapters, Chaps. 12 and 13, investigate the effective implementation of change from an organizational perspective. The first reviews various approaches to obtaining the best performance from sustainability teams, that is, how to capitalize on the intrinsically motivational power of do-good propositions. The second examines how to embed sustainability into the business core and, thereby, ensure its sustainability. The role of the sustainability portfolio analysis within different business units is examined.

Sources of Data and Methodologies

Since 1999, RobecoSAM, a Zürich-based asset management company, conducts an annual global sustainability assessment. RobecoSAM invites around 3400 of the world's largest publicly traded companies, measured by float-adjusted market capitalization based on the S&P global BMI Index,[5] from 60 different industries to participate in the survey. A questionnaire featuring between 80 and 120 questions is sent to participants, covering relevant economic, environmental and social factors. After due processing, the end product of the RobecoSAM assessment is arguably the globe's most reputed ESG benchmark: the Dow Jones Sustainability Index (DJSI).

As sustainability issues or materialities differ for each type of business, industry-specific questionnaires are used with different criteria and different weightings. Companies are given two to three months to complete the questionnaire. When companies do not respond, RobecoSAM retains the option to assess those companies based on publicly available data. Benchmarked companies receive a sustainability score between 1 and 100 and are compared to their industry peers. The top 10%, that is, top decile, within each industry are selected for inclusion in the DJSI World Index, which is published in the first half of September. After publication, the detailed company ratings can be accessed via Bloomberg terminals.[6]

To develop the concept of vectoring, the anonymized results from ten selected industries over a three-year period were examined, for companies that elected to actively participate in the DJSI benchmark between 2015 and 2017. The ten industries researched (automotive, banking, chemicals, construction materials, electric utilities, pharmaceuticals, food products, professional services, textiles and telecom) were chosen to generate a representative sample of the industries addressed by MSCI's Global Industry Classification Standard (GICS). The GICS is a four-tiered, hierarchical industry classification system that was established in 1999 by MSCI and Standard & Poor's (S&P) for use by the global financial community. It consists of 11 sectors, 24 industry groups, 68 industries and 157 sub-industries. As the GICS method-

---

[5] The S&P Global BMI (Broad Market Index), which comprises the S&P Developed BMI and S&P Emerging BMI, is a comprehensive, rules-based index measuring global stock market performance. It represents the only global index suite with a transparent, modular structure that has been fully float adjusted since its inception in 1989. Source: S&P Dow Jones Indices.

[6] The Bloomberg Terminal is a computer software system provided by the financial data vendor Bloomberg L.P. that enables professionals in the financial service sector and other industries to access the Bloomberg Professional service through which users can monitor and analyze real-time financial market data and place trades on the electronic trading platform. Source: Wikipedia.

ology is widely accepted as an industry analysis framework for investment research, portfolio management and asset allocation, the MSCI definition of sectors and industries is used in the rest of the book.

As part of the analysis, all company scores on all criteria have been restated as contributing to either risk reduction, opportunity seizing or both. To determine the company performance on risk reduction and opportunity seizing, two DJSI experts independently rated the DJSI criteria for their potential contribution to either risk or opportunity based on the questions in the questionnaire. In the follow-up stage, the expert assessments were compared, and the differences were settled. Not all criteria have equal importance for the various sectors. To accommodate this, individual criteria weightings per industry were applied, identical to those used by RobecoSAM for the composition of the DJSI for the years and industries researched.

The next step in the analysis required the construction of a separate risk–opportunity matrix for each industry and each year. That matrix enabled the identification of the top 10% of performers. A comparison was then performed at the level of each criterion between the top decile and the industry average. This comparison often yielded interesting insights when the gap between the top decile and the averages were statistically meaningful.

In addition to the anonymized data from DJSI on participants from 10 industries, two other sources of information were used extensively in the research.

1. Clinical case studies were conducted over the past decade with IMD business school in the area of value creation from sustainability and innovation. In total, 13 such in-depth studies were performed on companies such as Tumi, DSM, Renault and Unilever.
2. Practical examples and tools accumulated over 20 years of sustainability consulting with large corporations throughout Europe have been used to emphasize both the diagnostic and prescriptive application of the book.

Limitations of the Research

The research data exclusively contains companies that voluntarily participated in the DJSI. This means that a participation bias is to be expected, which should normally have positively skewed the results, on the assumption that strong sustainability players would be more incentivized to participate than laggards. Other eligible companies that do not actively participate in the DJSI are likely to be assessed by RobecoSAM but based on publicly available data. We acknowledge the fact that non-participating companies on average score significantly lower in the benchmark than participating ones due to the limited information available.

To the extent that a full peer industry review was not conducted in the identification of representative companies, a selection bias may also exist. Where possible, the example-based assertions are backed-up with additional research data from a variety of sources.

A final limitation to point out is due to the fact that the RobecoSAM questionnaires evolve each year to address new issues and emerging sustainability trends. Consequently, comparing results for specific industries at a criterion level, that is, governance, climate strategy or operational eco-efficiency, from year to year was sometimes not possible.

References

1. Kiron, D., Unruh, G., Kruschwitz, N., et al. (2017) *Corporate Sustainability at a Crossroads: Progress Toward Our Common Future in Uncertain Times.* Cambridge, MA: Sloan Management Review Association, MIT Sloan School of Management.
2. World Meteorological Organization (2018) *WMO Statement on the State of the Global Climate in 2017.* Retrieved from https://library.wmo.int/opac/doc_num.php?explnum_id=4453
3. Moore, G.A. (2006) Crossing the Chasm: Marketing and Selling High-Tech Products to Mainstream Customers. United States: Harper Business, HarperCollins Publishers.
4. Niculescu, M. (2017, July 13) Impact investment to close the SDG funding gap. *UNDP.* Retrieved from http://www.undp.org/content/undp/en/home/blog/2017/7/13/What-kind-of-blender-do-we-need-to-finance-the-SDGs-.html
5. WBCSD (2018) *Insights from the Reporting Exchange: ESG reporting trends.* Retrieved from http://docs.wbcsd.org/2018/02/Reporting_Exchange_Report_ESG_reporting_trends_2017.pdf
6. Kiron, D., Kruschwitz, N., Reeves, M., et al. (2015) *Joining forces: collaboration and leadership for sustainability.* Cambridge, MA: Sloan Management Review Association, MIT Sloan School of Management.
7. Ellen MacArthur Foundation (2018) What is a circular economy? https://www.ellenmacarthurfoundation.org/circular-economy. Accessed May 3 2018.
8. Farnworth, E. (2018, January 5) Why 2018 must be a pivotal year for climate action. *World Economic Forum.* Retrieved from https://www.weforum.org/agenda/2018/01/why-2018-must-be-a-pivotal-year-for-climate-action/

2

Patterns of Frontrunners

Peter Bakker, President of the World Business Council for Sustainable Development (WBCSD), is an expert with one of the best seats in the house to witness the evolution of the corporate world. WBCSD is a global, CEO-led organization of over 200 leading companies representing combined revenues of more than €9 trillion with more than 19 million employees. From that prime position, Bakker used powerful words to stress the mounting inevitability of sustainability-based transformation. In Bakker's view, companies simply need to start changing much faster.

> It is becoming ever clearer that for us to create a society that supports a healthy planet with happy people, we must change our course drastically.
> December 2017 insight blog of Peter Bakker [1]

In similar fashion, Feike Sijbesma, CEO of the Nutrition, Health and Sustainable Living giant DSM, referred to the term "Corporate Darwinism" in interviews with the authors back in 2012. When prompted, Sijbesma stressed that corporate success was increasingly a matter of survival of the most adaptive, emphasizing again the need for speed[1] in the adoption of sustainable practices.

Sustainability has made a resounding entry into the boardrooms of companies worldwide. Topics such as climate change and labor conditions are

---

[1] The term inspired the title of a case study published by the authors: "Darwinians at the Gate: Sustainability, Innovation and Growth at DSM." The case is available from www.thecasecentre.com and is referenced as IMD-3-2355.

© The Author(s) 2019
B. Leleux, J. van der Kaaij, *Winning Sustainability Strategies*,
https://doi.org/10.1007/978-3-319-97445-3_2

regularly part of board and shareholder meeting agendas and are now regarded as unescapable corporate responsibilities. Many organizations have established professionally staffed sustainability departments, often with direct reporting lines to the executive suite. As would be expected though, the speed of adoption of these leading-edge practices vary broadly by sector, industry and company, leading to interesting gaps between sustainability leaders and average performers. These variations of course provide an interesting terrain for examining the key drivers of sustainability strategies and their respective rollouts. Moreover, they represent an opportunity to develop interesting typologies and classifications of companies, with a view to helping them identify their relative sustainability shortcomings and very practical steps that can be taken to *upgrade* their sustainability scorecards and footprints.

At the same time, the cost of non-compliance has become astronomical. Look at what happened with Volkswagen in 2015 when the discovery of fraudulent software that enabled the manipulation of emissions tests led to some $30 billion in damages [2]. Some 5 million Volkswagens, 2.1 million Audis, 1.2 million Skodas, 700,000 Seats and 1.8 million commercial vehicles, were reported to have the fraudulent software installed, all adding to the bill [3]. Predictably, *Dieselgate* as the scandal was dubbed, also destroyed Volkswagens' reputation with consumers, employees, investors and other stakeholders. While the company had previously been an industry leader in automotive and a top performer in terms of fuel efficiency for more than a decade, the scandal led to the removal of Volkswagen from the Dow Jones Sustainability Index (DJSI). While the story is still unfolding, it is fascinating to note that the scandal barely made a dent in the company's sales. The group's revenues, on the right side of Fig. 2.1, were never seriously impacted; what little impact there was only lasted for a limited period. If penalties for such gross violations are so innocuous and short term, is there a bona fide business

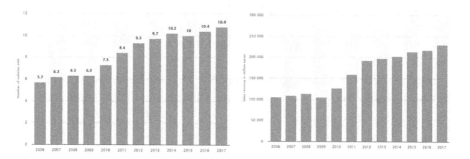

Fig. 2.1 Volkswagen worldwide vehicle sales (in million units) and revenues (in million Euros), 2006–2017 [4]

rationale for avoiding these incidents in the first place? Are consumers so impervious to these concerns that their pressure would not be enough to force major industrial companies into compliance? Philosophically then, what is enticing some companies to move aggressively in the adoption of sustainable practices while others to lag? Is it basic financial self-interest or a greater belief in the fact that doing what is good for society is ultimately good business?

While many companies have kick-started their sustainability journeys, the story above provides ample reason to dive deeper into the differences in attitude toward the discipline. It is critical to understand the characteristics and patterns of sustainability leaders and what enables them to justify and succeed in their approaches to sustainability. In particular, it is enlightening to study the specific elements of the sustainability spectrum they focused on and why, the strategies developed to capitalize on those focal points, the activities and structures put in place to implement them and the performance metrics used internally and externally to justify investing in them.

Climate Strategy: An Example of Data Analytics

The generic approach adopted in this book can be illustrated using the environmental, social and governance (ESG) benchmark scores of global companies on climate strategy. Climate change is often portrayed as one of the most important and truly global material issues, with the potential to destruct entire nations (think island submersions in the Pacific), kill wildlife in places such as the Great Barrier Reef, dramatically change agricultural practices or force massive migrations of people.

With most, if not all, industries likely to be impacted by climate change, albeit to varying degrees, companies face the need to design appropriate strategies to tackle the challenge. While most companies focus on the risks associated with a changing climate, some also seek to identify and seize the business opportunities linked to this global challenge. To realistically assess the performance of companies on climate change, DJSI[2] composer RobecoSAM developed a climate strategy criterion in collaboration with CDP, formerly known as the Carbon Disclosure Project. Since 2002, CDP has run a global disclosure system that enables companies, cities, states and regions to measure and manage their environmental impact. As a result, CDP claims to have built the most comprehensive collection of self-reported environmental data in the world [5].

---

[2] For more of an explanation about the DJSI, see "About Our Data and Research" in Chap. 1.

Table 2.1 Scoring on climate strategy criterion, 2015–2017 Dow Jones Sustainability Index, all companies, selected industries

	Industry average	Top 10%	Difference
Food products	72.92%	97.04%	24.11%
Pharma	82.10%	94.42%	12.32%
Electric utilities	80.33%	94.08%	13.75%
Telecom	51.89%	63.96%	12.07%
Chemicals	84.11%	98.40%	14.29%
Banking	69.54%	95.28%	25.74%
Construction materials	87.68%	97.97%	10.30%

The survey developed for the climate strategy criterion includes detailed questions on topics such as transparency in disclosure, emission targets, the presence of products and/or services classified as low carbon or that enable third parties to avoid GHG emissions and companies to assess their own financial risks and opportunities resulting from climate change. The climate strategy criterion is one of more than 20 criteria that make up the full RobecoSAM assessment, making it one of the most comprehensive of its kind. Other questionnaire criteria include corporate governance, operational eco-efficiency and human capital development. The relative weighting of each question and criterion is determined on an industry-basis by a RobecoSAM-appointed expert panel. For each criterion, companies receive a percentage of the maximum score; based upon the full set of questions in the climate strategy criterion, participating companies are awarded a score ranging from 0 to 100.

Comparing the average score on the climate strategy criterion with the marks of the top decile performers over the three-year research period provides some interesting insights. From the example in Table 2.1 on climate strategy, it is possible to infer that frontrunners outperform industry averages by some 16%—a meaningful difference.

Perhaps more striking is the difference in performance when comparing the selected industries with each other; the scores of the highest-scoring industry (Construction Materials) and lowest-scoring industry (Telecom) are different by a stunning 36%, on a topic that is relevant for both industries.

Not all companies see their icebergs as melting[3] at the same speed, and these different perceptions lead to more or less effective strategies for addressing climate change issues. In certain industries, such as food products and

---

[3] The metaphor of the melting iceberg is referring to the book about an emperor penguin colony in Antarctica that illustrates key truths about how to deal with the issue of change. *Our Iceberg Is Melting* by John Kotter and Holger Rathgeber.

banking, sustainability champions outperform their industry averages by as much as 25%. That situation makes it even more important to understand what these frontrunners' executives and their sustainability departments are doing differently, and why.

Sustainability-Based Transformations

Umicore: From Mining Bad Boy to Tesla Partner

Former mining company Umicore left its dark past behind to become a global leader in the circular economy movement, touted around the globe for its battery recycling technology. This spectacular turnaround was more than 10 years in the making and turned Umicore into a stock market darling, ultimately earning the company a place as the European partner in Tesla's Closed Loop Battery Recycling Program.

What was behind the magic that engulfed Umicore? Again, it was all about focus and speed. After a thorough portfolio analysis, Umicore's copper and zinc commodity businesses were spun-off and listed separately. Umicore adopted a radically new business model. The old mining–refining approach to developing material solutions was replaced by a leading-edge recycling-based model that relied on chemistry and metallurgy. By implementing the new business model, Chief Executive Officer (CEO) Marc Grynberg, Chairman Thomas Leysen and their fellow leadership team, managed to save the company from the financial abyss of its legacy businesses. The team succeeded in turning Umicore into a frontrunner in its industry in terms of innovation and sustainability, redefining the playing field for all parties. Recognition came not only from customers such as Tesla and Umicore's shareholders, but also from Corporate Knights, a leading global publisher on clean capitalism that awarded Umicore the overall number one position in its global sustainability benchmark in 2013.

Raising the Bar in Chocolate

We all love chocolate. As one expert said, "90% of the people love chocolate, the other 10% is lying." In 1737, renowned plant taxonomist Carl Linnaeus gave the cocoa tree its now famous name of *Theobroma*, or *Food of God*. As it appeals to millions of consumers around the globe, chocolate's €100 billion global market is one of the most competitive today. So how is it possible then for a startup company, initially run by amateurs with hardly any funding, to grow 50% year-on-year in a market dominated by global players such as Nestlé, Mondelez, Lindt and Mars? Too good to be true? That is what Tony's Chocolonely, a Dutch chocolate brand whose only purpose is to eradicate slavery from the chocolate value chain, has been up to over the past decade. With big brands struggling to effectively implement sustainability in their cocoa business, Tony's was created from scratch in 2005, and it developed into a €45 million company by 2017.

Tony's Chocolonely is not the only remarkable success story of purpose-driven growth in this industry. A singular chocolate producer also emerged in Australia. After much research and testing on local growing conditions, Daintree Estates was established in 2010 in North Queensland by a group of passionate chocolate aficionados and entrepreneurs. Together they created the first chocolate company in Australia that covered the entire supply chain from seedling nursery, cocoa plantations to post-harvest pod processing, chocolate production, marketing and selling. Focusing on the perceived health properties of antioxidants found in cocoa, their *plantation-to-plate* value chain enabled Daintree to capitalize on higher-yield cocoa beans while avoiding the old-style sustainability issues of smaller-sized farms.

Identifying Key Success Drivers

Umicore may be seen initially as an outlier—a *glorious accident* [6]—that neither proves nor disproves the case for sustainability in business. Each company is unique and faces different challenges and opportunities in its sustainability journey. But is it possible to identify the key genetic sequences in the DNA of frontrunners, that is, companies that shine in their sustainability approaches? Is it possible to identify patterns in the strategies and behaviors of those champions of the cause? Can those patterns, and the factors behind them, offer a clear methodology for the definition and implementation of effective sustainability programs? Can those elements truly provide the foundation for transformational journeys, that is, those that imbed sustainability at the very heart of a company's strategy, rather than simply providing decoration or greenwashing?

To extract the fundamental building blocks of transformational programs, we complement the ESG data study with extensive clinical case studies of sustainability champions. The research again was meant to be both descriptive and prescriptive. The cases provide the descriptive elements, that is, deep dives into the fine mechanics of sustainability leaders. How do they define the key issues on which to focus? How do they set objectives for their efforts? How do they organize for effective rollouts? What metrics do they consider for maintaining the momentum in their efforts? How do they define success, especially when success cannot be measured immediately in traditional financial terms? Of course, generalizing based on a small sample size may prove challenging, but with dozens of examples, patterns start to emerge, with clear commonalities. This is when the research turns prescriptive, identifying the factors that underlie and drive the success of the most ambitious sustainability transformations. These key drivers are then presented again in a clear action program, from sustainability strategy definition to implementation and follow-through, with appropriate worksheets provided to serve as roadmaps for the transformational journey.

The discovery of key genetic sequences in the DNA of leading sustainability programs supports our view that transformational companies are approaching sustainability differently. To summarize some of the key findings, transformational companies have a much higher sense of direction and accelerate execution by embedding sustainability into their core businesses, not adding them as appendices. This combination of direction and speed (or momentum) is what we refer to as vectoring. The book's objective is to aggregate into one single source the examples and tools derived from winning sustainability strategies around the globe. The aim is to help managers improve the effectiveness and impact of their sustainability programs, most notably through more purposeful targeting of their sustainability objectives (better bearings) and a more coordinated set of activities to accelerate their rollouts (more momentum).

In parallel to developing the concept of vectoring, instruments will be presented in great detail. For further clarification and application of these tools in your organization, additional online resources such as practical team exercises, canvases and worksheets are also available free of charge on the book website www.vectoring.online.

Vectoring Step 1: Getting the Bearings Right

Counterintuitively, less is more when it comes to selecting objectives. For companies developing sustainability programs, it can be incredibly tempting to support a vast number of sustainability causes. At first sight, a larger pool might improve a company's image and its attractiveness to employees, shareholders, local communities and other stakeholders because these causes or materialities are typically difficult to criticize. After all, how can one be against a company claiming to care about things such as child labor and biodiversity?

But as the sayings go, "He/she that too much embraceth, holds little," or simply, "grasp all, lose all." Focus helps in delivering a clearer story to stakeholders. And evidence suggests that shareholders react positively (by increasing the firm valuations) when companies deliver on key sustainability issues [7].

The evidence overwhelmingly supports the fact that frontrunners are obsessively focused on a limited number of critical, relevant and material sustainability issues. Focus is the key to proper implementation and ultimately capturing value from the efforts, particularly when addressing sustainability issues directly distilled from a well-articulated company vision, a longstanding family culture or a distinct statement of purpose.

To quickly illustrate the concept, a powerful example discussed later in the book comes from one of the globally recognized sustainability leaders in the wine industry—Bodegas Torres. During visits made by the authors to its headquarters in Vilafranca del Penedès in Catalonia (Spain), the Torres family clearly stated its deep personal commitment to combating climate change. This was re-affirmed repeatedly, even during the economic crisis of 2009 when many players within the wine industry were highly skeptical about the link between their businesses and sustainability. Miguel A. Torres, then CEO of the company, argued passionately about the fiduciary duty he felt toward the next generations to combat climate change. Besides the stewardship argument, a good business case could be made as well for taking care of that materiality, since faster ripening of grapes typically resulted in lower-quality wines.

> In the wine business one needs to think 15 years ahead. Forget weather statistics: facts are telling. In less than a decade, harvesting of the grapes in the Penedès region had to be brought forward more than 10 days on average [8].

By focusing on climate change, and not dozens of other sustainability causes, Bodegas Torres was named the World's Most Admired Wine Brand by *Drinks International* magazine in 2017, the ultimate recognition of its efforts in building brands with a clear societal purpose and conscience.

Vectoring Step 2: Accelerating Execution and Getting Momentum

Once the appropriate materialities have been selected, the concern turns to activities required to develop and roll out strategies to capture the opportunities that arise from these sustainability activities. Frontrunners rigorously implement sustainability programs that deliver value through reputation, cost reduction and/or growth, usually all three simultaneously. Laggards, on the other hand, often limit their efforts at reporting activities as part of their customary non-financial information cycle.

Reporting non-financial information can become addictive and very time-consuming. "We would like to have started to work on our action plan sooner, but we are still working on the sustainability reporting," is a much-heard comment during interviews with sustainability departments. Companies end up stuck in a reporting trap [9], occupied all year round delivering reports and communication and failing to turn ESG benchmark results into actions.

Compliance and reporting are indeed formidable tasks today, and they will likely get much worse. In 2017, the Reporting Exchange initiative by the World Business Council for Sustainable Development (WBCSD) [10] identified over 1750 reporting requirements, with a steep increase on climate disclosures since 2015. With reporting requirements on the rise, companies that fail to distinguish a business case for sustainability run an even higher risk of falling into the reporting trap.

Eco-efficiency can be a very good indicator of the maturity of the execution of sustainability programs. The direct benefits for sustainability programs can typically be found in areas such as reductions in waste, energy and water conservation, minimization of natural resource consumption and waste-generating activities, leading to lower costs and, in some cases, new business opportunities.

Going back to the DJSI data sample, an analysis of the operational eco-efficiency criterion sheds light on how well industries are capturing the *low-hanging fruit* in implementation. The key focus of the operational eco-efficiency criterion is on inputs and outputs of business operations and questions that include topics such as direct greenhouse gas emissions, energy consumption, water consumption and hazardous waste. During the 2015–2017 period, the players in the top decile of the ten industries researched outperformed the average of the fellow DJSI participants from their industries on the operational eco-efficiency criterion by almost 18%, as shown in Fig. 2.2:

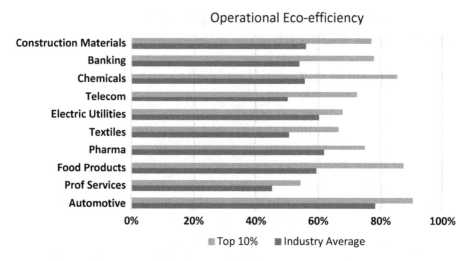

Fig. 2.2 Scoring on operational eco-efficiency criterion, 2015–2017 Dow Jones Sustainability Index, all companies

Within the group of ten industries researched, Food Products displays the biggest distance between the frontrunners and the industry average, with the frontrunners scoring 28% higher. This outperformance by the top 10% of companies is not simply a ranking artifact; it is grounded in reality, as the following Unilever example shows.

The *Unilever Sustainable Living Plan* (USLP), launched in 2010, is often lauded in sustainability circles as a best-practice example of vision and strategy. The USLP excelled not only through its clear corporate focus but also by fully integrating the underlying management structures into the organizational framework of Unilever. The in-depth case study of the Unilever production cluster in Tula (Russia) presented later in the book, illustrates how integrating the sustainability strategy into the existing reporting and management responsibilities led to successful execution, even in some of the toughest environments. At the food and ice-cream manufacturing cluster in Tula, one of the largest in Europe, local management was challenged with implementing a target of "zero non-hazardous waste to landfill" within ten months and without additional financial resources, and it delivered.

The Business Case for Sustainability

An intriguing discovery from the research is the sheer number of companies that lack direction and momentum in their sustainability efforts. In many instances, the business case for sustainability is so understated that it is hardly possible to muster the energy and resources necessary to engineer fast and decisive change. Interestingly, some 90% of global companies consider a sustainability strategy important to remaining competitive, but only 60% actually have a sustainability strategy! Even more damning, only 25% claim to have uncovered a clear business case for sustainability [11]. In plain language, of the 20 global companies, 18 believe that a sustainability strategy is a key competitive element, but only 12 have actually developed one, and 7 of those 12 have not yet figured out how to convincingly connect that strategy to profits in the future.

The absence of a clear business case for sustainability at the company level does not imply that one cannot be built. Ray Anderson, the legendary founder of Interface, a carpet producer that pioneered sustainability, made the case very vividly when he reformatted the question for his audience, asking them what the business case was for ending life on Earth [12].

Nevertheless, the absence of a clear business case puts many sustainability programs at risk of turning into pure communication exercises, handled by generalists and put on the low priority list at the corporate level. To state the point more powerfully, without the ability to connect sustainability to the bottom line, it is difficult to see how sustainability can be made sustainable!

So how can such a business case be constructed? According to the Integrated Reporting (IR) Framework,[4] a business case for sustainability can be assembled from four distinct building blocks:

- Cost savings from eco-efficiencies, for instance, by reducing waste, water usage or energy consumption
- Revenue growth from sustainable innovations
- Enhanced reputation with stakeholders, such as clients, employees and shareholders
- Lowering risk, for instance, by reducing the cost of capital or the dependency on scarce resources.

Novozymes, a Danish enzyme manufacturer with a global market share of over 40% in its field, is a recognized champion of sustainability. Shortly after its spinoff from sister company Novo Nordisk in 2000, Novozymes published its first integrated report in 2002. The company developed an original and effective way of assembling its business case for sustainability and product feasibility studies, combining financial and non-financial data from life cycle

---

[4] Refer to Exhibit 2.1 at the end of the chapter for a detailed description of the Integrated Reporting <IR> Framework.

studies. The approach is dubbed internally as the *enzyme window*, for business opportunities emerging from enzyme applications that can replace chemical substances in specific situations. Lifecycle data enables Novozymes' researchers to calculate the potential of their biosolutions for US agriculture in the "Acre Study." By applying biosolutions to one-acre corn fields, the study shows that in addition to feeding the 9 billion chickens already produced annually in the US, the corn could also yield 10 billion US gallons of bioethanol, save 120 million pounds of pure phosphorous and avoid over 87 million metric tons of CO_2 equivalents [13].

The numbers are impressive but perhaps not surprising if one considers Novozymes' corporate purpose:

Together, we find biological answers for better lives in a growing world—Let's rethink tomorrow.

Novozymes' *Partnering for Impact* strategy resulted in many new enzyme applications that significantly reduced the societal impact of incumbent solutions. As the case on Novozymes in Chap. 9 reveals, partnering and innovation—the core of Novozymes' strategy—and the ability to spot relevant micro-trends in sustainability have contributed significantly to the company's continuing success.

The Four Archetypes of Sustainability

According to the WBCSD, a clear disconnect exists in many firms between their enterprise risk management and their sustainability practices, leading to vastly understated sustainability risk exposures. A comparison between the material sustainability disclosures of 170 WBCSD members and the risk factors identified in their standard corporate reporting revealed that 71% of the sustainability issues that these businesses deemed material were not disclosed to investors as risk factors [14].

Part of the blame can be attributed to the fact that "enterprise risk" is a rather ambiguous term. And when translated into the sphere of sustainability, where risks and opportunities often overlap, it turns even more treacherous. To avoid falling into the open ditch, RobecoSAM attempted to provide some clarification. The description of risks and opportunities by the ESG specialist includes the following:

- Revenue opportunities and risks arising from changes in market growth, market share and competitive position
- Cost implications arising from expenses related to regulatory compliance, maintenance of social license to operate, environmental management, safety and human resources management
- Capital efficiency trends reflecting additional investments required to meet regulatory and other stakeholder requirements, environmental management, trends in the cost of installed capacity and in the operational life of assets
- Risk exposure arising from governance, regulatory, business conduct, environmental and social connection to non-investor stakeholders [15].

The anonymized data covers 275 companies operating in 10 industries. As Table 2.2 illustrates, each criterion is divided into economic, environmental

Table 2.2 Example of RobecoSAM criteria per industry (Telecom, 2017)

Dimension	Criteria	Weight %
Economic	Codes of business conduct	6
Economic	Corporate governance	7
Economic	Customer relationship management	5
Economic	Impact measurement & valuation	2
Economic	Information security & cybersecurity	3
Economic	Innovation management	2
Economic	Materiality	2
Economic	Network reliability	2
Economic	Policy influence	2
Economic	Privacy protection	5
Economic	Risk & crisis management	5
Economic	Supply chain management	4
Economic	Tax strategy	2
Environmental	Climate strategy	4
Environmental	Electromagnetic fields	2
Environmental	Environmental policy & management systems	4
Environmental	Environmental reporting	4
Environmental	Operational eco-efficiency	6
Social	Corporate citizenship and philanthropy	3
Social	Human capital development	6
Social	Human rights	4
Social	Labor practice indicators	4
Social	Occupational health and safety	3
Social	Social reporting	4
Social	Stakeholder engagement	3
Social	Talent attraction & retention	6
	Total	100

and social dimensions, adding up to a weighted total of 100% for each industry.

The data from RobecoSAM can be used to identify possible patterns in the development of sustainability programs. With sustainability becoming a bigger part of day-to-day business management, it is important to uncover how well large companies address the topic, particularly if they are more inclined to focus on sustainability risks or opportunities. More important than the focus is the real impact of their actions. After all, as stated by British economist Ronald Coase in his famous Warren Nutter Lecture "How Should Economists Choose?" (1981):

If you torture the data enough, nature will always confess.

In an effort to investigate the preferences of sustainability programs for risk or opportunity, the criteria in the list above were attributed to one or the other through an expert-opinion-based survey. For example, operational eco-efficiency was attributed 100% to opportunity seizing, meaning that the company's score on this criterion contributed to increasing the opportunity score. Not all criteria were identically distributed. For instance, climate strategy was attributed 75% to risk reduction and 25% to opportunity seizing (Table 2.3).

For the ten industries researched, all company scores on each criterion over the three-year research period were restated. By plotting all companies' XY scores within a matrix, an industry risk-reward map was generated displaying how industry participants were performing in terms of opportunity seizing and risk reduction. From this breakdown, four *archetypes* of company sustainability programs were extracted, each with its own characteristics: traditional, communicative, opportunistic and transformational. The chart is pictured in Fig. 2.3.

Table 2.3 Simplified example of the distribution of scores

Company A—chemical industry						
Criterion	Company score	Weighting	Criterion risk factor	Criterion opportunity factor	Risk score	Opportunity score
Operational eco-efficiency	88.10	8		100%	0.00	704.80
Climate strategy	61.70	7	75%	25%	323.93	107.98
				XY-score	323.93	812.78

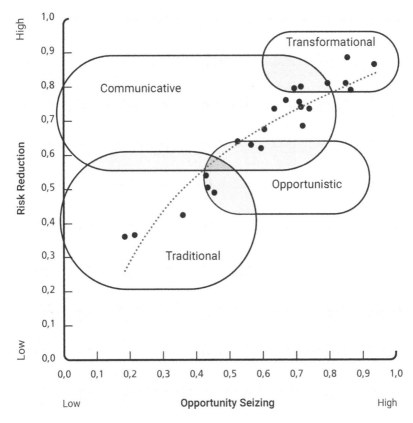

Fig. 2.3 Risk-reward mapping and the four archetypes of sustainability programs

Traditional

This sector encompasses many companies with a relatively high-risk profile and limited development of their business cases for sustainability. Sectors that feature on the negative screening lists of institutional investors and private equity firms with an inherent risk, such as tobacco and weapons, are likely candidates for the traditionalist quadrant. Traditional companies tend to be compliance-driven, leveraging regulations to justify and extend their licenses to operate. Most of them have sustainability departments reporting to regulatory affairs or investor relations.

Communicative

This sector covers companies with a limited capture of the opportunities provided by sustainability and high ESG compliance, such as corporate governance and codes of business conduct. A relatively high percentage of firms in the communicative sector are active in industries where opportunity seizing is complicated because, for example, sustainability measures are costly, impact is difficult to assess or the market is not mature enough for sustainable solutions. An example would be the automotive industry, where trailblazers such as Tesla and BYD[5] (Build Your Dream) have accelerated the momentum toward sustainable mobility. Risk reduction and compliance are often the first steps in the sustainability journey, and communicative companies can be found in almost all industries. Their sustainability departments are most likely to report into the corporate communications department.

Opportunistic

This sector includes companies that recognized the opportunities offered by sustainability but are still struggling with the relatively high-risk profile of their portfolios. Prevalent in this sector are diversified conglomerates, with portfolio companies at various stages of sustainability maturity. Opportunity seizing happens in part of the portfolio, but the risk profile overall remains high. These companies often suffer from a form of sustainability *schizophrenia*, where the *least-sustainable* parts of the company often end up being spun off. An example is the demerger of the zinc and copper commodity businesses from Umicore, the Belgian materials technology and recycling company. Other examples can be found in the energy sector, precipitated by the forced energy transition. Two German energy giants RWE and E.ON, encountered intense stakeholder pressure from the *Energiewende*, or energy turn, Germany's clean energy policy. Both companies decided to create separate renewable energy entities concentrating on innovation. The move returned the parent companies, who kept ownership of the legacy energy assets, to the *traditional* quadrant, while the renewable energy spinoffs emerged on the international scene as transformational entities, resolving their split personalities.

---

[5] BYD Company Limited, a leading high-tech multinational company founded in 1995 and listed on Hong Kong Stock Exchange and Shenzhen Stock Exchange, now operates in the four core fields of IT, automotive, new energy and rail transit having expanded from a company that only produced and marketed rechargeable batteries. The company employs approximately 220,000 people and has over 30 industrial parks and production bases worldwide.

Transformational

This last sector covers companies that have embraced sustainability in a holistic fashion, that is, both to capture opportunities and to reduce risk exposure. By focusing strongly on execution, transformational companies (re-)set the standard for their industry, as illustrated later with the examples of Bodegas Torres (Chap. 4) and Bolivian pasta producer Coronilla (Chap. 11). As will be discussed later, the sustainability programs of transformational companies are more closely tied to business operations, driving new opportunities for eco-efficiencies and revenue growth, with co-creation with external stakeholders a valuable source of new business development.

Red: A Backbone Provider with Some Real ... Backbone

Formed in 2008 to strengthen the separation and transparency of the regulated energy activities in Spain, the Red Eléctrica Group is an energy transmission agent, also known as a backbone provider. Its market focus includes not only Spain but also parts of Latin America. The company's mission is clearly stated as guaranteeing the correct functioning of the electricity system and ensuring the continuity and security of the electricity supply at all times. In other words, Red has a front row seat in the ongoing energy transition journey.

Red also looks for the maximum integration of renewable energy into its energy mix. The transition toward a new energy model required not only proper direction but also a lot of momentum. Red formulated an innovation strategy based on four pillars: people, sustainability, technology and digitalization. The strategy included a cultural change, which was needed to enable the company to take on future challenges. To help focus its efforts, a sustainability model was adopted for the entire company, taking into account the targets established by the United Nations Sustainable Development Goals (SDGs).

In its approach to sustainability, Red was covering both risk reduction and opportunity seizing. This holistic, pro-active stance toward the new energy future put the company squarely in the top transformational quadrant for electric utilities, as presented in Fig. 2.4, scoring over 90% on both counts, that is, risk reduction and opportunity seizing. The combination of actions generated an overall DJSI score in 2017 of 93 points for Red, making it the leader in the index for electric utilities.

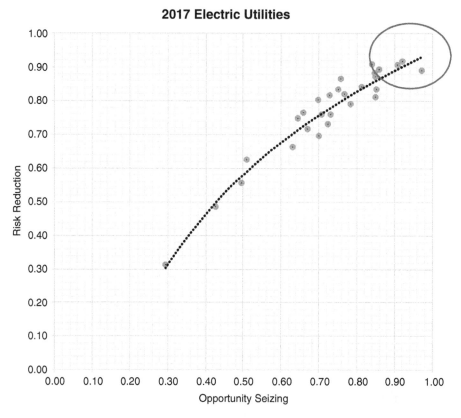

Fig. 2.4 Processed DJSI scores plotted in risk-reward map within the electric utilities sector (2017)

Fast Forward

The second part of the book elaborates on these sustainability archetypes, investigating in greater detail what constitutes proper direction in sustainability efforts, various sources of inspiration for this direction and relevant materialities for various types of companies. In this context, the contribution of various ESG ratings and the SDGs are also investigated, before analyzing how some of the most sophisticated investors, from venture capitalists to mutual fund managers, have been able to capitalize on the opportunities presented by sustainability as a modus operandi or investment theme.

The third part of the book will analyze various means to gain momentum in implementing sustainability strategies, including partnering, circular economy thinking, obtaining superior sustainability team performance and ultimately embedding it into the corporate strategy.

Exhibit 2.1: The Integrated Reporting SpiltIRSpigt Framework

As the topic of sustainability is maturing, so are the ways of measuring and benchmarking sustainability performance. One way of assessing your starting position is through applying the Integrated Reporting SpiltIRSpigt Framework. In order to facilitate the effective reporting of the impact companies have on society, the International Integrated Reporting Council (IIRC) was formed in August 2010 as a global coalition of regulators, investors, companies, standard setters, accountants and NGOs with the ambition of improving accountability, stewardship and transparency.

After much prototyping and co-design discussions among stakeholders, the IIRC came up with the Integrated Reporting SpiltIRSpigt Framework that helps companies report with a focus on value creation from financial as well as non-financial drivers. In doing so, the framework provides investors with improved information for investment decisions and drives further collaborative thinking in boards and strategy departments about objective setting.

The tool is centered around a model that focuses on capturing value through six forms of capital for value creation. The first two forms (financial capital and manufactured capital) are most commonly used in traditional, non-integrated corporate reporting. The other four capitals are new and represent the *softer* areas such as intellectual capital. In brief, the six standard capitals within the Integrated Reporting SpiltIRSpigt Framework can be defined as follows:

- **Financial Capital** The funds that are available to your organization for value creation such as debt, equity and grants.
- **Manufactured Capital** Your manufactured capital is made up of assets such as buildings, infrastructure and production equipment.
- **Intellectual Capital** The most common forms of intellectual capital are, for example, tacit knowledge, intangibles from brand and reputation and patents.
- **Human Capital** Human capital is created from your people's competencies, their capabilities and experiences.
- **Social and Relationships Capital** The relationships with your main stakeholders and how they ensure your social license to operate, create long-term value and support growth.
- **Natural Capital** Your natural capital can most often be defined from topics such as biodiversity, ecosystem health and your use of natural resources such as air, water, energy and minerals.

Applying the above forms of capital to corporate reporting, helps disclose matters that fundamentally affect an organization's ability to create value over the short, medium and long term. The disclosed matters, also known as materialities, can have both positive and negative impacts on your company's performance.

References

1. World Business Council for Sustainable Development website, Retrieved 01 April 2018. "We must reboot the financial system to deliver the SDGs" Bakker, P. (2017, December 1). Retrieved from https://www.wbcsd.org/Overview/News-Insights/Insights-from-the-President/We-must-reboot-thefinancial-system-to-deliver-the-SDGs

2. Riley, C. (2017, September 29) Volkswagen's diesel scandal costs hit $30 billion. *CNN Money.* Retrieved from http://money.cnn.com/2017/09/29/investing/volkswagen-diesel-cost-30-billion/index.html"

3. Calne, J. (2015, October 1) Volkswagen emission scandal: what "diesel-gate" means for VW owners. *The Independent.* Retrieved from https://www.independent.co.uk/life-style/motoring/motoring-news/volkswagen-emissions-scandal-what-diesel-gate-means-for-vw-owners-a6675376.html

4. Statistica (2017) Volkswagen's worldwide vehicle sales from 2006 to 2017 (in millions). Retrieved from https://www.statista.com/statistics/272049/worldwide-vehicle-sales-of-volkswagen-since-2006/

5. CDP (2018) About us. https://www.cdp.net/en/info/about-us. Accessed 16 April 2018.

6. Glauser, M.J. (1998, October 1) *Glorious Accidents: How Everyday Americans Create Thriving Companies.* Salt Lake City, UT: Shadow Mountain.

7. Khan, M., Serafeim, G., & Yoon, A. (2015, March 14) Corporate Sustainability: First Evidence on Materiality. *The Accounting Review*, Vol. 91, No. 6, pp. 1697–1724.

8. Source: MIGUEL TORRES: ENSURING THE FAMILY LEGACIES (IMD-3-2162).

9. Van der Kaaij, J. (2015, April 27) Steering Clear of the Sustainability Reporting Trap. *INSEAD Knowledge Blog.* Retrieved from https://knowledge.insead.edu/responsibility/steering-clear-of-the-sustainability-reporting-trap-3978

10. WBCSD (2018) *Insights from the Reporting Exchange: ESG reporting trends.* Retrieved from http://docs.wbcsd.org/2018/02/Reporting_Exchange_Report_ESG_reporting_trends_2017.pdf

11. Kiron, D., Unruh, G., Kruschwitz, N., et al. (2017) *Corporate Sustainability at a Crossroads: Progress Toward Our Common Future in Uncertain Times.* Cambridge, MA: Sloan Management Review Association, MIT Sloan School of Management.

12. Interface (2017, May 23) Let's start the climate takeback [PowerPoint slides]. Retrieved from https://www.slideshare.net/Interface/lets-start-the-climate-takeback

13. Kløverpris, J.H., Ahmed, N., & Hunter, M. (2017, March) *The Acre Study, Unlocking new potential in the agricultural value chain with biosolutions.* Retrieved from https://www.novozymes.com/en/news/news-archive/2017/03/more-from-one-acre-new-report

14. WBCSD (2017, January 18) *Sustainability and enterprise risk management: The first step towards integration.* Retrieved from https://www.wbcsd.org/Projects/Non-financial-Measurement-and-Valuation/Resources/Sustainability-and-enterprise-risk-management-The-first-step-towards-integration

15. GRI (2016). "Defining What Matters, Do companies and investors agree on what is material? *Mining, Metals and Electric Utilities.*" Retrieved from https://www.globalreporting.org/resourcelibrary/GRI-DefiningMateriality2016.pdf

Part II

Direction by Design

3

The Quest for Purpose

In this chapter, we introduce and discuss the first critical success factor for an effective sustainability effort—identifying the proper objectives for it. Through clinical observation, we discovered that many firms failed to successfully implement their sustainability strategies, not because they lacked the desire, the willingness or even the belief in the impact of sustainability on their businesses, but because they failed to identify proper objectives for their efforts. When firms become overly ambitious and select too many targets, their efforts tend to become dispersed and hence of limited impact. This creates demotivation and too often leads to the abandonment of meaningful and inherently valuable efforts. It definitely pays to focus but on the right targets.

In the next sections, we review the importance of purpose for an organization, and how it helps to coalesce various efforts and goodwill and gives a shared sense of direction. We then illustrate how sustainability can be a strong contributor to that sense of purpose by providing superior motives for business activities.

In later sections, we review how to identify and qualify the possible sustainability efforts and then to single out a small subset that would be most compatible with your business and hence best able to serve as guidance for your organizational efforts. We strongly emphasize the need to identify a small set of sustainability targets that clearly resonates with your organization's purpose.

© The Author(s) 2019
B. Leleux, J. van der Kaaij, *Winning Sustainability Strategies*,
https://doi.org/10.1007/978-3-319-97445-3_3

Providing a Sense of Purpose: In Search of the Why

Compasses, originally invented in China during the Han Dynasty between the second century BC and the first century AC, were first used to harmonize buildings in line with the principles of feng shui to attract positive energy. Only later during the Song Dynasty in the eleventh century AC were compasses adopted for navigation [1].

Viewing energy as a guiding source for direction has remained. Appreciative inquiry, the change management approach that focuses on the positive, is based on the heliotropic principle, that is, the notion that organizations and people move toward the source of positive energy similar to how sunflowers move in the direction of the sun to seek life and energy [2]. Company compasses, which have been designed as mission and vision or more exotically as *raison d'être* or *A Dream with a Deadline* [3], determine a reason for being and indicate the strategic direction to be followed.

Over the past two decades, a new compass—company purpose—has gradually made its way into the corporate boardroom. Today, many companies have some implicit or explicit form of a purpose statement for good reasons. A well-designed, clearly stated company purpose, also known as an organization's *why* [4], guides the company's strategies and defines its actions, and it has also been shown to help energize organizations, attract talent, win clients and improve reputations [5].

For purpose statements to be effective, it is essential they be both aspirational and specific. There is nothing wrong with stating that the company aims to "improve the lives of its clients," but it does not stand out from the crowd or provide clear direction to managers and employees. Nor does it signal deep commitment to outside stakeholders such as clients and suppliers.

Sustainability as a Source of Purpose

A company's purpose can also reflect the role it expects to play in society, that is, it can generate purpose explicitly from a sustainability focus. The purpose statement makes the brand more relevant to different stakeholders by connecting the *why*, the *what* and the *how*, and it focuses on addressing the business's impact on society. A purpose statement can take on a whole new dimension as demonstrated by Ecoalf—a fashion startup built on sustainability. As stated by Javier Goyeneche, the company's founder and President:

Ecoalf arose in 2009 from my frustration with the excessive use of the world's natural resources and the amount of waste produced by industrialized countries. Ecoalf symbolizes what I believe the fabrics and products of the new generations should be, a new fashion/lifestyle brand that integrates breakthrough technology to create clothing and accessories made entirely from recycled materials with the same quality, design and technical properties as the best non-recycled products. That way we show that there is no need to use our world's natural resources in a careless way. [6]

In a single swoop, Goyeneche's statement covers not only a higher purpose but also provides clear direction when it comes to product design and meaning as well as impact on society. Ecoalf's purpose has led to collaborations. For example, in partnership with Swatch, Ecoalf developed an exclusive collection of clothing for Swatch employees made from 100% recycled fabrics. Fabrics were processed from plastic bottles (about 41 recycled plastic bottles per Swatch uniform) and cotton leftovers and saved over 30 million liters of water. Similarly, Ecoalf collaborated with Starbucks, this time using recycled coffee grounds, to develop exclusive products such as backpacks, travel bags and accessory bags that are available for sale at the Starbucks Reserve Roastery and Tasting Room in Seattle.

When (re-)stating a company's purpose, finding the appropriate sustainability topics can amplify the chosen direction and help turn strategy into action, action that will materially affect the company's impact on society. And with increased societal impact comes extra trust from consumers. The Edelman Trust Barometer, for example, revealed 16 specific attributes that build trust, grouped into five performance clusters (integrity, engagement, products and services, purpose and operations). Attributes researched include ethical business practices, customer needs, treatment of employees and addressing society's needs in everyday business. In its 2015 version, the Edelman Trust Barometer exposed that by far the biggest reason for decreased consumer trust in business was the failure of companies to contribute to the greater good (53% of consumers) [7].

From Purpose to Business Impact: Talent Attraction and Retention

It is not easy empirically to tie purpose statements to specific sustainability programs and their impact on a company and its environment. Multiple factors intervene, and any evidence of correlation would likely be spurious.

Nevertheless, it may be possible to gain some interesting insights by creatively processing information that is commonly obtainable, for example, from the Dow Jones Sustainability Index (DJSI). While it is not possible to accurately isolate purpose statements for participating companies, company scores on measures such as talent attraction and retention can be used as proxies for *desirability* for current and potential employees, and hence as a measure of brand image. The concept of talent attraction and retention is operationalized in the DJSI rankings through a collection of metrics, including questions on long-term incentives for employees below the senior management level, employee engagement and turnover rates (i.e. churn). We analyzed 10 industries and compared the performance on this criterion for the top 10% of performers in the DJSI rankings versus their industry averages.

First notice in Table 3.1 that the industry averages in terms of talent attraction and retention are very similar and relatively high, meaning all industries seem to have found ways to address the issue. It is nevertheless interesting to point out that the top decile companies in the DJSI rankings are scoring on average 15% higher on that measure than average performers in their industry over the three-year period covered by the research. Even more telling is the difference between the top decile and the average within specific industries. In the Automotive industry, the difference between the top decile and the average performance on talent attraction and retention is only 5%, suggesting that top performers in terms of sustainability are only marginally better at talent attraction and retention than the rest of their industry.

At the other end of the spectrum, companies within the Food Products industry experience a very different situation. The top decile sustainability players in the DJSI rankings outperform their average competitors by a whopping 27% on talent attraction and retention, placing industry sustainability

Table 3.1 Scores on talent attraction and retention criterion, all sectors (DJSI 2015–2017)

	Industry average	Top 10%	Difference
Automotive	76.54%	81.36%	4.82%
Professional services	73.94%	81.57%	7.62%
Food products	64.02%	91.10%	27.07%
Pharma	70.21%	87.61%	17.41%
Textiles	61.90%	67.13%	5.23%
Electric utilities	74.01%	87.02%	13.01%
Telecom	69.51%	87.22%	17.71%
Chemicals	66.94%	86.69%	19.75%
Banking	68.20%	85.02%	16.82%
Construction materials	67.43%	84.10%	16.66%
		Average	14.61%

leaders such as Unilever, Nestlé and the Colombian Grupo Nutresa, miles ahead of their competitors on talent management. While the evidence is anecdotal and does not constitute proof of a connection between sustainability and definite business objectives, it does point to the importance of a higher sense of purpose, through ambitious sustainability programs, on definite business drivers, such as talent attraction and retention, at least in some industries.

From Why to What and How

The Ecoalf example illustrates the idea that sustainability can be a great source for company purpose. While it is not an exclusive source, it is still a rich one in its ability to tap fundamental human values and a large array of greater-good activities impacting the communities or the environment. These objectives tend to be inspirational, hence effective motivators of behaviors. Of course, using sustainability as a channel to define a stronger sense of purpose for a company would not have any impact unless we were able to identify the proper business drivers for the sustainability efforts. These business drivers, that is, the connection between the sustainability objectives and corporate objectives, are the ultimate enablers of the conversion of the company strategy into actions, including the impact the company is planning to generate in society.

The company purpose (the *why*) was the starting point of the journey to identify the *what* and the *how*; the business drivers are the practical stepping stones to answering these more pragmatic business questions, such as what market segments should be addressed, what key suppliers should be relied upon and what is the appropriate geographical footprint for the business.

Consider, for example, the mega-changes recently affecting the fast-food industry, with issues such as food security and obesity coming to the forefront and impacting business potential. In 2012, the city of New York became the first city in the world to officially outlaw large soft drinks when Mayor Bloomberg banned the sale of sugary drinks larger than 16 ounces, purposely to improve city residents' health [8].

Consumers were impacted too. In 2015, while on a research trip in Europe for this book, two researchers visited a fast-food restaurant at the local airport. After selecting their menu, one of them realized he did not have enough local currency to pay for his meal. Instead of using his credit card, he asked his colleague if he could settle the bill for him. After this awkward moment, he explained that the week before he had gotten into an argument with his wife when she discovered that he had visited a fast-food restaurant after reviewing the detailed statement provided by his credit card company. A recognizable story for some perhaps, and one that illustrates that at least a fraction of the consumer audience frames fast-food restaurants as places of mischief. Not the association you want when you are McDonald's, whose brand mission is "to be your customers' favorite place and way to eat and drink."

The McDonald's sustainability revolution is quite telling in this respect. After opening the first fast-food restaurant in 1948, the company went from strength to strength, all the way up to the middle part of the 2010s when sales numbers started to slip. As consumers started to become more aware of food-related health issues, fast-food restaurants slipped down the list as the eatery of choice.

The arrival of new CEO Steve Easterbrook in March 2015 meant vast change was looming at the golden arches. Just six months after starting in his new position, Easterbrook announced a comprehensive reform plan to his shareholders to make McDonald's relevant again (Easterbrook later referred to his actions as "How McDonald's got its mojo back") [9]. In the quest to improve brand relevance, the company's chief supply chain officer became responsible for sustainability—a move explained by the hefty societal impact of the choices the firm made in its supply chain with topics such as climate change, beef sustainability, packaging waste and recycling featuring highly on its list.

Soon after, McDonald's announced a new program for sustainability with its "Scale for Good" plan. Next to addressing climate action and the sustainability of its famous beef patties, Scale for Good also included topics such as serving 100% cage-free eggs and adding lower calorie choices to the menu. The fresh approach landed McDonald's on *Fortune's* Change the World List in 2016 because of the impressive changes it made to its supply chain—a recognition well deserved considering the magnitude of the changes the business needed with over 37,000 restaurants. The McDonald's network in Russia alone included some 650 restaurants and relied on about 160 long-term suppliers for some €350 million in purchases annually [10].

To illustrate the challenges of large-scale change in fast-food logistics, fellow restaurant franchise KFC and its celebrated Colonel Sanders can be called to the rescue. Upon changing its UK logistics provider early in 2018, the poultry specialist was forced to close many of its nearly 900 UK restaurants for several days, with others just offering limited menus [11]. Cause of the closure? No more chicken meat available! The negative consumer and press reactions caused the company to issue full-page apologies in newspapers showing an empty KFC bucket with the company logo creatively rearranged to read *FCK*.

At McDonald's, a redefinition of the company compass in terms of sustainability was inevitable, factoring in business drivers drawn from McDonald's *why*, *what* and *how*. The company found its way back to profitable growth, and after making it into *Fortune's* Change the World List, Easterbrook, a veteran of the company, commented, "What we're really trying to do is demonstrate that we want to use our size and scale for good, in helping egg farmers, in helping our agriculture practices, and clearly working on the agenda that our customers really care about [12]."

Bob Langert, the then vice president of corporate social responsibility and sustainability at McDonald's, was terribly accurate in his observations. In his retirement exit interview, barely a few weeks after Easterbrook took the top seat, he commented, "Our new CEO just spoke to all of us in a town hall meeting a couple weeks ago and gave a big shout-out to our mission to buy sustainable beef. We need to be a more relevant brand to consumers, to your point. And the work of sustainability is going to make us more relevant. Our actions for the future are going to be part of our growth [13]."

In the following section, we outline a straightforward burger-based workshop model that is most useful in learning how to define a sustainability-based purpose. Once applied to your own business, the tool supports identifying the key business drivers, and it will help you get started on the definition of a sustainability strategy and its effective rollout.

☞ Designing a Purposeful Business: Bob's Burgers

To help teams develop a better sense of purpose and make them more comfortable with the notion of thinking (and acting) beyond profits, it usually proves useful to disconnect them from their existing business setting and experiment in a safe and inspiring environment, easily recognizable for most. The tried and tested workshop format of Bob's Burgers, presented below, does exactly that.

The workshop takes 3 to 3½ hours and starts off by discussing an abridged version of the McDonald's business model visualized through the popular Business Model Canvas [14], as developed by Swiss business model guru Alexander Osterwalder and management information systems professor Yves Pigneur. The Business Model Canvas is a thinking tool for designing and enhancing business models by specifying nine categories, referred to as the

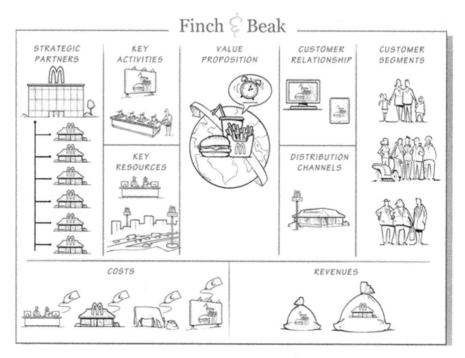

Fig. 3.1 Business Model Canvas designed by Business Model Foundry AG, adapted for McDonald's by Finch & Beak

building blocks of an organization. The building blocks include key partners, key activities, key resources, the value proposition, customer relationships, channels, customer segments, cost structure and revenue streams. According to Osterwalder and Pigneur's pioneering work, the performance of an existing organization can easily be improved using that simple model that forces users to address all key dimensions of a business in a visually attractive manner.

Applied to McDonald's, the Business Model Canvas key dimensions as depicted in Fig. 3.1 would be summarized as follows:

- The pivotal point and starting position in the canvas is the *value proposition*. In McDonald's case this is food of predictably high quality served quickly and consistently around the globe.
- The main *customer segments* targeted are families, youngsters, the elderly and some business people.
- McDonald's essential *strategic partners* are its franchise holders and their suppliers of food ingredients and equipment.

- The *key activities* are marketing communications and producing and selling fast food in its restaurants.
- The *key resources* McDonald's requires are the company's employees and its restaurants.
- On top of in-store interactions, the *customer relationship* also takes place online on the customers' preferred devices, be it a mobile phone, a tablet or a computer.
- For *distribution*, McDonald's depends on its own restaurants and those of its franchisees.
- The company's *cost* structure largely consists of employee salaries, restaurant construction costs, logistics expenses, raw materials and marketing communication costs.
- McDonald's *revenues* are generated at the restaurants owned by the company itself and those owned by its franchise holders.

With the company's impressive footprint globally, most if not all workshop participants will have abundant knowledge of the McDonald's experience, thereby guaranteeing lively exchanges. After introducing the McDonald's case in the plenary kick-off, participants are divided into groups of four to six individuals with an assignment to re-design the business. More specifically, they are asked to come up with an inspiring fast-food store concept in a city nearby, that maximizes its impact on society while running beyond break-even. The (non-exhaustive) list of ideas introduced by participants can become quite broad ranging from renewable energy, healthy menus and sustainable beef to a hangout for local youth or a training institute for restaurant employees.

The full description of Bob's Burgers workshop format can be downloaded from www.vectoring.online, including high-resolution files.

🗁 Purpose Statement Formulation: Interface's Mission Zero®

Building a purpose statement explicitly connected to a contribution to society definitely helps to build trust. On the other hand, companies with a strong sense of purpose do not necessarily have to focus on a specific sustainability issue. The sense of purpose can come from a more holistic approach, as long as the formulated purpose is differentiated enough to give a strong sense of direction to the organization.

Take a look for example at Interface, the global manufacturer of modular carpets. Founded by the late Ray Anderson in 1973, the company has grown from its original factory in LaGrange, Georgia, into a stock-listed corporation with some 3500 employees, an annual turnover of about $1 billion, sales offices in 110 countries and 6 manufacturing facilities.

As one of the world's pioneers in sustainability, Interface was able to change its strategy from a traditional approach toward a clear focus on sustainability without sacrificing business goals. As early as 1994, after 20 years of business as usual, Interface's legendary founder set the company on a completely different path, focusing on "Climbing Mount Sustainability," that is, the creation of additional value, not only for economic purposes, but also for society and the environment.

Ahead of his time, Anderson instilled the vision that Interface would be the first company that, by its deeds, showed the entire industrial world that sustainability could be imbedded in all its dimensions (people, process, product, place and profits) by 2020—and in doing so would become restorative through the power of influence. This vision was reflected in Mission Zero®—the company's focused commitment to eliminate any negative impact Interface may have on its environment. Over the years, Interface implemented this sustainability strategy by working as an innovative ecosystem and closing both technological and biological cycles in a circular economy model.

The results have been astonishing. By 2017, Interface had reduced its Greenhouse Gas emissions by 95%, water use by 86%, energy inefficiency at manufacturing sites by 43% and waste-to-landfill by 91% compared to 1994 [15]. Moreover, 58% of all raw materials were bio-based or made from recycled materials and the company used 87% renewable energy leading to a total carbon footprint reduction of 60%. These impressive numbers gave Interface a spot as one of the top five most sustainable corporations, alongside giants such as Unilever and Patagonia [16].

Mission Zero® not only gave them reputation mileage but also inspired employees and partners to come up with several game-changing innovations:

- Inspired by the gecko, the small nocturnal tropical lizard better known for its toe pads that can cling to smooth surfaces, Interface came up with an original way to eliminate toxic glues used in carpet installation. It developed the TacTiles, adhesive stickers that fix carpet tiles to the floor, a more durable and faster carpet installation system that makes replacements and recycling easier, leading to less waste. TacTiles created a brand-new market for Interface, with more than 40 million square meters of carpet installed with TacTiles since 2006 [17].

- Interface pioneered the development of recycled nylon. Based upon a partnership with the Zoological Society of London and Aquafil, an Italian yarn supplier, the company launched an initiative to tackle the issue of fishing nets being discarded in the ocean in poor regions of the world. The initiative, Net-Works, delivered both social and commercial benefits, by improving the livelihoods of local fishermen while providing Interface with recycled nylon as input for carpet tiles. Recycled nylon product is now globally used as a replacement for virgin nylon, which contributes to the climate action list. Since 2012, 142 metric tons of waste fishing nets have been collected, providing alternative income to 1500 families.

With the original, ambitious targets within sight, Interface has had to refresh and update its vision. It came up with the *Climate Take Back* vision, moving from restorative to regenerative, from *learning from nature* to *acting as nature*. Largely based on the research results of Paul Hawken and a coalition of more than 200 scientists, writers, architects, NGOs and other experts in its Project Drawdown,[1] the new program has been designed with the ambitious focus of decarbonizing society. The *Climate Take Back* program was formulated around four basic pillars:

- Live Zero—Doing business in ways that give back whatever is taken from the Earth.
- Love Carbon—Stop seeing carbon as the enemy and start using it as a resource.
- Let Nature Cool—Support the biosphere's ability to regulate the climate.
- Lead Industrial Re-revolution—Transform industry into a force for climate progress.

📂 Purpose Statement Formulation: adidas's Performance with Purpose

In some cases, the absence of a corporate purpose statement explicitly pinpointing the role the company expects to play in society is compensated at the

---

[1] Project Drawdown is a climate change mitigation project initiated by Paul Hawken and climate activist Amanda Joy Ravenhill. Central to the project is the compilation of a list of the "100 most substantive solutions to global warming." The list, encompassing only technologically viable, existing solutions, was compiled by a team of over 200 scholars, scientists, policymakers, business leaders and activists; for each solution the carbon impact through the year 2050, the total and net cost to society, and the total lifetime savings were measured and modeled. Source: Wikipedia, accessed 28 March 2018.

portfolio level. Some firms in effect let their products and services do the talking. A sustainability leader from the fast-moving fashion industry presents a useful example. DJSI textiles industry leader adidas formulated a corporate statement of purpose that could be regarded as non-specific in its address of societal impact:

We believe that, through sport, we have the power to change lives.

As a high-level pitch, the statement of purpose may ring authentic but it may lack specifics to be effective in vectoring, that is, instigate direction and speed.

Yet, this did not prevent the company from transitioning effectively from strategy to action. In its 2017 product portfolio, adidas introduced Parley editions of running footwear under the newly created sub-label of *Performance with Purpose*. Parley is a collaboration network where creators, thinkers and leaders come together to raise awareness for oceans and collaborate on solutions. One of the prime activities is ensuring that other waste plastic streams are not accidently blended with ocean plastics. Using a lifecycle approach across the whole value chain to assess its impact, adidas recognized that raw materials accounted for half of its environmental impact, and 68% of the company's overall water consumption. Partnering with associates, adidas pioneered new ways of reducing material wastage, for example, using 3D printing [18] (also known as additive manufacturing, whereby 3D objects are constructed by depositing material in layers until the predesigned shape is formed versus traditional manufacturing, now referred to as subtractive manufacturing, whereby 3D objects are constructed by cutting material away from a solid block of material or through the reuse of waste plastic).

adidas and Parley began their partnership under the Ocean Plastic Program with a common goal: transforming marine plastic pollution into performance sportswear, while reducing the sourcing of virgin raw materials and addressing waste in the value chain. According to adidas, each pair of adidas Parley sports shoes contains on average the raw material of 11 PET bottles recovered from the ocean. With a story that was engaging enough to resonate, consumers responded enthusiastically: adidas exceeded its ambitious sales target of selling one million adidas Parley shoes in 2017, with expectations of more to come, creating a substantial spin-off from the firm's *Performance with Purpose* sub-label [19].

☞ Developing a Purpose Statement: The Cover Story

The Cover Story is a visioning tool designed to help firms generate a company purpose. Similar to the dream stage in appreciative inquiry, which invites you to take an aspirational look at the future of the organization or service, Cover Story uses a technique called *back-casting*. Back-casting commences with defining a desirable future and then works backwards to identify actions that will connect the dreamed-up future to the present.

In essence, the Cover Story approach entails the development, in less than two hours, of a future cover page. This is usually conducted in a workshop format with a maximum of 20 participants with as many diverse backgrounds and roles as possible. To apply the tool, make sure to start by dividing the workshop participants into groups of three to four individuals. Ask the groups to write an article for the cover of *Fortune Magazine* five years from now, featuring the company, its purpose statement and its outstanding achievements in society, starting with the headline of the article. The obligatory components of the frontpage, next to the central headline, are a suitable picture and a (short) story of what contributed to the company's success. Most importantly, the story needs to contain the description of the secret ingredient that made the company's sustainability program into a gigantic success.

Ask some of the groups to quickly present their solutions and start working on a plenary version of the headline. After completion of the plenary version, challenge the audience to turn this attractive foresight into reality by generating a 100-day action plan. To facilitate the implementation of a Cover Story workshop and its 100-day corollary, you can download additional material, including the workshop instructions, from www.vectoring.online.

🗁 Pursuing Purpose: Tony's Chocolonely's Slave-Free Chocolate [20]

Tony's Chocolonely started as a business with a clear-cut higher purpose: to be 100% slave- and child-labor free. While making a television documentary in 2003 on labor conditions in the cocoa industry, Dutch reporter Teun van de Keuken was shocked to discover that most of the chocolate in the global marketplace was harvested using child labor—and that the problem was well known to major chocolate makers. In reaction, Teun felt obligated to bring this horrible stain on the chocolate industry to the attention of a much wider audience by turning himself in to the police as an accomplice to a felony: he had consumed a well-known contraband by eating a couple of chocolate bars that were produced with illegal child labor. When that protest did not work satisfactorily, Teun decided to create his own brand—Tony's Chocolonely.

Conquering the Market with Slave-Free Chocolate

As the Dutch law enforcement system was figuring out how to handle the case, Teun (a.k.a. Tony) produced a small batch of 5000 chocolate bars. Tony's Chocolonely—the world's first guaranteed slave-free chocolate—was born. The first batch was sold out in a single day. After this success, the very first Fair-Trade Tony's Chocolonely bars hit the shop shelves on November 29, 2005.

In the first few years of its existence, Tony's grew slowly but steadily to a turnover of around €1 million in 2009. Despite this early success, the company needed to renew its energy to reach its stated objective of making a difference for the long term. So, it hired an experienced marketer—Henk Jan Beltman—whose former stint at Innocent Drinks gave Henk Jan the much-needed hands-on experience to make a difference at Tony's. Henk Jan also understood the benefits of combining a clearly defined company purpose with a valid social enterprise model that would make a profit and generate a positive impact on society. After six months at Tony's, Henk Jan became the company's majority shareholder, and he took full responsibility with the title of chief chocolate officer (CCO).

Serious Business Benefiting All Stakeholders

Based on its mission "Together we make 100% slave free chocolate," the company clearly communicated that Tony's was "crazy about chocolate, serious about people." Tony's concern for people applied predominantly to cocoa farmers and their employees in the supply chain, but it did not stop there. End consumers were also critical stakeholders. Tony's efforts toward achieving its mission were recognized when the company became a member of the global B Corp community in 2013.[2]

---

[2] Started in the US in 2006 as a tool for impact assessment, B Corps had grown by 2017 into a global movement of companies that were pursuing the shared purpose. All B Corps were purpose-driven and created benefits for stakeholders at large, not just shareholders. Individually, B Corps met the highest standards of verified social and environmental performance, public transparency, and legal accountability, and aspired to use the power of markets to solve social and environmental problems.

In the beginning, Tony's was dealing with trading companies in Ghana and the Ivory Coast. To increase its impact and to make sure its chocolate was as *slave free* as possible, Tony's engaged in a long-term partnering agreement to buy cocoa beans directly from the farmers, providing them with a fair premium price for their product while combating child slavery. A third cooperative in Ghana was added to Tony's supply chain to spread its impact to over 1200 farmers.

Growing with Purpose

Innovations kept the brand relevant and helped maintain the energy that came with the purpose-driven model, as shown in Fig. 3.2. Tony's chocolate bars were designed to mimic the landscape of Western Africa. No equal rows and chunks: Tony's bars were not divided equally, as the world's wealth itself is not divided equally. To the delight of Henk Jan, at times this triggered customer complaints as the split of the bar was deemed unfair.

Fig. 3.2 Supply chain process—Tony's Chocolonely

Table 3.2 Net revenue (€ Millions)

2009	2010	2011	2012	2013	2014	2015	2016	2017
1.0	1.6	2.4	4.5	7.4	9.6[a]	17.6	29.3	44.9

Source: Tony's Chocolonely Annual Fair Report 2016–2017
[a]In 2014 Tony's Chocolonely changed its' annual reporting from calendar years to reporting from 1 October to 30 September

Because of the high level of public exposure generated, Tony's did not have to spend any money on advertising other than keeping the brand viral by generating stories on a regular basis. Fans also supported Tony's purpose. When the company introduced its "Good News" campaign to support retail price increases to pay additional premiums to farmers, many consumers reacted with delight. This enthusiasm enabled Tony's Chocolonely to keep growing. Net revenues increased by an average of 59% each year between 2013 and 2017 as shown in Table 3.2. In 2015, the company decided to expand to the US, opening its first international office in Portland, Oregon. Other markets targeted for distribution included Sweden and Germany.

Testing Dilemmas with the Rocking Chair Test

The establishment of a value-based business model has created potent dilemmas, as faced by many companies with mixed-purpose models. When push comes to shove, do you fall back on business principles or ethical values? Henk Jan approached these dilemmas with what he referred to as the rocking chair test—he imagined himself at the ripe age of 90, sitting in a rocking chair and looking back at his life. In a perfect world, what should he have done, what way and with whom, when the dilemma presented itself?

This peaceful scenario was viciously disrupted in 2013, when Henk Jan, still in his early forties, had a stroke. This caused him to think more carefully about his own succession. He was convinced the company's growth was rapidly exceeding his own capabilities; he was definitely happier as an early-stage entrepreneur than as the chairperson of a company with €50+ million in turnover. Henk Jan considered stepping down entirely when he turned 50. That left him seven years to ensure that Tony's would leave a lasting legacy on the cocoa supply chain.

Accelerating the Cocoa Supply Chain While Maintaining Purpose

In the meantime, the more traditional players in the chocolate industry were not sitting still. The global awareness of corporate social responsibility increased with investors and consumers driving large multinationals to increase their sustainability program efforts. Most big players in the chocolate market started addressing the slavery topic with renewed vigor. A 2016 master's thesis from the University of St. Gallen [21] revealed the six major Swiss chocolate manufacturers that were investigated (Barry Callebaut, Chocolat Frey, Chocolats Halba, Lindt & Sprüngli, Mondelēz and Nestlé) clearly showed signs of structurally engaging in the topic of illegal forced labor.

As the topic of sustainability gained more attention among mainstream competitors, Tony's Chocolonely received lots of international attention, and potential suitors showed up unannounced, both from inside and outside the chocolate arena. Henk Jan and his team realized there was still a lot of work to be done to eradicate slavery from the cocoa supply chain; teaming up with or becoming part of a larger entity would translate into a larger impact, but it could potentially also threaten Tony's purpose.

Henk Jan's own experience had taught him it was no easy feat to sell the company and continue with the same level of purpose as part of a large multinational. When his former employer Innocent Drinks sold its shares to Coca-Cola, the purpose of the company was definitely diluted. Besides, Henk Jan had seen telling examples from similar situations where purpose was diluted due to a change of ownership such as Ben & Jerry's (to Unilever), Stonyfield Farm (to Danone) and the Body Shop (to L'Oréal). The question was whether Tony's Chocolonely would be able to overcome that paradigm, or should it continue to scale on its own terms.

Tips, Traps and Takeaways

✋ Tips

- Test the companies' purpose statement for the correct aspirational levels and make sure it is explicit enough to give direction.
- Look for business drivers in the value chain to help determine the company's role in society.
- Measure awareness of the company's purpose as a degree of talent attraction and retention.

☄ Traps

- Beware of purpose statements that are overly shallow; for instance, avoid statements that resemble "improving the lives of our clients by selling our products."
- Deploying purpose statements on only a part of the business or portfolio; make sure that the connection to the company's strategy is prominently present.

☝ Takeaways

The presence of a purpose statement connecting the *why*, the *what* and the *how* with a well-defined impact on society is essential for developing a company direction equipped with a surplus of purpose. By making the business's impact on society as tangible as possible, that surplus of purpose reinforces the firm's appeal to stakeholders. Based on the DJSI data from the ten sample industries, top decile performers outperformed their peers by as much as 27%. Correspondingly, examples from companies leading in sustainability demonstrated an explicit formulation of a purpose statement with a narrow societal scope, that is, concentrating on just a few sustainability issues as is the case with Tony's Chocolonely and Ecoalf. As an alternative to this narrow societal scope, a broad focus is equally potent as exemplified by Interface and its Mission Zero® approach, as long as the business impact is energizing and unambiguous.

In the absence of such an explicit purpose statement, companies can generate compasses from their company values and, as the adidas Parley example illustrated, the development of a specific *Performance with Purpose* product group reinforced the existing company purpose. Last but not least, the McDonald's example illustrated that, even in a major company transformation, sustainability can play an important part through its contribution to the relevance of the brand, again generating surplus purpose.

References

1. Wikipedia contributors (2018) History of the compass. *Wikipedia, The Free Encyclopedia.* https://en.wikipedia.org/w/index.php?title=History_of_the_compass&oldid=845919581. Accessed 11 March 2018.
2. Subirana, M. (2016) *Flourishing Together: Guide to Appreciative Inquiry Coaching.* Winchester, UK: O-Books.

3. Horovitz, J. & Ohlsson-Corboz, A. (2007) *A Dream with a Deadline: Turning Strategy into Action*. Harlow, UK: Pearson Education.

4. Sinek, S. (2009) *Start with Why: How Great Leaders Inspire Everyone to Take Action*. United States: Penguin Books.

5. Groscurth, C. (2014) Why your company must be mission-driven. *Gallup Business Journal*.

6. Ecoalf (2017) Ecolaf homepage. https://ecoalf.com. Accessed 23 March 2018.

7. Edelman (2015) 2015 Edelman trust barometer global results [PowerPoint slides]. Accessed 5 April 2018.

8. Parks, A. (2012, September 13) Goodbye, Big soda: New York becomes first city to ban large-sized soft drinks. *Time*. Retrieved from http://healthland.time.com/2012/09/13/goodbye-big-soda-new-york-becomes-first-city-to-ban-large-sized-soft-drinks/

9. Whitten, S. (2017, July 26) Interview with McDonald's CEO Steve Easterbrook: How McDonald's got its mojo back. *CNBC*. Retrieved from https://www.cnbc.com/2017/07/26/mcdonalds-ceo-you-have-a-choice-to-either-be-the-disrupter-or-the-disrupted.html

10. Zaitseva, N. et al. (2016) *Sustainable Russia: A Guide for Multinational Corporations*. Moscow: Moscow School of Management.

11. Pasha-Robinson, L. (2018, February 23) FCK: KFC issues full-page apology for "chicken crisis". *The Independent*. Retrieved from https://www.independent.co.uk/news/uk/home-news/kfc-chicken-shortage-crisis-stores-closed-apology-advert-newspaper-a8224791.html

12. Kowitt, B. (2016, August 20) The full transcript of McDonald's CEO interview with Fortune. *Fortune*. Retrieved from http://fortune.com/2016/08/20/mcdonalds-ceo-easterbrook-transcript/

13. Makower, J. (2015, March 2) Exit interview: Bob Langert, McDonald's. *GreenBiz*. Retrieved from https://www.greenbiz.com/article/exit-interview-bob-langert

14. Osterwalder, A. & Pigneur, Y. (2010) *Business Model Generation: A Handbook for Visionaries, Game Changers and Challengers*. United States: Wiley.

15. Interface (2018) Mission zero: Measuring our progress. http://www.interface.com/US/en-US/campaign/climate-take-back/Sustainability-Progress-en_US. Accessed 20 March 2018

16. GlobeScan SustainAbility Survey (2016) *The 2016 Sustainability Leaders*. Accessed 15 March 2018

17. Interface (2018) TacTiles—The easy way to install modular flooring without glue. http://www.interface.com/EU/en-GB/about/modular-carpet-tile/TacTiles-en_GB. Accessed 20 March 2018

18. Wilson, M. (2017, September 11) How adidas cracked the code of 3D-printed shoes. *Fast company*. Retrieved from https://www.fastcodesign.com/90138066/how-adidas-cracked-the-code-of-3-d-printed-shoes

19. adidas (2018) adidas Parley: Run for the oceans. http://www.adidas.com/us/parley. Accessed 13 April 2018

20. This case is an abridged version of TONY'S CHOCOLONELY: THE PURSUIT OF GROWTH WITH PURPOSE (IMD-7-1982) Copyright © 2018 by IMD—International Institute for Management Development, Lausanne, Switzerland (www.imd.org). No part of this publication may be reproduced, stored in a retrieval system or transmitted in any form or by any means without the prior written permission of IMD.

21. Wettstein, M. (2015) Cocoa sourcing: Sustainability challenges and emerging corporate response. Master's Thesis, University of St. Gallen.

4

Focusing on Materialities That Matter

After introducing the importance of adopting a clear statement of purpose, and the role sustainability can play in identifying the various facets of a firm's contribution to society, we proceed in this chapter to develop a better understanding of the tools available to focus the sustainability efforts on elements that contribute the most, that is, impactful materialities. Once the statement of purpose has been established, companies and individuals frequently must cope with limited bandwidth in terms of attention and resources. Hence, the importance of selecting a limited number of high-impact efforts, instead of the all-too-common machine gun approach of spraying efforts large and thin. Effective implementation requires sniper precision in the definition of sustainability targets and dedicated efforts in execution. Therefore, in the first sections of this chapter, materiality is first precisely defined, then the importance of gaining alignment between enterprise risk, company strategy and materiality is highlighted. Finally, some practical do-it-yourself (DIY) tools for materiality analysis and the development of a company materiality matrix are introduced and explained in detail.

Materiality and Sustainability

"Materiality" is potentially a confusing term, especially since it tends to cover territories of variable geometries for financial and sustainability specialists. Before embarking on a thorough journey to discover the materiality universe, it is important to clarify the meaning ascribed to in this book. When the

© The Author(s) 2019
B. Leleux, J. van der Kaaij, *Winning Sustainability Strategies*,
https://doi.org/10.1007/978-3-319-97445-3_4

World Business Council for Sustainable Development (WBCSD) conducted its meta-analysis of sustainability and risk, its startling conclusion was that only 29% of the materiality issues presented in the sustainability reports of the respondents were also included in the companies' legal disclosures of risks. For 35% of the companies analyzed, the disclosure percentage was precisely zero(!), demonstrating the feeble link between materiality, in its sustainability acceptance, and enterprise risk management [1].

Fortunately, the report also included some good news. Increasingly, executives are coming to terms with the fundamental concepts surrounding sustainability, in particular materialities. With additional pressure for non-financial reporting, the materiality matrix has become a familiar sight in corporate reports. Nonetheless, quite frequently clarifications for the C-suite are required on questions such as:

- What is the relevance of identifying sustainability issues, and which ones deserve to be labeled material?
- How do you perform a quality materiality analysis?
- What is the end result of such a process?

More Is Not Better: Evidence from Data

Quantitative research [2] on environmental, social and governance (ESG) performance supports the view that concentrating on a limited number of relevant sustainability issues tends to improve the performance of such activities, measured, for example, by shareholder returns. Researchers from the Harvard Business School, for example, set out to examine if and how sustainability investments enhance the value for investors, distinguishing investments in material versus immaterial sustainability issues. In total, 45 industries were examined across six major sectors: healthcare, financial, technology and communications, non-renewable resources, transportation, and services.

To perform their tests, the researchers compiled a synthetic *materiality index*, constructed by mapping the individual sustainability issues as defined by the Sustainability Accounting Standards Board (SASB),[1] to the MSCI KLD 400 Social Index, cataloguing each MSCI KLD data element as either material or immaterial. Formerly known as the Domini 400 Social Index, the

---

[1] The Sustainability Accounting Standards Board or SASB is an independent standards-setting organization for sustainability accounting standards that meet the needs of investors by fostering high-quality disclosure of material sustainability information.

MSCI KLD was created in the early 1990s by pioneer Amy Domini and contains sustainability data from 1992, enabling long-term panel data analyses. SASB, for its part, considered material issues to be those with evidence of wide interest from a variety of user groups and evidence of financial impact, the same evidence used by the SEC in determining the materiality of financial information.

The study results were surprisingly conclusive. Companies that concentrated their efforts on *material* sustainability issues outperformed their peers in terms of total shareholder returns, as measured by annualized alpha, by a stunning 4.83%, as shown in Fig. 4.1.

While the research supported the hypothesis that high performance on material issues paid off, it also showed that companies that worked diligently on immaterial issues did not significantly outperform their peers who performed poorly on those same issues (−0.38% versus −2.20%). More arresting was the fact that companies performing highly on *both* material and immate-

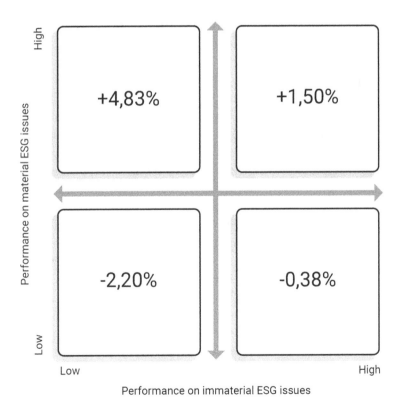

Fig. 4.1 Shareholder returns, as measured by annualized alpha (Source: Table 7, p. 46, Performance on Material and Immaterial Sustainability Issues, Annualized Alpha)

rial ESG issues were shown to perform worse (+1.50% versus +4.83%, a 3.33% shortfall) than those focusing only on material ESG issues. In other words, there was a negative return on investments in immaterial ESG issues!

The conclusion to be drawn from this important piece of research is that it pays to identify the proper ESG issues on which to focus a sustainability strategy. Additionally, a properly defined sustainability program performing well on high-material issues strongly connected to business activities can create significant value for investors. Again, more is not better. Better is better!

The Evolving Reach of Boards' Fiduciary Responsibilities

A board of directors is trusted to run the company in the best interest of the shareholders. This principle is often referred to as a fiduciary trust, that is, the legal obligation of one party to act in the best interest of another. The duty-bound party, the fiduciary, is entrusted with the care of the owners' assets. Over the past decade, this principle has extended to include the longer-term impacts of sustainability risks and opportunities. In other words, shareholders and other providers of capital are now accepted as stakeholders contributing to the list of material topics.

With the rise of integrated reporting, where a firm's annual report is combined with its sustainability report, the reference to six different forms of capital (financial, manufactured, intellectual, human, social and relationship and natural capital) defined by the International Integrated Reporting Council (IIRC),[2] has increased correspondingly. The set of *relevant* stakeholders has grown, each with its vested interests to defend. For a firm, positively or negatively impacting these interests could have a considerable influence on the long-term shareholder value of the company, thereby becoming material.

With the launch of a public consultation on fiduciary duties and sustainability by the European Commission in November 2017, the interest in this matter is set to further expand. In the view of the European Commission, clarification and thereby emphasis on these duties could motivate investors to allocate capital more efficiently by taking into account longer-term sustainability risks and opportunities, rather than simply seeking short-term financial returns.

While looking to comply with the principles of fiduciary trust, firms might struggle with the question of when a sustainability issue turns into a material

---

[2] The International Integrated Reporting Council (IIRC) is a global coalition of regulators, investors, companies, standard setters, the accounting profession and NGOs. The coalition is promoting communication about value creation as the next step in the evolution of corporate reporting.

topic from a legal perspective. To obtain an answer to this question, the US-based SASB tried to provide a point of reference. Its legal framing of materiality originates from a ruling of the US Supreme Court:

> Information is material if there is a substantial likelihood that the disclosure of the omitted fact would have been viewed by the reasonable investor as having significantly altered the 'total mix' of information made available. [3]

Rephrased, the ruling implies that sustainability issues that could have a long-term shareholder value impact must be regarded as financially material. RobecoSAM, for its part, supports the qualification of material sustainability issues as seen through an investor's eyes. As the composer of the Dow Jones Sustainability Index, RobecoSAM invites companies to apply their hands-on working definition of the financial materiality of sustainability issues for reporting purposes:

> A factor is deemed financially material if it might have a present or future impact on a company's value drivers, competitive position, and thus on long-term shareholder value creation.

Three observations on applying the latter definition:

* It insists on using an investor's perspective only when defining materiality.
* It considers a timeframe factor in assessing sustainability, including not only short-term impacts but, more importantly, long-term ones on value creation.
* It stresses the impact of sustainability factors on a company's core business value drivers—namely growth, profitability, capital efficiency and risk exposure [4].

The Creep of Corporate Responsibility

At the turn of the century, the range of corporate responsibilities started to widen, from stand-alone issues to all value chain drivers. Where in the past, companies were mostly concerned with their own behaviors, they now also had to take responsibility for the conduct of suppliers, clients and other stakeholders, which resulted in a radical rethink of their scope of accountability. And this scope is continuously growing as transparency increases and science uncovers fresh facts about the impact of products on health, well-being and the environment.

In the past decade, the food and beverage industry, for example, has had to come to terms with a bittersweet surprise. Robert H. Lustig, a well-reputed Professor of Pediatrics who specializes in neuroendocrinology with an emphasis on the regulation of energy balance by the central nervous system, picked a fight with sugar. Based on his research and clinical practice on childhood obesity and diabetes, one of his medical lectures—"Sugar: The Bitter Truth"—went viral in 2009 reaching an audience of almost eight million viewers. Over the years, Professor Lustig became a global figurehead for the science-based combat against sugar, resulting in him being heralded with the following statement:

> No scientist has done more in the last fifty years to alert Americans to the potential dangers of sugar in the diet.

According to Professor Lustig:

> Sugar's not dangerous because of its calories, or because it makes you fat. Sugar is dangerous because it's sugar. It's not nutrition. When consumed in excess, it's a toxin. And it's addictive. [5]
> Robert Lustig, The Toxic Truth About Sugar

In response to the growing pressures and demands by consumers, governments and public figures, such as the prominent television chef Jamie Oliver, to reduce sugar levels and produce *real food*, food companies have worked hard to address this emerging materiality. In 2016, global food giant Nestlé announced a revolutionary innovation that enabled a 40% reduction in the amount of sugar it uses. The new process was said to make sugar dissolve faster, so consumers experience an identical level of sweetness even at lower doses. The first product containing this innovation, Milkybar Wowsomes hit the shelves in the spring of 2018 [6].

Other industries are showing similar developments. Consider the example of one of the largest companies in the world—Apple. As recently as 2012, the *New York Times* featured an article describing the harsh labor conditions for workers assembling iPhones, iPads and other devices. Based upon information gathered from factory employees, worker advocates and documents published by technology suppliers themselves, the story unveiled common practices such as using under-age workers, improperly disposing of hazardous waste and falsifying work records, to name just a few. Moreover, two big chemical explosions at iPad factories reportedly killed four people and injured 77. Apple could not even claim ignorance as a defense: it had been alerted beforehand about these perilous conditions by a Chinese NGO.

The article exposed the company from Cupertino for the deficiencies of its outsourced supply system, deficiencies that were deemed unethical. Similar working conditions were found at factories producing for Dell, Hewlett-Packard, IBM, Lenovo, Motorola, Nokia, Sony, Toshiba and others. However, as the largest player in the field, Apple caught the brunt of the fall-out generated by the article, prompting an emergency response from the Californian powerhouse. It promised to vigorously increase its efforts to "clean up" its supply chain and take responsibility for all suppliers. It fully redesigned its approach to the outsourced supply chain, looking beyond traditional buying relationships for partnerships and collaborations on key responsibility topics. Apple also strengthened its reporting efforts by agreeing to publish annually a supplier progress report that would document the progress. Since 2007, Apple reportedly trained 14.7 million people in its supply chain on workplace protections. In 2017 alone, the company conducted 756 assessments in 30 countries, covering 95% of its total purchase spend. Process chemicals at its final assembly facilities were verified to be a 100% compliant with its newly developed Apple Regulated Substances Specification [7]. A telling example of the power of vectoring, the Apple story also illustrates the necessity of including sustainability topics in the enterprise risk management systems.

Apple's newfound commitment did not stop at labor conditions. At a shareholder meeting in 2014, CEO Tim Cook, in response to questions, stated that return on investment was not the company's primary consideration when addressing issues such as renewable energy. As he commented:

> When we work on making our devices accessible by the blind, I don't consider the bloody ROI.

Similar comments were made by the CEO about addressing environmental issues, worker safety and other areas that did not appear to have an immediate profit. The company does "a lot of things for reasons besides profit motive. We want to leave the world better than we found it."

> If you want me to do things only for ROI reasons, you should get out of this stock. [8]

Reporting on Sustainability: The Materiality Matrix

The Apple example not only highlights the rapid ripening of corporate responsibility around the world; it also emphasizes the fact that sustainability issues are often addressed at the behest of stakeholders, or by the impact these issues might have on the business. To communicate the focus of the company's sustainability program, firms often use the *materiality matrix*, a simple graphic that visually presents on one axis the importance of an issue to stakeholders and on the other axis its impact on the company's business. As described by the WBCSD [9], the purpose of a materiality analysis can be fourfold:

1. Aligning sustainability strategy with corporate strategy
2. Identifying and prioritizing business opportunities
3. Improving decision-making processes by incorporating key sustainability criteria
4. Reporting relevant information concisely.

But what does a materiality matrix look like in real life? How can the various materialities be identified and quantified in terms of their impact on the business? Consider, for example, the beer business, a multi-faceted industry as far as sustainability and materiality are concerned. In 2012, the European brewers committed to addressing alcohol abuse with their *European Beer Pledge*. This voluntary initiative by brewers did not prevent the topic of alcohol abuse from becoming one of the documented targets in the UN Sustainable Development Goals,[3] making it a red-hot issue for the industry and snowballing the market for 0% alcohol beers. Next to this prime focus, producers are also facing various other topics such as water efficiency, energy use and the CO_2 impact from packaging.

Three Business-Induced Complexities

Typically, each industry faces its own specific sustainability challenges. Within an industry, individual companies can have significantly different profiles, which complicate sector benchmarking. Consider the comparison between Walt Disney Co, JCDecaux, the world's largest out-of-home advertising com-

---

[3] SDG target 3.5 aims to strengthen the prevention and treatment of substance abuse, including the harmful use of alcohol.

pany, and cable company Liberty Global. All three companies are classified in the Media sector according to the MSCI Global Industry Classification Standard (GICS),[4] but each of them has a different type of operation leading to different material topics. How can you ever expect to compare their sustainability performances?

Clearly, the process of developing a credible, extensive materiality matrix is not simple for any company. The process of materiality assessment itself is at best cumbersome, at worst a time-devouring mishmash of external and internal opinions. In addition to the regular difficulties that occur when organizing a multiple stakeholder process, the sustainability materiality assessment can suffer from several business-induced complexities, that is, complications generated by the specifics of the business model of the company. Three of the most common business-induced complexities are:

1. **The Mixed-up Chameleon Complexity** [10] Material issues do not stop at the company's back door. Or at the front door, for that matter. But to what degree do companies adjust their sustainability material topics to suit their value chain partners? The analogy with the classic children's collage book by Eric Carle, *The Mixed-up Chameleon*, springs to mind. It features a chameleon that discovers it can change not only its color but also its shape and size and tries to imitate all the animals at the zoo—all at once. Service industries such as consultancies and banks are strong candidates for focusing on the material issues within their client portfolio, rather than on their own (relatively small) footprint. With a potentially very diverse client base, the range of material topics that needs to be addressed can easily become huge and unmanageable.
2. **The Geography Complexity** As definitions of material issues might differ by region, global operators face an extra challenge compared to local competitors. The dairy sector provides ample evidence for this, as the example of the Dairy Sustainability Framework demonstrates. Devised after 100 individual interviews, several global meetings and workshops, and reviews of more than 80 dairy and 20 non-dairy sustainability initiatives from all over the world, the Dairy Sustainability Framework came to life. In total, the Dairy Sustainability Framework included 11 global criteria such as waste, water and greenhouse gas emissions. These criteria were allowed to be interpreted differently across 11 regions around the globe, enabling a prioritization of the issues relevant to

---

[4] GICS is a four-tiered, hierarchical industry classification system. It consists of 11 sectors, 24 industry groups, 68 industries and 157 sub-industries. The GICS methodology is widely accepted as an industry analytical framework for investment research, portfolio management and asset allocation and was established in 1999 by MSCI and Standard & Poor's (S&P) for use by the global financial community.

a region, while connecting them at a worldwide level. For instance, water availability, as well as water quality, might not be very relevant to dairy farmers in Western Europe but it figures much higher on the priority list of Southeast Asian farmers, giving the global criterion of water a higher weighting in the regional comparison of farmer performance.

This geographic differentiation of material issues not only applies at the country level, it can also become relevant on a regional or even local level. To illustrate the local influences, an example from an unusual type of industry emerges: the business of golf-course management. In 2010, the Sustainable Golf Project was created to design a sustainability benchmark on the European Tour Events for professional golfers with the ambition of accelerating the adoption of sustainability in the golf industry. To demonstrate its effectiveness, the Sustainable Golf Project conducted an exploration of sustainability on golf courses in Catalunya. Five top-of-the-range Catalan courses such as PGA Catalunya, Emporda and Real Club de Golf El Prat were asked to input their basic data on water use, energy use and waste management. The courses were compared based on the triple bottom line model (people, planet, profit) according to the methodology developed by the Sustainable Golf Project. To the point of local influences on materiality, the study unveiled that the Catalan golf courses located in the region of Girona consumed significantly more water than those from the Barcelona region, where the water was twice as expensive [11]. In essence, it demonstrated that local pricing of raw materials could make a difference in setting business priorities for material issues.

3. **The Hodgepodge Complexity** Conglomerates with a broad array of portfolio businesses face a correspondingly large number of potentially material topics. This diversity makes it difficult to focus the efforts on a small subset of issues. In the absence of one central business driving materiality, much is left to the individual portfolio businesses. Decentralized businesses are leading to decentralized sustainability, but this is creating extra complexity for reporting and corporate alignment and it can stand in the way of implementation on a transformational level.

To return to the previously cited example of the beer industry, Heineken's 2016 materiality matrix, shown in Fig. 4.2 serves as an illustration of some of the complexities encountered as well as an outstanding example of a vectoring approach to sustainability. Their matrix displays 16 individual topics and singles out six areas that Heineken wants to concentrate on. In addition, the difference between locally and globally managed topics is made apparent. Topics all have clear labels and a clarifying statement is made on the topic of waste and packaging, connecting readers to the previous version of their materiality matrix.

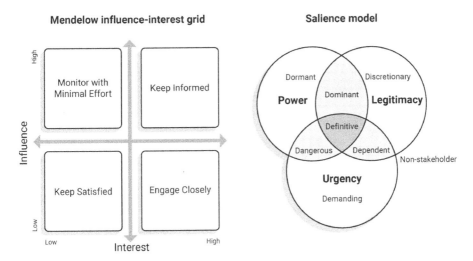

Fig. 4.2 Materiality matrix 2016, Heineken

Building Your Own Materiality Matrix

Developing a robust materiality matrix is an intensive exercise that requires involving a broad array of stakeholders. Generally, the process is repeated every three to five years, with smaller intermediate updates in some instances. But it is not just the matrix that matters; for the most relevant ESG standards, such as the Global Reporting Initiative (GRI),[5] it is sometimes also required to publicly disclose the materiality analysis process that was applied and its outcomes, as well as associated targets and progress toward achieving those targets. With reporting standards and fiduciary responsibility on the line, a robust and transparent process becomes indispensable to guarantee a high-quality materiality matrix with a limited number of sustainability issues.

Designing the process and, more importantly, sticking to it, can be daunting. Securing the involvement of senior management from diverse parts of the company and keeping the rules to a minimum is often the key to success. The immaturity of materiality as a subject within organizations does not make this an easy challenge, which emphasizes the need for a structured process with buy-in from the top. In its background paper on materiality, the IIRC recognizes the importance of the role of management in the final composition of the list of material topics:

---

[5] The Global Reporting Initiative—GRI—helps businesses and governments worldwide understand and communicate their impact on critical sustainability issues such as climate change, human rights, governance and social well-being.

Another unique feature of materiality for Integrated Reporting purposes is that the definition emphasizes the involvement of senior management and those charged with governance in the materiality determination process in order for the organization to determine how best to disclose its unique value creation story in a meaningful and transparent way. [12]

To generate a materiality matrix that embraces the principles of vectoring, a straightforward six-step approach is recommended as outlined below. Later in this chapter, an application example within a mid-sized European bank is included, with further details on the six-step process.

1. **Select and Assess the Relevant Stakeholders** Before starting the development of a materiality matrix, it is imperative to obtain a solid overview of the impacted stakeholders and their sustainability priorities. A robust

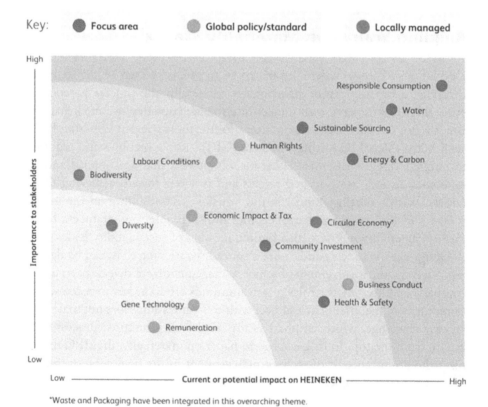

*Waste and Packaging have been integrated in this overarching theme.

Fig. 4.3 Two methods of classifying stakeholders: The Mendelow influence-interest grid and the Salience model [13]

stakeholder assessment process helps companies focus on the right issues with the right stakeholders, bringing improved adaptiveness to stakeholders such as customers, employees and investors.

Two of the most frequently used methods of classifying stakeholders are the *Mendelow influence-interest grid* and the *Salience model* as shown in Fig. 4.3. The Mendelow influence-interest grid provides a straightforward way of visualizing stakeholders by classifying them according to their influence over your activities and their interest in them. The subsequent matrix prioritizes stakeholders in four action quadrants [14].

A more elaborate classification is provided by the Salience model that is rating the relative importance—the salience—of stakeholders by looking at the cumulative score on three elementary stakeholder attributes: power, urgency and legitimacy [15]. Most commonly, the classification is obtained by qualifying each of the stakeholder groups on each of the three attributes as high, medium or low. By combining the outcomes of the three attributes, seven sections emerge as possible classifications for stakeholders. The low salience classes are *latent* stakeholders that possess only one of the attributes. The moderately salient stakeholders exhibit two of the attributes and are referred to as *expectant* stakeholders. The combination of all three attributes delivers the *definitive* stakeholders. The desired outcome of both methods is the prioritization of stakeholders and the desired relationship from the organization's perspective.

2. **Define the Long List of Sustainability Topics** Frequently scanning the company landscape on stakeholders' positions on sustainability topics helps identify rapidly evolving issues and increases the success rate of potential solutions. From various standardization and reporting initiatives such as GRI and SASB,[6] lists with predefined topics exist for most sectors. Together with sector publications from ESG rating agencies, trend analysis and desk research on stakeholders, these predefined topics form a solid basis for creating long lists with relevant topics for the selected stakeholders. These lists typically include more than 30 possible topics.

3. **Rank the Topics and Create a Short List** The desired vectoring can only be achieved if topics are pruned and possibly clustered into a shorter list of maybe 15 important issues, as shown in the Heineken example. Research

---

[6] SASB: Sustainability Accounting Standards Board/SASB is the independent standards-setting organization for sustainability accounting standards that meet the needs of investors by fostering high-quality disclosure of material sustainability information.

is applied to prioritize the topics with the help of stakeholders. Focus groups are frequently used as well as online consumer and employee surveys. The wide availability of data on sustainability topics and their associated risks and opportunities is reducing the need for company-specific research. When identifying sustainability topics for the materiality matrix, it is most effective to feature non-financial and non-operational issues.

4. **Rate the Business Impact of the Short List in Terms of Both Risks and Opportunities** When looking at topics that are relevant to stakeholders and potentially have a significant impact on the company, it is important to understand that the impact could be both positive and/or negative. The four building blocks of the Integrated Reporting (IR) Framework created by the IIRC provide an interesting tool to determine the impact of the investigated issues. It looks at four ways of creating value from sustainability:

- Cost savings from eco-efficiencies
- Revenue growth
- Enhanced reputation
- Lowering risk.[7]

5. **Construct a Concept Materiality Matrix** From the researched stakeholder information, the first version of the materiality matrix can be constructed. We refer to this first draft as the concept materiality matrix, since it will endure further rounds of validation and consolidation. To design a visually attractive materiality matrix, a number of practical questions have to be answered:

- Are color markings required for local and global issues, as is the case with Heineken?
- Is it possible to display the link between company strategy and the materiality matrix?
- How will the selected topics be displayed?
- Should the standardized actions, such as monitor, be included in the matrix quadrants as with the Mendelow influence-interest grid?

6. **Fine-Tune the Materiality Matrix, Get Sign-Off by Senior Management and Document the Process** In the last stage of the development, final checks are conducted before obtaining a definitive sign-off by top management on the materiality matrix. Do not forget once the sign-off has been obtained to document the process for potential use in the annual report.

---

[7] Refer to Exhibit 2.1 at the end of Chap. 2 for a description of the Integrated Reporting <IR> Framework.

🗁 An Example Process: Materiality Matrix Development at Bank Alpha

At the start of the materiality assessment, the stakeholder landscape was mapped, and stakeholders were prioritized by using the Salience model. A big data tool[8] was applied to capture the reporting practices and emerging trends in the banking industry and look more closely at the material topics of the bank's main peers. This part of the analysis was complemented with an overview of material issues found in ESG frameworks, such as the Dow Jones Sustainability Index, the Global Reporting Initiative Standards and the Sustainability Accounting Standards Board. Based on the findings from these ESG frameworks and trends, a long list of 27 material topics was composed.

As the next step, five internal interviews were conducted with a selection of (executive) board members to obtain their opinions on the 27 selected topics and their expected impact on the bank's current and future business. Based upon the interviews, the sustainability team was able to shorten the list to 15 top sustainability topics.

To rank and prioritize the different issues and to define the business impact of each issue, a workshop was organized at the company headquarters. Several business directors participated in the workshop together with representatives from different staff departments such as human resources. Most participants were physically present, others participated remotely. Workshop participants were invited to rank the material issues based on the perspective of stakeholders such as customers, employees, investors and policy makers. Supported by a prepared impact assessment as shown in Table 4.1, the participants also categorized the business impact of each issue.

To facilitate the discussions in the workshop and help the off-site participants take part effectively in the discussion, an online quiz tool[9] was introduced and participants were asked to forward their opinions on the potential business impact of each sustainability topic by casting an online vote.

After the workshop, the relevant material issues were ranked based on the interest of all key stakeholders through additional desk research, interviews and surveys. The material issues were then mapped to those in the Sustainable

---

[8] Datamaran is a solution based on Artificial Intelligence technology for tracking Environmental, Social and Governance (ESG) issues.

[9] The online quiz tool used in this instance was Kahoot, a game-based platform that creates a playful, engaging environment. More information can be found at www.kahoot.com.

Table 4.1 Sample of sustainability issues and a potential impact assessment table

Material issue definition	Examples of opportunities	Examples of risks
Privacy & data security		
Secure IT-systems to preserve and protect personal information from being accessed by unauthorized parties	• Reputation • Customer trust • Compliance with existing & future regulations	• Technological developments and cyber threats • Limiting innovation capability • Impact of breaches (costs, business continuity)
Enhancing financial capabilities		
Deploying educational activities to stimulate financial empowerment and help customers make smarter financial decisions	• Customer loyalty and trust • Compliance • Access to new markets • Positive impact on local economies	• Reputation, credibility • Conflicts of interest • Lower incomes
Diversity and inclusion		
Heterogeneity of the staff. Equal opportunities for employees of different backgrounds, genders and cultures	• Employer reputation • Improving employee engagement & capacity to attract new talent • Compliance with corporate governance regulation	• More resources required to find right profiles • Cultural conflicts within workforce

Development Goals (SDG)[10] framework and compared to the companies ESG performance on these topics. In the final stage, a renewed materiality matrix was created based on the stakeholder rankings of material issues, strategic priority setting and the business impact of these issues. This new matrix was presented to the Sustainability Committee of Bank Alpha for final approval including the intermediate outcomes. As a last step in the development, the matrix was given to corporate communications to add visual appeal and the development process of the materiality matrix was documented.

---

[10] The Sustainable Development Goals (SDGs), otherwise known as the Global Goals, are a universal call to action to end poverty, protect the planet and ensure that all people enjoy peace and prosperity. These 17 Goals build on the successes of the Millennium Development Goals, while including new areas such as climate change, economic inequality, innovation, sustainable consumption, peace and justice, among other priorities. The goals are interconnected—often the key to success on one will involve tackling issues more commonly associated with another. Source: United Nations Development Programme, March 2018.

☞ Applying a Quick-and-Dirty Materiality Scan: The Materiality Map

In a competition analysis or an M&A process, the resources for a full material-ity analysis might be insufficient and a *leaner* solution may be called for. In that case, the Materiality Map, which is essentially a quick-and-dirty materiality scan, is a useful alternative (refer to Fig. 4.4). The Map is applied during a two-hour workshop with a group of three to eight participants. As preparation, the competitors of the organization are to be identified and researched on their sustainability programs and their associated targets.

To start the workshop, begin by identifying the scope of the organization considered. Next determine, through a plenary brainstorm, what stakeholders are relevant and solicit examples from the audience of sustainability initiatives within the scope of the organization or similar organizations that seemingly have a positive business impact. Share the prepared analysis of the main competitors and discuss the implications and list the most relevant sustainability issues.

Plot the sustainability issues on the map considering the relative business impact and relative importance to stakeholders. Once completed, take the seven most important *material* issues and score the organizations' performance,

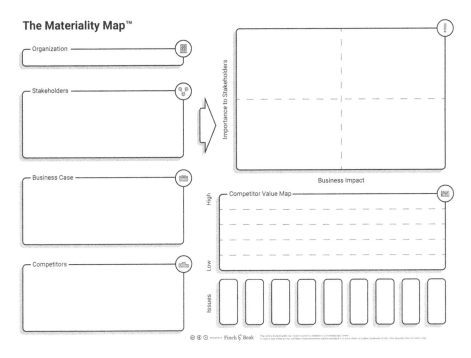

Fig. 4.4 Materiality map

from hands-on experience, as well as from that of the main competitors and plot it on the competitor value map. Wrap up the workshop by concluding in a plenary format.

To apply the tool, download the Materiality Map poster and the associated workshop instructions from www.vectoring.online.

In the final section of this chapter on the materiality of sustainability issues, we introduce you to the sustainability journey of the Spanish Torres family, one of the leading winemakers in the world. Their groundbreaking sustainability efforts from generation to generation is an exemplary example of a company that has found its vector direction and is executing it.

🗀 Miguel Torres Wines: Focus on Climate Change [16]

Back in 2010, Miguel A. Torres faced a formidable task. With a mere two years to go before retiring as president of Miguel Torres S.A., one of the largest and most reputed Spanish winemakers and distributors in the world, he wanted to ensure that the values the firm espoused would not be lost. Moreover, he sought to convince his family, employees and the rest of the wine industry of the importance of climate change issues and their impact on the wine industry. In his view, environmental responsibility would have to become an even bigger part of the Torres family legacy. By focusing relentlessly on the material issue of climate change, Bodegas Torres had turned sustainability into a key defining element of its wines and a long-term competitive advantage, creating new opportunities in the very competitive global wine industry.

> The better we care for our earth, the better the wines we make.
>   Miguel A. Torres

The Emergence of a Family Wine Business

The roots of the Torres family in the Penedès region of Spain, in Catalonia, could be traced back to the seventeenth century, with the very first written records of wine trading in the family going back to 1628. It was not until two centuries later that the family firm was officially incorporated. Jaime Torrès Vendrell, an entrepreneurial soul and the second son with no chance of inheriting any of the family fortune, decided to try his luck abroad and emigrated to

Cuba in 1855. After making his fortune in shipping and petroleum, Jaime returned to Catalonia in 1870 to start the Torres company with his father and his brother Miguel. From the outset, a shared sense of creating a company with a strong value system was key to the Torres family as is still exemplified by their company logo: the three towers (Torres) representing the founding family members. Considerable effort was put into familiarizing each employee with the family tradition and company legacy, and what it meant to work at Torres.

A New Generation with New Ideas

In 1962, at age 21, fourth generation member Miguel A. Torres joined the family business bursting with new ideas. From his first day in office, Miguel focused on a clever mix of innovation and tradition. In particular, he wanted to implement the most modern techniques to enhance the overall quality of Torres wines, for instance, by progressive conversion of all vineyards to ecological viticultural practices, eliminating pesticides and herbicides, and converting to organic alternatives whenever possible.

In 1991, Miguel followed, as intended, in his father's footsteps, with the support of his mother Doña Margarita. In line with his previous work in the firm, he continued to grow the company, balancing both innovation and tradition with a long-term perspective. Not long after becoming CEO and long before many of his peers were convinced, Miguel recognized climate change was a substantial risk and major material issue for the company.

Achieving Leadership in Environmental Performance

Environmentally responsible vineyard practices had already been meticulously applied by Torres for more than 30 years, and several local environmental protection programs had been implemented. To further address climate change, the Torres & Earth program was launched in 2007. It was a program where environmental initiatives were bundled and expanded. Various actions were taken to react to the changing climate and market conditions, including investments in renewable energy solutions, lowering the weight of bottles to reduce the operational carbon footprint and vehicle electrification.

The company also developed new scenarios to adapt vines to the evolving climate reality. Vintners were encouraged to change procedures and take counter measures, such as modifying their planting techniques, changing their canape management and exploring new regions that were becoming favorable for wine production because of the progressive increase in temperature.

Based on these efforts, Torres was receiving mounting recognition and, in 2010, the company received the coveted International Green Company of the Year award from the prestigious magazine *The Drinks Business*. And Responding to Climate Change, an official observer to the United Nations Framework Convention on Climate Change process, named Miguel Torres as the world's leading sustainable winery.

The Relevance of Sustainability to Wine Consumers

Even though end consumers were not yet putting a high premium on sustainability as an attribute of the wine they purchased at the local store, sustainability increasingly has been featured higher on the agenda of retailers across the globe since the mid-2000s. Larger merchants, such as Walmart and Tesco, have pioneered new sustainability standards, focusing on issues such as reduced packaging, optimized logistics and communicating the carbon footprint of products more visibly to consumers.

The Torres company's involvement with sustainability issues runs a lot deeper than most companies' efforts, which often focus on the reputational benefits of adherence to norms, standards and regulations. Building on its company values, Torres's approach to sustainability involves a profoundly ingrained belief that the economy, society and environment are so intertwined that they can only be conceived of as an integrative system.

This has, for example, been demonstrated by the fact that Torres has always tried to treat its employees fairly. In its Chilean winery, Miguel A. Torres's father Don Miguel surprised many in the industry by insisting on paying all farm hands *decent* wages, not simply *market* rates. As the responsibility for moderate consumption of alcohol slowly made its way into the value chain, Torres innovated their category once more. More than five years ahead of the adoption of the SDG's Goal 3 (Target 3.5) that aimed to prevent the harmful use of alcohol, the company launched a range of no alcohol/low alcohol (NALA) wines called Natureo.

A New Generation of Leadership: Continued Focus

Fifty years after joining the company, Miguel A. Torres stepped down and in 2012, his son Miguel Torres Maczassek was named as the new managing director of the Torres group, while daughter Mireia started overseeing the company's research, development and innovation function in 2014.

Under Miguel Jr.'s leadership, the Torres company continued to practice its values, which are especially visible in its sustained environmental commitments. Torres has updated its carbon target for 2020 to reducing CO_2 emissions per bottle by 30%. To achieve these ambitions, the company reinvests 11% of its profits into environment and climate-related initiatives, an accumulated investment that was expected to surpass €12 million in 2017.

The company's resolute efforts showed substantial results. For 2015, it reported an increase in turnover of 9.7%, reaching €263 million, highlighting particularly the positive performance of its international subsidiaries in China, Chile and Sweden. The Torres & Earth program initiatives equally delivered: by 2016, the company had reduced its own carbon emissions by 40%,[11] and in 2017, Torres was named the World's Most Admired Wine Brand by *Drinks International* magazine.

While Miguel A. Torres is no longer concerned about the company's daily operations, he remains an active member of the family business as a shareholder and brand ambassador. His crowning achievement was when he was honored with a Lifetime Achievement Award by the Institute of Masters of Wine and Drinks Business in June 2017.[12] In particular, Miguel's commitment to conserving the environmental, investing in research and development, implementing initiatives and disseminating these best practices to encourage others was praised. Although retirement is not yet in his future, Miguel A. Torres can look back on a successful, long-spanning career of building a family business with a strong legacy including an outstanding environmental responsibility.

Tips, Traps and Takeaways

☞ Tips

- Put extra emphasis on the governance of the materiality analysis process and its documentation.
- Map the high-importance sustainability topics with the company's must-win battles and its enterprise risks, identify gaps and develop an action plan to overcome them.
- Link the Sustainable Development Goals to your materiality matrix. See also Chap. 5 for more tools and backgrounds on targeting the Sustainable Development Goals.

---

[11] Torres (2017). Torres & Earth: Results, Inventory 2016.

[12] Torres (22 June 2017). Miguel A. Torres wins Lifetime Achievement Award by the Institute of Masters of Wine and Drinks Business.

- Use the correct jargon to describe material sustainability topics as they will resonate better in the organization.
- Once the choice of material sustainability topics is finalized, focus on the attractive presentation of the matrix. After all, one of its purposes is to communicate to stakeholders.

💣 Traps

- Make sure to obtain the attention of senior management. Unsupported processes generally lead to generic materiality matrixes with little added value.
- Beware of the *reporting-purpose-only materiality matrix* that is too distant from the business to really engage colleagues and outside stakeholders.
- In composing the long list, do not confuse material issues with operational topics or financial indicators such as revenue growth.
- When comparing your selected sustainability focus with that of your peers, be aware that official reports provide a projected image. Check the actual peer performance where possible before drawing conclusions.

👉 Takeaways

In this chapter, the importance of an authoritative materiality matrix was brought forward. The examples from Heineken and Torres illustrated that, in the case of identifying, weighing and selecting sustainability topics, a broader range is not necessarily better. On the contrary, less is more and better is better. Focusing on a concise set of sustainability issues that are unmistakably material to stakeholders is fundamental to success; it will not only increase the energy of participants in the sustainability program but also reduce reporting efforts and make the external communication more comprehensible. Once the company's materiality matrix is in alignment with those design principles, forging the link between the materiality matrix and the enterprise management system becomes much more straightforward.

To determine the relevance of the various stakeholders considered, two methods for stakeholder classification were presented:

1. The Mendelow model that categorizes stakeholders into one of four quadrants through its Influence-Interest grid;
2. The Salience model where the relative importance of stakeholders depends on the scoring of three stakeholder attributes: power, urgency and legitimacy.

Managing and documenting the process for the development of the materiality matrix is another key to its success. When developing a materiality matrix, several business-induced complexities need to be taken into consideration. Geographic scope, diversity of activities and the company's business model are described as the most impactful business-induced complexities.

The example process of Bank Alpha, a mid-sized European bank, typified the importance of timely support from senior management. Composition of an impact assessment table describing materialities, example opportunities and example risks helps prepare the C-suite for their assessment of the business impact of material issues.

References

1. World Business Council for Sustainable Development (2017) *Sustainability and enterprise risk management: The first step towards integration.* Retrieved from https://www.wbcsd.org/Projects/Non-financial-Measurement-and-Valuation/Resources/Sustainability-and-enterprise-risk-management-The-first-step-towards-integration
2. Khan, M. Serafeim, G., Yoon, A. (2015) *Corporate sustainability: First evidence on materiality.* Boston, MA: Harvard Business School.
3. TSC Industries, Inc v. Northway, Inc., 426 U.S. 438, 449 (1976) Accessed March 6, 2018.
4. Global Reporting Initiative and RobecoSAM (2016) *Defining what matters: Do companies and investors agree on what is material?* Retrieved from https://www.globalreporting.org/resourcelibrary/GRI-DefiningMateriality2016.pdf
5. Lustig, R., Schmidt L.A., Brindis, C.D. (2012) Public Health: The toxic truth about sugar. *Nature*, Vol. 482, pp. 27–29. https://doi.org/10.1038/482027a
6. Reid, D. (2018, March 27) Nestlé launches a new chocolate bar using sugar-reduction technology. *CNBC.* Retrieved from https://www.cnbc.com/2018/03/27/nestle-chocolate-bar-uses-science-technology-to-restructure-sugar.html
7. Apple Inc. (2018) *2018 Progress report.* Retrieved from https://www.apple.com/supplier-responsibility/pdf/Apple_SR_2018_Progress_Report.pdf
8. Denning, S. (2014, March 7) Why Tim Cook doesn't care about "the bloody ROI." *Forbes.* Retrieved from https://www.forbes.com/sites/stevedenning/2014/03/07/why-tim-cook-doesnt-care-about-the-bloody-roi/#5d16067855f2
9. World Business Council for Sustainable Development (2014) *Journey to materiality, A guide to achieve corporate goals by applying materiality to environmental, social and governance issues.* Retrieved from http://wbcsdservers.org/wbcsdpublications/cd_files/datas/capacity_building/flt/pdf/WBCSD_FLP_2014_Journey%20to%20materiality.pdf

10. Carle, E. (2010) *The Mixed-up Chameleon*. New York, NY: Harper Collins.
11. WILL BROWN BECOME THE NEW GREEN? SUSTAINABLE GOLF IN THE OLD AND NEW WORLD (IMD-7-1579). Copyright © 2018 by IMD—International Institute for Management Development, Lausanne, Switzerland (www.imd.org). No part of this publication may be reproduced, stored in a retrieval system or transmitted in any form or by any means without the prior written permission of IMD.
12. International Integrated Reporting Council (2013) *Materiality background paper for SpiltIRSpigt*. Retrieved from https://integratedreporting.org/wp-content/uploads/2013/03/IR-Background-Paper-Materiality.pdf
13. Stamsnijder, P. (2016) *Stakeholder Management*. Amsterdam: Boom Uitgevers
14. Mendelow, A.L. (1981) *Environmental scanning: The impact of the stakeholder concept*. ICIS 1981 Proceedings. Paper 20.
15. Mitchell, R.K., Agle, B.R., Wood, D.J. (1997) *Toward a theory of stakeholder identification and salience: Defining the principle of who and what really counts*. Briarcliff Manor, NY: Academy of Management Review
16. This case is an abridged version of MIGUEL TORRES: ENSURING THE FAMILY LEGACIES (IMD-3-2162) Copyright © 2018 by IMD—International Institute for Management Development, Lausanne, Switzerland (www.imd.org). No part of this publication may be reproduced, stored in a retrieval system or transmitted in any form or by any means without the prior written permission of IMD.

5

Sustainable Development Goals

In earlier chapters, we introduced the contributions sustainability could make to the definition of effective statements of purpose, that is, the self-definition of the company's impact on its environment and society. We then proceeded to develop the argument further and highlighted the fact that, while sustainability offers a broad palette of meaningful objectives to choose from, this very diversity can be its Achilles' heel, that is, too many choices often leads to the wrong choices. We developed the concept of materiality, to distinguish those material sustainability issues that have meaningful business impact, from immaterial ones. Evidence was provided supporting the view that sustainability investments only make financial sense when targeting relevant material issues, and it also stressed the importance of focus in that selection. Focusing on a limited set of material issues facilitates the alignment of resources toward the objectives, the communication of results and impacts, and the link to the business's bottom line.

Vectoring is thus gradually coming into perspective as a concerted corporate effort to properly set the moral compass through a pertinent sustainability-driven statement of purpose focusing on a limited number of material sustainability issues. In this chapter, we develop a better understanding of an outside source of drive and inspiration for many organizations and individuals, namely the United Nations Sustainable Development Goals, a unique initiative in voluntary global responsibility with clear targets and deadlines.

© The Author(s) 2019
B. Leleux, J. van der Kaaij, *Winning Sustainability Strategies*,
https://doi.org/10.1007/978-3-319-97445-3_5

Target 2030: The Sustainable Development Goals

The biggest call to action for sustainability was launched on September 25, 2015, when the leaders of 193 nations adopted an ambitious set of global goals to combat poverty, inequality and climate change in the United Nations General Assembly. That day, the United Nations called for governments, businesses, NGOs and citizens around the world to join forces in achieving the 17 Sustainable Development Goals (SDGs) and its associated targets by 2030 (refer to Fig. 5.1). In preparation, over a million people were involved in the unique dialogue to develop the SDGs.

> But I would like to quote the famous philosopher Elvis Presley. In one of his timeless hits he asked for "A little less conversation, a little more action."
> Prime Minister of Norway Erna Solberg on the Sustainable Development Goals [1]

To realize the immense ambition of this global agenda, goals were set to cover a broad set of topics in three main dimensions of sustainable development: economic growth, social inclusion and environmental protection. The goals were meant to be universal and had to apply to all countries.[1]

Fig. 5.1 The sustainable development goals, source United Nations

---

[1] Refer to Exhibit 5.1 at the end of the chapter for a specimen of the challenges and the impact achievements for SDG 6 (Clean Water & Sanitation) and SDG 7 (Affordable & Clean Energy).

With an estimated $5–7 trillion required to finance the realization of the goals on an annual basis [2], the private sector was tasked with the crucial role of becoming the engine for innovation and technological development behind the SDGs. Described at its introduction by the Secretary-General of the United Nations as "a to-do list for people and planet," the SDGs were a non-legally binding set of objectives.

Since action and progress on the SDGs was the most important feature of the goals, governments, civil society, the private sector and other stakeholders were all expected to contribute to their realization. To keep a healthy pressure on implementation, the responsibility to monitor progress toward the SDGs on the road to 2030 was primarily given to countries.

As an overarching sustainability effort, these SDGs have become another source of inspiration for companies. As they continuously develop and refine their materiality matrices, sustainability leaders are also incorporating these new objectives into their vectoring approach, concentrating their efforts on the SDGs where they can make a difference and that fit best with their business strategies. In the next section, we illustrate how this *co-optation* of the SDGs can take place in a harmonious way, looking at food waste as a source of SDG-driven opportunities and risks.

Food Waste: Gems in the Garbage?

Roughly 30% of our global food is wasted. As a result, food waste is accounting for an estimated $940 billion in losses worldwide and approximately 8% of global Greenhouse Gas emissions (refer to Fig. 5.2) [3]. At the same time, the United Nations Food and Agriculture Organization calculated that about 795 million people of the 7.3 billion people on our planet were suffering from chronic undernourishment [4]. Responsible consumption and production, also referred to as SDG 12, belong to the list of the 17 strategic goals. Its ambitious target (labeled 12.3) states:

> By 2030, halve per capita global food waste at the retail and consumer levels and reduce food losses along production and supply chains, including post-harvest losses.

Awareness of food waste opened an array of opportunities in the marketplace, based on concepts such as waste stream valorization and supply chain reconfiguration. As an example, in 2014, a year before SDGs were even formally adopted, Intermarché, the third largest supermarket chain in France,

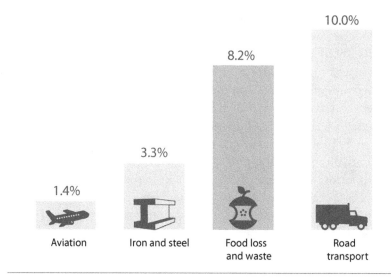

Greenhouse Gas Emissions from Food Loss and Waste
Approach the Levels from Road Transport

10.0%

8.2%

3.3%

1.4%

| Aviation | Iron and steel | Food loss and waste | Road transport |

SHARE OF GLOBAL GREENHOUSE GAS EMISSIONS (2011/12)*

http://champions123.org/   CHAMPIONS 12.3   WORLD RESOURCES INSTITUTE   UNEP

Fig. 5.2 Impact of food waste on climate change. Source: World Resources Institute

decided to start selling imperfect fruits and vegetables at its stores. Selling for 30% less than regular products, Intermarché recognized the window of opportunity in educating consumers' views on misshapen food products. The French food retailer launched its "inglorious fruits & vegetables" campaign, celebrating the "ugly" produce that often ended up in the trash bin at farms, distributors and retail stores.

Fighting Food Waste on a Local Scale: Pep Lemón

Always on the lookout, the opportunity also attracted a host of startup entrepreneurs looking for other gems in the garbage. Pep Lemón, an innovative, locally sourced and refreshingly bittersweet lemonade, launched in 2014 on the beautiful island of Mallorca. The local surplus in citrus production, mostly lemons and oranges, resulted in tons of waste every year. Elaborated by German designer Christoph Hafner and his Mallorcan wife Carmen Verdaguer in their home, Pep Lemón made use of these excess local lemons, putting the saying, "If life serves you lemons, make lemonade," into good practice. Their compassionate business model fueled much buzz around the brand, making Pep a local favorite in a flash. To source their raw materials, Christoph and Carmen made a deal with the local agricultural cooperative to source fruit that was not perfect enough for supermarkets. For packaging, the Pep team opted for retro glass returnable bottles—a rarity in Spain but practical on an island like Mallorca. Other local partners included the last independent bottling plant in the Baleares—a social enterprise that was employing disabled youngsters to press and process the lemons.

A couple of months after Pep Lemón burst onto the scene, other soft drinks were introduced: Pep Orange, Pep Toni (tonic) and Pep Cola. Unfortunately, Pep's success did not just attract friends. The launch of Pep Cola was a wake-up call for giant PepsiCo and its team of corporate lawyers. Not because of the fear of a new competitor—Pep's annual turnover was around $152,000 [5] at the time, hardly worrying for a company with a reported global citizenship giving of $100.9 million in 2016 [6]. It was the perceived brand name infringement that triggered a chilly PepsiCo response. After unsuccessful negotiations, Pep Lemón struggled and finally closed its doors in early 2018, ending the career of a promising startup and an inspiring example of a circular, social and collaborative economy, leaving much of Mallorca's citrus fruit to rot again.

Closing their business to go on a "creative break," the Pep Lemón founders learned a valuable lesson with a bittersweet aftertaste; even as a social startup with an admirable business model, one must be careful not to wake the *sleeping giant*. Romanticism does not survive in a highly competitive environment and many attempts at business model innovation fail. A better understanding of how business models evolve over time, and action on that knowledge, increases the chance of success. In the words of Professor Clayton M. Christensen of Harvard Business School:

> There are currently a lot of 'lemons' being produced by the business model innovation process—but it doesn't have to be that way. [7]

Fighting Food Waste on a Global Scale: Champions 12.3

Halving food waste worldwide before 2030 is a formidable assignment requiring scaling support. Enter Champions 12.3, a coalition of nearly 40 pioneering CEOs, ministers and other global leaders committed to achieving the SDG target on food loss and waste. Supported by the Dutch government and the World Resources Institute, the Champions frequently meet to assess progress on achieving SDG target 12.3. Moreover, the Champions share best practices and analyses on food loss and waste reduction and how to overcome barriers to the application of those best practices.

Unique in its approach of being advocated by a coalition of heavyweights from a broad range of sectors, Champions 12.3 represents an exceptional example of vectoring toward the SDGs. Early on, the Champions realized that firms aspiring to contribute to target 12.3 depend on clear direction and effective implementation. A well-structured road for deployment was compulsory for mobilizing action. Approaching the challenge through a three-step principle (refer to Table 5.1) provided the solution and the basis for a call to action in which Champions 12.3 encouraged leaders to "target, measure, and act" to develop the business case in their own environment:

Annually, Champions 12.3 releases its progress report containing vital information on the advancements of combating food waste around the globe. The report also covers more generic data on the roadmap to halving the food wasted. Quantifying food loss and waste helps business managers better understand and respond to how much, where and why food is being lost or wasted. Individually, 12.3 Champions, such as Kellogg Company and Nestlé, publicly report their food loss and waste inventories.

Table 5.1 Three-step principle as applied by the Champions 12.3

Step	Explanation
Step 1. Target	Targets set ambition, and ambition motivates action. Champions 12.3 recommends that every government (national and city) and company set a target for reducing food loss and waste that is aligned with SDG Target 12.3
Step 2. Measure	What gets measured gets managed. Champions 12.3 recommends governments and companies measure their food loss and waste to understand how much, where and why it is occurring, and monitor progress over time. The Food Loss and Waste Accounting and Reporting Standard (www.flwprotocol.org) can help countries and companies do so
Step 3. Act	What ultimately matters is action. Champions 12.3 recommends leaders start implementing practices, programs and policies that reduce food loss and waste. The business case report showcases a number of proven approaches

Source: Call to Action by Champions 12.3, champions123.org, retrieved April 15, 2018

Embedding the SDGs

So how can firms apply their version of target, measure, act to plot their way toward the actual embedding of the 17 SDGs and their related 169 targets and 304 indicators in their own activities? Champions 12.3 showed how focus and structured action planning were essential for achieving impact. Its three-legged approach of target, measure and act is applicable to various companies set on capturing more value from their sustainability activities. To compose a vectoring approach grounded in the SDGs, the first required step is simply to take stock, that is, comparing the existing sustainability program with the full list of 17 SDGs and their respective targets. Firms need to check for SDGs that are considered relevant but are still unaddressed in their current sustainability program.

As the relevance of SDGs is in part sector-driven, comparing a firm's SDG analysis results with its main peers based on public information uncovers additional understanding in most cases. Peer comparison typically provides a useful overview of sector activities as the pattern that emerges can be used to complete the list of sustainability topics the firm may want to concentrate on. Given that sustainability performance is often measured relative to peers, SDG peer analysis can be valuable to investors as well once a clear connection is made to the firm's core business strategy.

SDGs from an Industry Perspective

A vivid example of the insights gained from an SDG peer analysis can be found in the pharmaceutical industry. By actively working on the SDGs, pharmaceutical companies can capture value in terms of brand image and reputation as well as possibly gain new business opportunities, such as entrance into new markets and expansion of the consumer base. When comparing the reported activities of a European pharma firm (highly regarded as a sustainability pioneer) with some of its industry peers, interesting variances appeared. As displayed in Fig. 5.3, the firm seemed far ahead on some of the SDGs, such as No Poverty and Clean Water & Sanitation. The deep-dive workshop that followed the peer analysis resulted in an action list for improved communication and led to changes in the firm's SDG-focus. Again, a successful SDG implementation is constructed around targets, measures and actions.

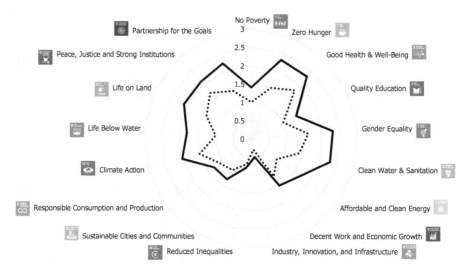

Fig. 5.3 Communication intensity of SDG's in pharma industry. Company X (*regular line*) versus industry peers (*dotted line*). Source: Finch & Beak/Datamaran

Once the peer analysis is complete, the selection of appropriate SDGs and associated targets is back on the table. To turn this into action, a measurement system is to be put in place by converting the SDG targets into a dashboard with key performance indicators for daily measurement and periodic reporting. With the target and measure stages firmly in place, the formulation of the action plan is the natural next step.

Forward-thinking companies have been mapping their selected SDGs with their strategic must-win battles, to increase boardroom relevance of the SDGs. A good example of this translation can be found at Dow Chemical. Dow plans to lead the transition to a sustainable planet and society, and this lofty target for 2025 has been translated into seven specific goals to achieve this. To turn these sustainability goals into actions, Dow concentrated on three themes (1) unlocking the potential of people and science, (2) valuing nature and (3) building courageous coalitions. By mapping the SDGs on its seven 2025 goals, Dow ensured that its sustainable development efforts became fully integrated into the firm's strategy. In line with the target-measure-act phasing, the SDGs also have been included in the company's integrated annual reports.

Partnering Required: Access to Medicine and Sanitation

Peer analysis would seem to support the view that competition is a source of energy for effective sustainability efforts. At the same time, so is cooperation and partnering because the world's biggest challenges cannot be solved in isolation [8]. To reach ambitious sustainability goals, global partnerships are nothing less than unavoidable. Again, we can look at the fields of pharmaceuticals and personal hygiene for valuable lessons.

For the pharmaceutical industry, SDG 3 (Good Health and Wellbeing) is a natural focus of attention. GlaxoSmithKline (GSK) is a pharmaceutical company that has been successful in incorporating SDG 3.8—achieving access to safe, effective, quality and affordable essential medicines and vaccines for all— within its business strategy. In fact, GSK has been ranked by the Dutch independent initiative Access to Medicine Index [9] as the best research-based pharmaceutical company for its effort to improve access to medicine in 107 low- and middle-income countries.

Thanks to its equitable pricing strategies, through intellectual property leniency in poorer nations, GSK has been able to act upon one of the most pressing health issues, thereby building tremendous goodwill and a strong market presence. Partnerships have been crucial for GSK's success. Scalability has been achieved by partnering with academic institutions across Africa, local governments and at times even competitors, such as Johnson & Johnson. These partnerships helped GSK leverage its R&D capabilities, ensure better access to products and ultimately facilitates commercialization in new markets. By establishing a scalable access-to-medicine strategy with a large impact on high-priority needs, GSK developed its business in developing countries, which now accounts for approximately 25% of its global sales, opening up new markets and engaging a vast new pool of consumers often referred to as "the other 6 billion" people by GSK CEO Andrew Witty.

SDG 6 (Clean Water and Sanitation) resonates with Unilever, which owns brands such as Lifebuoy, Domestos and Signal. The Unilever Sustainable Living Plan is aimed at improving the handwashing habits of one billion people, reducing the incidence of child deaths by 44%, and enhancing sales of its products in India and Pakistan, two countries with the highest rates of diarrhea-related child deaths. To scale the impact and deliver the message, partnerships with local entities and governments were crucial as they had local knowledge and expertise. A program called the *Perfect*

Village [10] was created to drive awareness, knowledge and adoption of Unilever products in hard-to-reach rural communities. The program included product education sessions and health, beauty and hygiene workshops for the community on, for example, the importance of handwashing to prevent the spread of disease. While delivering hygiene to hard-to-reach rural areas, Perfect Village sowed the seeds of development in local retailing, creating growth for years to come.

According to Unilever, sustainable living brands, internally defined as products with positive social and environmental purposes at heart, are growing 30% faster than conventional brands, indicating benefits on two dimensions—business and societal. Unilever's definition of what makes a true Sustainable Living brand was not only based on having a clear purpose that helped tackle a social or environmental concern, but also it had to contribute to one or more of the targets set in the Unilever Sustainable Living Plan, which, in turn contributed to the 17 SDGs [11].

Local and Global: Not Just the Developing Countries

As part of the UN 2030 agenda, SDG 6 aims to ensure the availability and sustainable management of water and sanitation for all. With water scarcity and flood resilience becoming growing issues in many countries, partnerships to address SDG 6 are no longer the exclusive preserve of developing countries. Once regarded as a "distant" problem, water has become a topic on a global scale with many, if not most, major cities around the globe facing fresh water challenges.

Global topics within the SDGs do not always require large-scale, global initiatives. Take the example of a centuries-old industry—brewing. Making beer requires a lot of water—UK brewers on average consume 4.1 liters of water to produce a liter of brew. And that is after the brewers have managed to squeeze a 39% reduction in that number since 1990 [12]. Not surprisingly, as the scarcity and prices of fresh water rise, breweries are spending ever more efforts on reducing water usage by investing in water-efficient technology. Dutch brewer Bavaria presents an interesting example with its "Boer, Bier, Water" (Farmer, Beer, Water) initiative in the Netherlands. In this local small-scale initiative, Bavaria collaborates with local farmers, banks, government and other stakeholders to preserve resources. With farmers incentivized to use less pesticides to grow the brewer's barley, the main results of the program are centered around water efficiency, crop protection and soil quality. The promotion of locally sourced brewer's barley as a crop also offers a reputational premium for the brewer.

☞ Defining a Vectoring Approach to Sustainable Development: The SDG Proposition Workshop

When a firm contemplates the development of an SDG initiative but does not have the resources to conduct full-fledged research on this, a simple workshop version of the SDG analysis can be helpful. The workshop takes about three hours and can be held with a group of approximately 8–12 people, preferably with diverse backgrounds. Some participants might even be outside experts on specific topics such as climate change or water preservation.

To apply the tool, make sure to start with the definition of material sustainability topics for the firm. This is the time to pull back the previously constructed materiality matrix if it exists. If not, a solid brainstorming with the participants can set the proper base for the exercise. If needed, these topics can be organized in categories of importance, from high to low.

Next, you can ask the participants to each create up to five Post-it Note items containing the company's most relevant strategic initiatives. Discuss the initiatives and cluster them if necessary. As a last step in the preparation phase, determine in plenary the geographies best targeted by the SDG initiatives.

Once the premises for the exercise have been laid out (materiality matrix + strategic initiatives + target geographies), the main portion of the workshop can start. Participants are then asked to conduct a brainstorm (in pairs) on potential SDG initiatives, again with Post-it Notes. Once there is a decent number of initiatives displayed on the wall, have the participants present their ideas, and cluster them if necessary. Once the exercise is completed, sort the proposed initiatives into the quadrants of potential societal and business impacts through plenary discussion and select jointly the top five initiatives through voting. Draw lines between the individual SDGs and the selected ideas. Finally, connect the ideas to the sustainability topics, must-win battles and geographies (refer to Fig. 5.4).

Download the SDG Proposition poster in A0 format, the associated facilitator guide and proposed workshop agenda from www.vectoring.online.

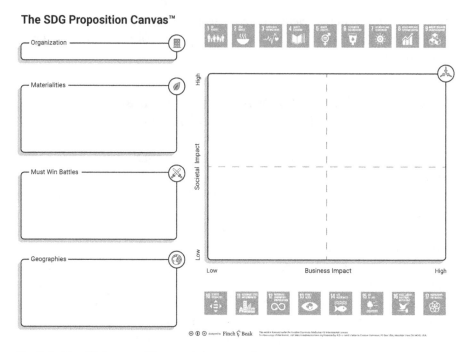

Fig. 5.4   The SDG proposition workshop template

🗂 How Umicore Integrates Sustainability and SDGs into Its Strategy [13]

Umicore, a Belgium-headquartered global materials group, has undergone a remarkable transformation over the last three decades, from a stagnant mining company with a dreadful environmental and social track record to a true global leader in the emerging global circular economy. Umicore's heritage dates back to 1805, when Napoleon Bonaparte granted Jean-Jacques Dony control of the valuable Vieille-Montagne zinc mine located between Liège and Aachen. Vieille-Montagne became the first building block of the group. A century later, the Union Minière du Haut Katanga was formed to mine mineral deposits in that province of the Belgian Congo.

Following this turbulent colonial past, the merger of four Belgian mining and metals companies in 1989 laid the foundation for what would soon become Umicore. Going through a global economic slump and a change of parent company during the 1990s, the merged organization was eager to make some big changes. When Thomas Leysen became the new CEO in May

2000, he set out on a path to transform the company, at this point essentially a non-ferrous mining company, into an international materials-technology group. The new name, Umicore, also enabled it to divorce itself from its controversial role in the Belgian Congo.

All member states committed to helping achieve these goals, which advocated among others environmental sustainability, reversing the loss of environmental resources and reducing CO_2 emissions.

Ready for the Future: Environment, People and New Business

Umicore's new strategic choices kickstarted a major reshuffling process. The copper and zinc businesses were divested and spun-off, and several large strategic acquisitions were made, including Precious Metal Group, a leading global producer of car catalysts, and specialty chemicals company Hall. Vigorously addressing its legacy and showing pro-active environmental management leadership, Umicore embarked on a massive clean-up and site-remediation effort, with €174 million in investments spread across major sites in Flanders, Wallonia, Bulgaria, the Netherlands and France.

As a formal commitment to employees and other stakeholders, Umicore signed a Global Framework Agreement in collaboration with workers' unions and federations, covering an array of issues such as human rights, working conditions and environment. This also included the company's commitment to the UN Declaration of Human Rights and the International Labour Organization's core labor standards. In line with its new strategy and company culture, Umicore upgraded its corporate communication standards to display its improved practices better. The company's first integrated annual report was released in 2007, combining both financial and non-financial information.

Competing with Clean Technologies

What emerged of the transformation was a global materials technology giant focused on application areas where its expertise in materials science, chemistry and metallurgy could provide competitive advantages. In November 2010, Umicore's reformulation of its strategy was launched as *Vision 2015* [14] to generate a new wave of growth to reap the fruits of the heavy investments made during the prior five years. The company increased its concentration on clean technologies, aligning its growth focus with long-term megatrends including resource scarcity, emissions control, renewable energy and electrification of the automobile. Not accidentally, these new objectives were perfectly in line with the ambitions of the Millennium Development Goals.

The company's commitment to clean technologies did not go unnoticed. In 2013, Umicore was named "the world's most sustainable company" by Corporate Knights, receiving praise for its focus on clean technologies, including emission-control catalysts, materials for rechargeable batteries and photovoltaics, and advanced recycling. But awards are no substitute for profits and from a shareholder perspective, Umicore was urged to monetize its sustainability efforts better, in terms of market share and positive press but also by truly leveraging its prime position in competitiveness. Umicore started to look even more intensely for value-creating opportunities to turn its sustainability advantage into clear financial gains.

Strategy for Profitable Growth: Horizon 2020

The importance of sustainable innovation was reinforced again in Umicore's *Horizon 2020* strategy, launched in September 2015. It targeted accelerated growth and performance, aiming by 2020 to [15]:

- Achieve clear leadership in clean mobility materials and recycling
- Double the size of the business in terms of earnings
- Rebalance the portfolio and earnings contributions
- Turn sustainability into a lasting competitive edge.

That same month, the successors to the Millennium Development Goals, the UN Sustainable Development Goals, were announced. For Umicore, with its years of involvement in environmental and social leadership, it was an easy step to align its business model to these new SDGs and document how its activities contributed to achieving the goals. In the company's Annual Report 2016, the link between megatrends, their impact on Umicore businesses and Umicore's contributions to the various SDGs were elegantly explained (refer to Table 5.2) [16]:

Pay Off Time: Flourishing in a Volatile World

With the fast-increasing global production of lithium batteries, the price of one of its main raw materials, cobalt, continued to flare up, tripling in 2016 and 2017. This inspired the Democratic Republic of Congo, the world's leading

Table 5.2 Link between megatrends, their impact on Umicore businesses and Umicore's contributions to the various SDGs

Megatrend	Potential impact	Umicore's contribution	Related to SDGs
Resource scarcity "Trends such as continued population growth, urbanization and more affluent lifestyles are driving ever-higher demand for resources. This poses the question: how will we meet future demand?"	"Demand for most metals will increase as a result of population growth and urbanization and also because of their use in technologies that aim to reduce society's environmental impacts"	"Our closed loop business model ensures that we extract the valuable metals from industrial residues and end-of-life materials enabling them to be reused"	• 8: Decent Work and Economic Growth • 12: Responsible Consumption and Production
Clean air "Regulation has gradually led to a reduction in air pollution in many countries and regions over the past 30 years. However, much more needs to be done and there are still major challenges to human health from poor air quality."	"Recent data analysis revealed that air pollution is the fourth deadliest health risk worldwide"	"We are one of the world's leading producers of catalysts and catalytic filters used in emission abatement systems for light-duty and heavy-duty vehicles as well as off-road equipment"	• 3: Good Health & Well-being • 11: Sustainable Cities and Communities
Vehicle electrification "Worldwide, the transport sector causes 14% of all greenhouse gas emissions due to human activities and this is still growing. Electrified mobility will play a key role in reducing CO_2 emissions, improving air quality and reducing dependence on fossil fuels"	"The transport sector is the fastest growing source of greenhouse gases, mainly via CO_2 emissions from road vehicles"	"Umicore is one of the world's leading producers of cathode materials for lithium ion batteries. Cathode materials are key in determining the power and energy density of rechargeable batteries, and hence the driving range in the case of electrified vehicles"	• 11: Sustainable Cities and Communities • 13: Climate Action

Source: Umicore's Annual Report 2016

cobalt producer, to raise its taxes and royalties on metals, including copper and cobalt in early 2018. And to protect its electric-vehicle industry, China began aggressively buying controlling interests in the largest mines in the Congo. Companies such as Apple, Tesla and others were experiencing shortages in the supply of sustainable cobalt [17]. Unsurprisingly, all these market developments favored Umicore, with the window of opportunity for recycled cobalt growing bigger and bigger [18].

Umicore's shareholders, for once, were more than satisfied. In February 2018, Umicore reported record performance for the 2017 financial year. Growth was strongly driven by its Energy & Surface Technologies business group, which increased its revenues by 46%, mostly due to volume growth in rechargeable battery materials. As the company reported in its FY2017 results [19]:

> Global demand for Li-ion rechargeable batteries used in electrified vehicles will continue to grow fast as automotive OEMs[2] roll out their electrification strategy. Further strengthening of emission targets, particularly in China and Europe, is pushing OEMs to put more electrified models with longer driving ranges on the road. NMC[3] is the chemistry of choice for batteries used in plug-in hybrid and full electric vehicles and demand for this chemistry is growing rapidly. Umicore is benefiting disproportionately from this trend due to its competitive offer of a wide range of high-quality transportation grade NMC-products, a unique ability to scale up fast, and the early qualification with a large number of cell manufacturers and automotive OEMs.

Market developments and the company's financial results underline the relevance of the choices the company has made in previous decades and demonstrates that integrating sustainability into strategy is paying off for Umicore.

Tips, Traps and Takeaways

👍 Tips

- Follow the Champions 12.3 example of taking a target-measure-act approach.
- Address only the most relevant SDGs and concentrate on turning plans into actions with the help of clear monitoring.

---

[2] Original equipment manufacturers (OEMs) are companies that produce parts and equipment that may be marketed by another manufacturer. Source: Wikipedia.
[3] Nickel Manganese Cobalt.

- Link the Sustainable Development Goals to your existing materiality matrix, solve potential conflicts and complete the program where gaps appear.
- Consider building a coalition of the willing in your value chain with fellow stakeholders for the realization of action plans.
- The complete overview of the 17 SDG and its 169 targets is downloadable from the www.vectoring.online website.

☀ Traps

- Beware of insufficient pruning of SDGs on relevance resulting in a lack of focus (and subsequently lack of results).
- Challenge and test the relationship of the selected SDGs with the company strategy and/or the materiality matrix.
- Avoid looking for isolated approaches, with little partnership and collaboration. No man is an island.[4]
- A paternalistic framing, viewing the SDGs as a faraway challenge, is a set-up for failure. If your business is solely local, make your SDG program local.

☝ Takeaways

This chapter highlighted the need to base the design of the SDGs on actionability. Successful deployment of SDG activities requires a method similar to the one applied to materiality analysis in the previous chapter. Together with the inspiring advocacy of the Champions 12.3 on food waste, the cases of GlaxoSmithKline and Unilever confirmed the need for direction and speed, that is, vectoring, when addressing the SDGs. For effective deployment of SDG initiatives, Champions 12.3 suggests applying a three-step principle: target-measure-act to develop business cases contributing to the realization of the SDG targets. The SDGs offer opportunities in many forms and sizes; the key concern for companies is to actively contribute to some of these goals.

The chapter also highlights two leading prerequisites crucial to success:

1. The alignment of the selected SDGs and the intended solutions with the existing priorities in the company's strategy and sustainability program. A

---

[4] "No man is an island" refers to a poem by John Donne (January 22, 1572–March 31, 1631), a Jacobean metaphysical poet. His works include sonnets, love poetry, religious poems, Latin translations, epigrams, elegies, songs and sermons. Source: Wikiquote.

mapping exercise to scrutinize the SDG alignment is therefore recommended.

2. Notwithstanding the suggested SDG peer analysis to come to grips with the overall SDG landscape within the industry, the development of partnerships within the value chain, big and small, global or local, are indispensable. Partnering can be developed in a horizontal sense (with peers), a vertical sense (with value chain partners) or both. Sustainability leaders researched for the book were all inclined to involve a mix of stakeholders such as policy makers, companies, investors, academics and startup innovators. The problems with partnering are specifically addressed in Chap. 9.

The SDG proposition tool introduced in this chapter presents an easy-do-deploy workshop model that can be used to generate ideas on SDG initiatives, design productive partnerships, align relevant sustainability topics with the firm's must-win battles and geographies, and bring forward initiatives that impact both society and business.

Capturing the business opportunities that emerge from the SDGs is frequently facilitated by the engagement born out of working on topics aimed at creating a better world together. In the words of one of the great Greek tragedians Sophocles:

To be doing good deeds is man's most glorious task.

Nevertheless, the rules of competition and business still apply, and the presence of a legitimate business case is essential, as the story of Pep Lemón painfully illustrated.

Exhibit 5.1: The Sustainable Development Goals: Examples SDG 6 and 7 [20]

To illustrate the challenges the United Nations Sustainable Development Goals (UN SDGs) are addressing, and to convey some of the inspirational value that is encapsulated within its definitions, two example SDGs are detailed below. The challenges and the impact achievements are sourced from the UN's first accounting of where the world stands at the start of the collective journey to 2030, the Sustainable Development Goals Report 2016. The targets are directly taken from the UN's sustainable development knowledge platform.

Goal 6: Clean Water & Sanitation

Challenges and Impact Achievements

Goal 6 goes beyond drinking water, sanitation and hygiene to also address the quality and sustainability of water resources. Achieving this Goal, which is critical to the survival of people and the planet, means expanding international cooperation and garnering the support of local communities in improving water and sanitation management.

- In 2015, 6.6 billion people, or 91% of the global population, used an improved drinking water source, compared with 82% in 2000. However, in 2015 an estimated 663 million people were still using unimproved sources or surface water.
- Between 2000 and 2015, the proportion of the global population using improved sanitation increased from 59 per cent to 68 per cent. However, 2.4 billion were left behind. Among them were 946 million people without any facilities at all who continue to practice open defecation.
- Water stress affects more than 2 billion people around the globe, a figure that is projected to rise.
- Integrated Water Resources Management plans are under way in every region of the world.

The Road Ahead: Targets

6.1   By 2030, achieve universal and equitable access to safe and affordable drinking water for all

6.2   By 2030, achieve access to adequate and equitable sanitation and hygiene for all and end open defecation, paying special attention to the needs of women and girls and those in vulnerable situations

6.3   By 2030, improve water quality by reducing pollution, eliminating dumping and minimizing release of hazardous chemicals and materials, halving the proportion of untreated wastewater and substantially increasing recycling and safe reuse globally

6.4   By 2030, substantially increase water-use efficiency across all sectors and ensure sustainable withdrawals and supply of freshwater to address water scarcity and substantially reduce the number of people suffering from water scarcity

6.5   By 2030, implement integrated water resources management at all levels, including through transboundary cooperation as appropriate

6.6   By 2020, protect and restore water-related ecosystems, including mountains, forests, wetlands, rivers, aquifers and lakes

6.a   By 2030, expand international cooperation and capacity-building support to developing countries in water- and sanitation-related activities and programs, including water harvesting, desalination, water efficiency, wastewater treatment, recycling and reuse technologies

6.b   Support and strengthen the participation of local communities in improving water and sanitation management

Goal 7: Affordable & Clean Energy

Challenges and Impact Achievements

Goal 7 seeks to promote broader energy access and increased use of renewable energy, including through enhanced international cooperation and expanded infrastructure and technology for clean energy.

- The proportion of the global population with access to electricity increased steadily, from 79% in 2000 to 85% in 2012. Despite these improvements, 1.1 billion people were still without this essential service in 2012.
- In 2014, some 3 billion people, over 40% of the world's population, relied on polluting and unhealthy fuels for cooking.
- Modern renewables grew rapidly, at a rate of 4% a year between 2010 and 2012.
- Global energy intensity improved by 1.3% a year from 2000 to 2012. About 68% of the energy savings between 2010 and 2012 came from developing regions, with Eastern Asia as the largest contributor.

The Road Ahead: Targets

7.1   By 2030, ensure universal access to affordable, reliable and modern energy services

7.2   By 2030, increase substantially the share of renewable energy in the global energy mix

7.3   By 2030, double the global rate of improvement in energy efficiency

7.a   By 2030, enhance international cooperation to facilitate access to clean energy research and technology, including renewable energy, energy efficiency and advanced and cleaner fossil-fuel technology, and promote investment in energy infrastructure and clean energy technology

7.b   By 2030, expand infrastructure and upgrade technology for supplying modern and sustainable energy services for all in developing countries, in particular least developed countries, small island developing States, and land-locked developing countries, in accordance with their respective programs of support

A comprehensive overview of all 17 SDGs with the complete 168 targets can be found on www.vectoring.online.

References

1. Solberg, E. (2015, September 25) From Global Conversation to Global Action, Statement by Prime Minister Erna Solberg, UN Sustainable Development Summit 2015, New York, September 25, 2015. https://www.regjeringen.no/en/aktuelt/from-global-conversation-to-global-action/id2454205/

2. Niculescu, M. (2017, July 13) Impact investment to close the SDG funding gap. *UNDP*. Retrieved from http://www.undp.org/content/undp/en/home/blog/2017/7/13/What-kind-of-blender-do-we-need-to-finance-the-SDGs-.html

3. Champion 12.3 (2017) *The business case for reducing food loss and waste.* https://champions123.org/the-business-case-for-reducing-food-loss-and-waste/

4. Food and Agriculture organization of the United Nations (2015) *The State of Food Insecurity in the World.* http://www.fao.org/3/a-i4646e.pdf

5. Garcia Bustos, J.A. (2018, March 17) Pep Lemon cierra vendiendo más. *Diario de Mallorca.* Retrieved from http://www.mallorcadiario.com/pep-lemon-cierra-vendiendo-mas

6. PepsiCo (2016) 2016 Annual Report. Retrieved from https://www.pepsico.com/docs/album/annual-reports/pepsico-inc-2016-annual-report.pdf

7. Christensen, C.M., Bartman, T., van Bever, D. (2016) *The hard truth about business model innovation.* Cambridge, MA: Sloan Management Review Association, MIT Sloan School of Management.

8. Kroll, C. & Annan, K.A. (2015) *Sustainable Development Goals: Are the rich countries ready?* Germany: Bertelsmann Stiftung. Retrieved from http://www.sgi-network.org/docs/studies/SDGs_Are-the-rich-countries-ready_2015.pdf

9. Access to Medicine Index (2018) 2016 Access to Medicine Index Overall Ranking. https://accesstomedicineindex.org/overall-ranking/. Accessed April 15, 2018.

10. Unilever (2017) Improving lives in rural Vietnam. https://www.unilever.com/news/news-and-features/Feature-article/2017/nguyen-hieu-tho.html. Accessed April 15, 2018.
11. Unilever (2018) Embedding sustainability. https://www.unilever.com/sustainable-living/our-strategy/embedding-sustainability/. Accessed April 15, 2018.
12. British Beer & Pub Association (2015) *Brewing green 2015: Our commitment towards a greener future for Britain's beer and pubs.* Retrieved from http://s3.amazonaws.com/bbpa-prod/attachments/documents/uploads/23857/original/Brewing%20Green%202015%20website%20copy.pdf?1450438083
13. This case is an abridged version of UMICORE: URBAN MINING AND THE MONETIZATION OF SUSTAINABILITY (IMD-7-1708) Copyright © 2018 by IMD—International Institute for Management Development, Lausanne, Switzerland (www.imd.org). No part of this publication may be reproduced, stored in a retrieval system or transmitted in any form or by any means without the prior written permission of IMD.
14. Grynberg, M. (2010, November) Vision 2015 [PowerPoint slides]. Retrieved from Umicore website http://www.umicore.com/storage/migrate/2010CMD_Vision2015.pdf
15. Grynberg, M. (2015, September) Strategic update [PowerPoint slides]. Retrieved from Umicore website http://www.umicore.com/storage/migrate/2015CMD_StrategicUpdate.pdf
16. Umicore (2017) *Annual Report 2017*. Retrieved from http://annualreport.umicore.com/our-business/global-trends/
17. Hermes, J. (2017, May 31) Shortage of ethically sourced cobalt from Congo causes trouble for GE, Apple, Tesla … and more. *Environmental Leader*. Retrieved from https://www.environmentalleader.com/2017/05/shortage-ethically-sourced-cobalt-congo-causes-trouble-ge-apple-tesla/
18. Clowes, W. (2018, January 25) Congo raises cobalt, copper taxes amid opposition from miners. *Bloomberg*. Retrieved from https://www.bloomberg.com/news/articles/2018-01-25/congo-raises-cobalt-copper-taxes-amid-opposition-from-miners
19. Umicore (2018, February) Umicore announces record results, growth acceleration and capital increase [Press release]. Retrieved from http://www.umicore.com/storage/main/2017fypressreleaseen.pdf
20. United Nations (2016) *The Sustainable Development Goals Report 2016*. Retrieved from http://www.un.org.lb/Library/Assets/The-Sustainable-Development-Goals-Report-2016-Global.pdf

6

ESG Ratings and the Stock Markets

After introducing the primary components of a proper vectoring approach, namely a sound company purpose, a focus on a small set of relevant materialities synchronized to the Sustainable Development Goals, we endeavor to explore the connection between sustainability and the environmental, social and governance (ESG) ratings and how the latter are evaluated by stock markets. With the help of several company examples, this chapter first examines the increasing awareness of ESG factors within the investment community, then moves on to suggest an approach for designing a company-specific ESG ratings game plan. An overview of the most influential ESG ratings is also provided, including a summary of their background, methodology and typical usage.

Darwinians at the Gate[1]: Shareholders and Sustainability

Make no mistake, around the globe, shareholders big and small have started to pay attention to sustainability as a driver of value creation. In the past, investor relations departments could safely ascertain that shareholders paid very limited attention to the sustainability issues of their investments, but the story today is radically different and *ignorance-is-bliss* strategies have outlived their usefulness.

---

[1] Darwinians at the Gate is a play on words taken from the title of the IMD 2013 case on DSM (IMD-3-2355) of which an abridged version is included in this chapter. The phrase is referring to "Barbarians at the Gate: The Fall of RJR Nabisco," which is a book about the leveraged buyout of RJR Nabisco by raiders, written by investigative journalists Bryan Burrough and John Helyar (1989).

© The Author(s) 2019
B. Leleux, J. van der Kaaij, *Winning Sustainability Strategies*,
https://doi.org/10.1007/978-3-319-97445-3_6

Table 6.1 Signatories and assets under management (2006–2017) of principles for responsible investment

Year	Assets under management (US$ trillion)	Number of asset owners	Assets under management (US$ trillion)	Number of signatories
2006	2.0	32	6.5	63
2007	3.2	77	10	185
2008	4.2	135	13	361
2009	3.6	172	18	523
2010	4.8	203	21	734
2011	5.5	229	24	890
2012	7.6	251	32	1050
2013	10.5	268	34	1186
2014	11.2	270	45	1251
2015	13.2	288	59	1384
2016	13.9	307	62	1501
2017	16.3	346	68.4	1714

Source: PRI website, retrieved March 10, 2018

To validate that assertion, one can look, for example, at the UN Principles for Responsible Investment (PRI),[2] which expects its signatories to incorporate ESG issues in their investment analysis and decision-making processes. The PRI purports to turn investors into *active* owners incorporating ESG issues into ownership policies and practices. The statistics on PRI signatories over the last decade, shown in Table 6.1, support the sizable increase in awareness and concern among investors and asset managers around the world.

To stress the tangible commitment represented by joining the movement, the PRI coordinating body announced in 2018 that it had put 185 of it signatories on a watchlist after growing criticism that they were not taking their commitments seriously enough [1]. Companies on the watchlist were given two years to make improvements and fulfill PRI's minimum requirements.

The ESG concerns have also evolved from simple negative screening, that is, the practice of excluding whole sectors, individual companies or certain practices from investment portfolios based upon negative ESG factors, toward a more pro-active position on sustainability. Active ownership [2] is on the rise, with more shareholders exercising their rights as investors to influence company ESG policies. Active owners, through voting and engagement, encourage companies to improve their ESG results. Of course, the vested interest or expecta-

---

[2] The PRI is the world's leading proponent of responsible investment. It works to understand the investment implications of ESG factors and to support its international network of investor signatories in incorporating these factors in their investment and ownership decisions. The PRI acts in the long-term interests of its signatories, the financial markets and economies in which they operate and ultimately the environment and society.

tion is that such an improved ESG profile will lead to decreased costs, enhanced competitiveness and ultimately better profitability for the investments.

🗁 The CADMOS Engagement Funds and the Buy and Care Strategy [3]

As an example, let us look at CADMOS, one of the pioneer funds created by de Pury Pictet Turrettini & Cie S.A. (PPT) [4], a Geneva-based wealth management boutique. In 2006, PPT launched the CADMOS European Engagement Fund aimed at going beyond what the general socially responsible investments (SRIs) were offering and promoting active engagement between shareholders and companies. It was followed in 2009 by the CADMOS Emerging Markets Engagement Fund, then by the CADMOS Swiss Engagement Fund in 2014. By the first quarter of 2018, PPT had reached CHF 3.8 billion in assets under management on behalf of institutional and individual clients.

Over the period, PPT developed a sophisticated approach for its engagement funds, which it labeled the Buy & Care investment strategy. The process was built around three founding principles:

- Promoting deeper company analyses
- Better portfolio management
- Fostering more active ownership.

> We put in extra efforts to ensure a holistic view on the companies and sounder assessment models to ascertain the companies' competitive advantages. We ensured an active engagement at all levels to deepen our understanding of the companies and their needs to develop new social impacting strategies. [5]

The team at CADMOS expanded the standard assessment by establishing 14 criteria to gauge the quality of the ESG corporate efforts and reports. An additional complexity of course was to evaluate the adherence of a company to its stated ESG principles. A four-step company assessment ensued.

Step 1 gathered the company's sustainability data, condensing it into nine topics. Together, these topics encompassed the issues identified by classic sustainability frameworks, such as the UN Global Compact, the Global Reporting Initiative, the UN Guiding Principles and the Sustainable Development Goals. From these nine material topics, the team would select three for each company, depending on that company's characteristics and industry sector.

Step 2 developed a company-specific analysis using Michael Porter's Five Forces model, creating a link between the companies' competitive advantage and their social responsibility.

Step 3 involved benchmarking the companies' preparedness, gauging the quality of ESG-driven reports and weighting the maturity of the company's social-impact strategies. Preparedness was assessed according to five criteria (materiality & salience, commitment & strategy, objectives & actions, indicators & monitoring, achievements & remediation). Reporting quality was assessed on six criteria (accessibility, clarity, comparability, accuracy, reliability and integration). Maturity of the strategies involved four criteria as well: impact commitment, adherence to standards & bodies, leadership commitment and proof of past partnerships.

Step 4 required compiling a summarized version of the assessment, aimed at highlighting a company's strengths and weaknesses and addressing its main sustainability gaps.

A key element of the strategy was to establish and maintain an active dialogue with the portfolio companies and engage with them to improve their profile. The proximity with the executive board of each company facilitated regular reviews on preparedness and the quality of the reports. The secondary goal was to actively contribute to the definition of areas of potential improvement.

From Engagement to Results

Active engagement does not necessarily lead to results; it is a long road from getting institutional investors to *consider* integrating ESG variables into their investment decisions to *actually factoring* ESG parameters directly into their valuations. A number of obstacles stand in the way of this transition.

First comes the issue of identifying ESG issues that are material to the valuation. Sector analysts often have difficulty interpreting the information provided by company reports and ESG rating agencies and translating those into their valuation models. To overcome this problem, investment firms have started to demand higher-quality information on ESG issues from the companies they cover. An example of this evolution is the 2018 annual letter by CEO Larry Fink of investment behemoth BlackRock[3] aimed at CEOs of large corporations. The letter, suitably titled, "A Sense of Purpose," stressed the need for companies to include societal impact in their decision making:

[3] BlackRock is a leading publicly traded investment management firm with $6.288 trillion of assets under management at December 31, 2017. With approximately 13,900 employees in more than 30 countries, BlackRock provides a broad range of investment, risk management and technology services to institutional and retail clients worldwide (Source: BlackRock website).

Society is demanding that companies, both public and private, serve a social purpose. To prosper over time, every company must not only deliver financial performance, but also show how it makes a positive contribution to society. Companies must benefit all their stakeholders, including shareholders, employees, customers, and the communities in which they operate.

Your company's strategy must articulate a path to achieve financial performance. To sustain that performance, however, you must also understand the societal impact of your business as well as the ways that broad, structural trends—from slow wage growth to rising automation to climate change—affect your potential for growth.

Larry Fink, CEO BlackRock [6]

Larry Fink's letter was not totally unexpected; it was the natural next step in a long string of annual letters and the confirmation of BlackRock's commitment to *long-term sustainability*. More surprising though was the fact that in March 2018, barely two months after Larry's letter was made public, his points found a new resonance with the emergence of the Cambridge Analytica scandal. Specialists had sounded the alarm about the limited governance and risk exposure of data-harvesting firms for over a decade, but it was on March 16, 2018, that it exploded into full public view when Facebook announced it was suspending Strategic Communication Laboratories (SCL), the parent company of political data analytics firm Cambridge Analytica [7]. The reason? Potential misuse of personal information of more than 50 million Facebook users by Cambridge Analytica. Facebook's share price plunged on the news as investors factored in the implications for a key component of the company's business model, that is, the sale of personal user information. For large investors, the short-term stock market correction was a worry for sure; even more worrisome was the impact of the breach on lawmakers from the US, Europe and other regions of the world who saw some of their worst fears confirmed and who jolted into action, calling for tighter regulation for data sharing and usage.

Within the media sector, data security had been discussed as a key materiality for years, but it was the Cambridge Analytica scandal that put the spotlight on the possibility that new privacy laws could permanently impede Facebook's license to operate. Just 11 days later, at the end of March 2018, it was reported that Facebook had lost a little over $100 billion in market valuation [8]. With celebrities such as Apple co-founder Steve Wozniak and Tesla's Elon Musk joining the *Delete Facebook* movement, the risk of long-term brand damage had become a harsh reality.

The Increasing Burden of Non-Financial Reporting

With the rising importance of ESG data and increasing stakeholder demands, companies are often overwhelmed by the sheer volume of reporting now expected from them. Besides annual (integrated) reports, they are now expected to respond to ESG benchmarks, sustainability ratings, and supply chain surveys, tasks that can drain the energy of even the best-intentioned sustainability team.

To cope with the increasing reporting demands, a number of avenues are available. First, a solid integration of the sustainability key performance indicators (KPIs) within the regular management structure helps reduce the extra burden. Next, the establishment of a selective set of sustainability issues to report about decreases the necessary efforts. But the growing demand for non-financial reporting keeps acting as a magnet for resources, sometimes to the point of putting the sustainability compass at risk and precipitating companies into what is sometimes described as the *Reporting Trap* [9]. With so much expected on the reporting front, what is actually left in terms of resources to effectively improve the business impact of the company on society?

New legislations on ESG disclosures continue to be adopted rapidly around the world. For instance, the EU Directive [10] on non-financial and diversity information established a roadmap for corporate ESG reporting in Europe. After its original announcement in 2014, all EU member states have incorporated it into national legislations, requiring compliance from fiscal year 2017 onwards. All companies with 500+ employees, a balance sheet exceeding €20 million in assets and/or a net turnover of €40 million fall within the scope of the directive and have to report on the objectives of their sustainability policies, how they are applied, as well as the results of the implementations as an integral part of their corporate governance statement. Companies are also obliged to publish a diversity statement for age, gender and professional and educational background of their board members.

The Evolving Landscape of ESG Ratings

With sustainability taking hold and becoming ever more multi-faceted, institutional investors, asset managers and financial institutions have been forced to rely increasingly on third parties to assess ESG performance, creating a whole new industry of service providers. The ESG rating agency arena has developed into a global business, even bringing in big names such as

Bloomberg, MSCI and Thomson Reuters. For companies, obtaining ESG ratings has many implications beyond just the cost and time needed to participate; these include understanding the specifics of each rating, such as their business model and the way the ratings are published, distributed and applied [11]. Companies need to make sure they do not end up being rated on issues that are not material to them and thus unfairly downgraded in the ratings. On the flip side, participation in ESG ratings can bring additional attention for sustainability from the C-suite, provide useful analysis and feedback to improve sustainability programs and become a welcome source of peer information.

The ESG ratings market has enjoyed considerable growth with many newcomers, local and global, trying to claim their share. In a marketplace set for consolidation, ESG rating agencies have been forced to innovate and improve their services continuously. Take the previously introduced case of Volkswagen's *Dieselgate*. Volkswagen had been included in the DJSI automotive industry listing for 13 years in a row. After 2015, when the uncovering of manipulated emissions tests at the German car manufacturer led to the loss of some $30 billion of the company's value, ESG raters were forced to respond. Since Volkswagen had been showcased as an industry leader in terms of fuel efficiency prior to the scandal, the reputation of the data accuracy from the various ESG raters was considered to be at stake.

This response by ESG agencies is well exemplified by what happened to the automotive industry in the DJSI. The 2017 DJSI data for automotive showed a noticeable decline in the overall industry score compared to previous years (refer to Fig. 6.1). The 3% drop in the overall score between 2015 and 2016 and the subsequent 10% plunge between 2016 and 2017 were in part thought to be driven by *refinements* to the annual ESG questionnaire for the automotive industry and the adjustments of the applicable weight factors.

Fig. 6.1 DJSI score drop in the automotive industry from 2015–2017 (restated for research purposes)

Designing an ESG Ratings Game Plan

ESG ratings are complex and getting more so. Hence, it is crucial for companies to develop an appropriate game plan to deal with them. The first question is whether they should bother to participate in the first place. When answered positively, then the question turns to sorting through the various ESG rating schemes for the one that is most appropriate. In this section, we elaborate on our initial theme of vectoring, showing that it provides solid predictions in this arena, strongly suggesting that companies are wise to opt for ESG benchmarks that have material impact for them, prioritizing their limited resources for relevant benchmarks and ratings only. It is all too easy to lose focus when contributing to society, but focus is the key to sustainable implementation.

Commencing projects with the *why* question is never a bad idea. Is the company participating in the ESG ratings to learn from its benchmarking or does it want to tell the investment community how well it is performing on ESG issues, or both? Learning and communicating are perfectly valid as objectives, but it is still essential to define precisely which is/are being pursued to ensure the proper measurement of success. Companies that are novel to the topic and have just started to devise a sustainability strategy, define targets and implement sustainability measures may find a lot of value in the extensive feedback provided by some rating agencies. The learning alone may justify the investment of an ESG rating and may help redirect future efforts. Companies with a solid history of sustainability engagement and a public listing might be more inclined to select better communication platforms to underline their excellence toward the institutional investors and asset managers. Most companies, though, are likely to opt for a mix of objectives to capture two different benefits—richness and reach.

Value from Learning: Richness

Richness refers to the need to gain insights on the company's ESG performance, not only through feedback from the rating agencies but even more so from comparison with competitors and peers. Some of the most significant aspects to consider from the *eager student* perspective are:

- **Focus** Does the rating focus solely on one specific issue (e.g. climate change, access to medicine), or does it assess the company's sustainability performance from a wider perspective? Companies should determine whether they are looking for an in-depth review of a single aspect, or a more general overview that can deliver insights on stronger and weaker performance areas.

- **Depth of the Questionnaire** How broad or specific are the questions in the rating? Generic assessments will not lead to specific recommendations. When a company's main objective is to learn from the rating's process, in-depth, detailed questions with quantified requests for data are more valuable than high-level reviews.
- **Level of Personalized Feedback** What kind of feedback on the company performance is provided at the end of the process? Feedback is only relevant as a tool for optimizing performance if it is detailed and insightful, particularly when dealing with areas prone to improvement. Comprehensive results, such as partial scores on sub-criteria, can be useful tools to design and plan interventions to improve the company's sustainability efforts.

Value from Communication: Reach

Reach refers to the ability to demonstrate leadership in sustainability through a credible third party. Some of the important ESG ratings characteristics to assess from the *seeking influence* perspective include:

- **Initiator and Target Group** What is the organization behind the assessment and for whom are the insights being collected? What are the target audience and the communication channels? Companies looking for a strong reach need to prioritize stakeholder relevance and impact. Selecting the most suitable ESG ratings might be a case of determining which stakeholders are most deserving of your attention.
- **Recognition** It is essential to conduct a proper audit of the reputation and trustworthiness of the ESG ratings agency. That assessment often starts with the key stakeholders; just ask them which third-party source they trust and work with. They have every reason to be quite open about their preferences in that domain.
- **Communication Channels** Publications such as the RobecoSAM Sustainability Yearbook, which includes complete listings of leading companies for 60 industries, are useful for demonstrating your company's performance from an independent expert perspective. However, some rankings only provide survey results to paying customers, leaving valuable opportunities for public recognition unleveraged. Therefore, take note of the rating agency's business model and how it communicates its results.

When adding in estimates of the efforts and costs required to participate in these ESG ratings, companies can start to design their own ESG ratings game plan by prioritizing their reasons to participate. Combining motivation with an assessment of the rating's richness and reach, provides a solid base for vectoring forward efficiently in the complex world of ESG ratings.

As a starting point in those efforts, Table 6.2 below provides a basic overview of some of the most-popular global ESG rating agencies.

☞ Turning ESG Results into Actions: The ESG Canvas

For companies looking to improve their ESG ratings over the long term, a clear course of action is not always easy to identify. To help companies unravel the complexities associated with the outcomes of ESG ratings, the *ESG Program Canvas* (refer to Fig. 6.2) has been developed. In a 2½-hour workshop with about four to eight participants, the canvas aims to determine how the current ESG rating outcomes relate to the company's sustainability approach and determine effective interventions and actions.

As groundwork for the workshop, the facilitator prepares an analysis to summarize the existing company's ESG scoring on the provided criteria such as climate change strategy, labor conditions or governance. Typically, this is accomplished by creating a simple heatmap that exhibits the company's backlog on the individual criteria to the industry sustainability leaders. In the exceptional case that the industry leader's score is not readily available, the relative score level can be estimated by developing a rough industry ceiling from the annual reports and sustainability programs of selected competitors.

The workshop itself starts by filling in the sustainability strategy (refer to Table 6.3) checklist in a plenary brainstorming format. Once the checklist has been completed, the results can be compared against the heatmap score of the industry sustainability leaders and the ESG criteria that are emerging as weak spots can be determined. This two-way mapping process uncovers the main ESG performance gaps from both data analysis as well as team experience.

To start planning for improvement, identify possible causes of the ratings outcome from the sustainability strategy checklist in groups of two to four participants and ask the groups to come up with ideas for improvement. In a plenary format, all interventions and actions can be shared and then clustered and mapped in the *Interventions & Actions* section by jointly estimating their impact and feasibility. In some cases, the group was able to reach a consensus

Table 6.2 ESG ratings agencies overview

ESG report provider	Background	Rating scale	Methodology	Usage and reputation
Bloomberg ESG Data	Collects ESG data for over 9000 companies Integrated into Bloomberg Equities and Intelligence Services International scope	Out of 100 Provides scores from third-party rating agencies	Looks at 120 ESG indicators	In 2016, Bloomberg had over 12,200 ESG Customers
Corporate Knights Global 100	Publishes an annual index of the global 100 most sustainable corporations in the world	Out of 100 Ranked against other companies in their industry group	14 key performance indicators Companies only scored on relevant performance indicators for specific industry	Out of the top 10 corporations listed on the 2017 "Global 100," 4 out of 10 companies had published a press release regarding this listing
DJSI	First global index to track sustainability-driven companies based on RobecoSAM's ESG analysis Broken down into: DJSI World, DJSI Regions and DJSI Country International scope	Out of 100 Ranked against other companies in their industry	Industry-specific questionnaire, covering relevant economic, environmental and social factors 80–120 questions Updated annually	Partnered with RobecoSAM Out of 10 Industry Group Leaders listed on the 2016 DJSI, all 10 companies published a press release regarding this listing

(*continued*)

Table 6.2 (continued)

ESG report provider	Background	Rating scale	Methodology	Usage and reputation
ISS	Acquired Ethix SRI and partnered with RepRisk to provide ESG and SRI research ISS's solutions also include climate change data and analytics from its recent acquisition of Climate Neutral Investments International Scope	ISS QualityScore: 1–10 Climetrics Score: 1 to 5 green leaves	ISS QualityScore: Covers board structure, compensation/remu-neration, shareholder rights, and audit & risk oversight Updated on an ongoing basis ISS-Ethix: Provides research, screening and analysis on SRI topics	A leading provider
MSCI ESG	Provides ratings for over 6000 companies and 350,000 equity and fixed income securities International scope	AAA to CCC	Looks at 37 key ESG issues Data collected from publicly available sources Companies monitored on an ongoing basis Annual in-depth review	iShares MSCI EAFE ESG Select ETF and MSCI EM ESG Select ETF institutional investors, including Legal and General Investment Management, Morgan Stanley, Northern Trust Asset Management, and PIMCO

(continued)

Table 6.2 (continued)

ESG report provider	Background	Rating scale	Methodology	Usage and reputation
RepRisk	Founded in 1998 Provides ESG reports for more than 84,000 private and public companies across 34 sectors International scope	AAA to D	Looks at 28 ESG issues, which map onto the Ten Principles of the UN Global Compact Also looks into "Hot Topics" (currently a list of 45) Updated daily	Partnered with the United Nations-supported Principles of Sustainable Investment and Institutional Shareholder Services Inc. (ISS) Institutional investors, including Amundi and APG
Sustainalytics	2008 consolidation of DSR, Scoris and AIS Covers over 6500 companies across 42 sectors International scope	Out of 100 Sector/industry-based comparison	Looks at industry-specific ESG indicators, covers at least 70 indicators in each industry Also looks at systems to manage ESG risks and disclosure of ESG issues and performance	Strategic relationships with BNY Mellon, City of London Investment Management (CLIM), Columbia Threadneedle, Norwegian Government Pension Fund, and Prudential Fixed Income
Thomson Reuters ESG Research Data	Thomson Reuters acquired Asset4 in 2009 Provides ESG data on over 6000 companies International scope	Percentile rank scores (available on both percentages and letter grades from D− to A+)	Covers 400 different ESG metrics, electing 178 of the most relevant data points Categories are weighted Updated every 2 weeks	Comprehensive database ESG Scores are available on Thomson Reuters Eikon platform

Adapted from Huber, B. M. (2017). ESG Reports and Ratings: What They Are, Why They Matter? Davis Polk & Wardwell LLP. Accessed April 21, 2018.

The ESG Program Canvas™

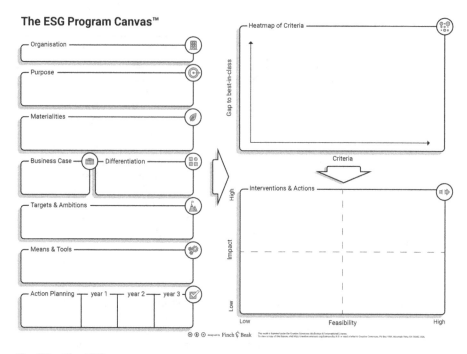

Fig. 6.2 The ESG program canvas

Table 6.3 Sustainability strategy checklist [9]

Element	Question
Purpose	What is the company purpose and in what way is it interlinked to the existing sustainability program?
Materialities	Are the most relevant sustainability topics identified and have drivers, such as geographical areas of operation, customer segments served, structure of the value chain, products and services and key stakeholders, been factored in?
Business case	What is the business case for sustainability and in what way is it connected to the overall company strategy?
Differentiation	What are the areas of industry-wide collaboration and what strategic areas will make the company enlarge its competitiveness, for instance, through enhanced reputation, product cost reduction or innovative products and services?
Targets & ambitions	Is the present set of key performance indicators (KPIs) covering our business case and differentiation focus? Was there a senior management commitment to the objectives and were they externally communicated?
Means & tools	Are the appropriate tools available to implement the required changes within the company and toward our stakeholders?
Action planning	Is there a concrete multi-year roadmap for the implementation of the sustainability program and is it actionable enough?

on the priorities, so only a few interventions were required. One illustration is that of a company in the building materials sector where, during the application of the ESG Program Canvas, the team decided to bundle their efforts on improving the structure of health and safety reporting in their industry and on the impact measurement of their business.

After the workshop, a summary of the most appropriate interventions is prepared including the ownership of the action points and timing. The complete instructions for the tool can be downloaded from the www.vectoring. online website together with the poster version of the canvas.

Integrating SDGs into Investment Portfolios

ESG ratings are increasingly taken into consideration by investors in their company assessments. Some of the leading institutional investors have started explicitly integrating SDGs into their investment strategies, providing another practical incentive for companies to pay even more attention to their ESG profiles.

Pioneering in this field, APG, a Dutch asset management company with a reported €44.5 billion invested in sustainable development investments and PPGM, a pension fund service provider with pension assets worth €218 billion, joined forces on this topic in 2017. As a first result of the partnership, APG and PGGM published a common methodology to identify investment opportunities derived from the SDGs. By hand-picking 13 of the most *investable* SDGs from the original set of 17 [12], the partnership developed an original taxonomy to create clearer guidance on what type of investments qualify as sustainable development investments. For example, in the case of SDG 6 (Clean water and sanitation), four out of six sub-goals have been categorized as investable sub-goals such as "6.1: Access to safe and affordable drinking water for all" and "6.4: Increase water-use efficiency and reduce the number of people suffering from water scarcity." Each of these investable sub-goals was carefully mapped to the most relevant themes such as water supply and distribution, wastewater discharge and hygiene. To highlight the investment opportunities, the relevant themes were connected to the most likely investment areas such as water saving systems, network construction and personal hygiene products. Both partners have affirmed that they intend to further develop the methodology in the years ahead and continue their efforts to embed it into their regular reporting structures. For companies with a strong sustainability profile looking for institutional investors, the APG/PPGM development emphasizes the case for a thorough implementation of the SDGs and their associated targets.

Some companies were remarkably quick to respond to the maturation of ESG factors and the incorporation of the new dimension of SDGs as was described in the previous sections. The story of Dutch life-science giant Royal DSM (DSM) and its approach to ESG factors is an outstanding illustration of such a company.

🗁 DSM: From Coal Mining to Leading the ESG Indices [13]

DSM is a global science-based company active in health, nutrition and materials with roots that could be traced back to a humble Dutch state-owned coal mining company started in 1902. With a heavy focus on innovation, the company completed its transformation from a commodity chemicals producer to a global life sciences and materials sciences company at the leading edge of technology. Through its Nutrition and Materials businesses, DSM was involved in a broad variety of industries, such as animal feed, food and beverages, pharmaceuticals, personal care, electronics, automotive and consumer goods. In 2017, DSM employed approximately 21,000 people worldwide and generated net sales of more than €8.6 billion [14].

Sustainability as a Business and Innovation Driver

At DSM, sustainability became a fundamental driver for future business and the entire innovation agenda. As early as 2010, DSM formulated a strategy to build on its strength in life and materials sciences, capitalizing on what it saw as the most promising global megatrends, notably health & wellness, global shifts and energy & climate change. Based upon these megatrends, all business activities were challenged to identify major issues for DSM and its customers, and then solving those issues through scientific innovation.

By 2017, DSM's sustainability strategy was focused on delivering science-based, sustainable and scalable solutions that had the potential to transform markets. Through its initiatives, DSM focused on making a tangible contri-

Table 6.4 DSM's SDG focus [15]

SDG	DSM activities
SDG 2 End hunger, achieve food security and improved nutrition and promote sustainable agriculture	"DSM works to improve nutrition via initiatives such as the Nutrition Improvement Program and Africa Improved Foods, providing fortified food solutions and micronutrient products, as well as through partnerships such as with World Food Programme (WFP). DSM supports the Base of the Pyramid with fortified food solutions and programs and provides micronutrients through products such as MixMe sachets. DSM continues to support the now independent nutrition think-tank, Sight and Life"
SDG 3 Ensure healthy lives and promote well-being for all at all ages	"DSM's health, nutrition, biomedical and high-performance materials portfolios are geared for maintaining, protecting or regenerating health in all age groups (e.g. by reducing salt and sugar levels in processed foods or by reducing emissions associated with chemical manufacturing processes). DSM's First 1000 Days Program supports mother and child health. We employ the DSM Life Saving Rules to protect employees from harm and the DSM Vitality Program to promote awareness of good health and healthy living options among employees"
SDG 7 Ensure access to affordable, reliable, sustainable and modern energy for all *SDG 13* Take urgent action to combat climate change and its impacts	"In partnership with RE100, DSM is increasing the use of renewables in our energy mix, reducing our carbon footprint. DSM enables solar and bio-based energy solutions and supports the move toward a low-carbon economy through solutions such as POET-DSM advanced biofuels and high-performance materials for solar panels. DSM's Bright Minds Challenge is identifying innovative solutions and new materials that will fast-track the movement toward 100% renewable energy. The DSM advocates responsible action on climate change in combination with our stakeholders"
SDG 12 Ensure sustainable consumption and production patterns	"DSM contributes to a bio-based, circular and low-carbon economy with products such as Akulon® oil pans and Arnite® car lighting. DSM-Niaga enables the manufacture of carpets that can be recycled, again and again. Food waste is reduced through DSM food solutions such as Pack-Age®. Bio-based chemicals such as bio-succinic acid replace fossil-fuel-based alternatives in applications from packaging to footwear. Through the Brighter Living Solutions program DSM considers the impact of products throughout the value chain"

bution to achieving the UN Sustainable Development Goals[4] (refer to Table 6.4). In DSM's view, all 17 of the SDGs were important, but the company recognized its limited capacity to support all goals in an equal fashion. To generate speed and impact, DSM concentrated on just five SDGs:

Benchmarking Sustainability: The Dow Jones Sustainability Index

Growing awareness in the investor community of the value of sustainability led to the creation of a number of benchmarks to track the progress of companies on sector-specific economic, environmental and social drivers. One of the most reputed is the Dow Jones Sustainability Index (DJSI), established in 1999, with the aim of tracking the performance of the world's largest companies in terms of corporate sustainability to generate attractive long-term investment returns. The index is compiled annually by RobecoSAM, a subsidiary of asset management firm Robeco, and subsequently co-published with S&P Dow Jones Indices.

Each year RobecoSAM invites over 3400 publicly traded companies to participate in its Corporate Sustainability Assessment based on their free-float stock market value. The Corporate Sustainability Assessment includes queries on social, economic and environmental topics such as occupational health and safety, corporate governance, operational eco-efficiency and customer relationship management. Companies provide input on their performance through 90+ questions, approximately half of which are sector-specific, with answers accompanied by supporting documentation and disclosures.

Based on the outcomes of the company assessment, compiled into a sustainability score between 0 and 100 points for over 20 ESG criteria, the DJSI World Index tracks the largest companies in the S&P Global Broad Market Index universe and publishes a ranking on the top 300+ performers. Regional and country indices are also compiled to accommodate more local companies. The DJSI encompasses many celebrated brands such as BMW, Coca-Cola and Nike. In total, the DJSI covers 60 industries, collated into 24 *industry groups* such as materials, consumer services and energy.

---

[4] The Sustainable Development Goals (SDGs) are a collection of 17 global goals set by the United Nations to end poverty, protect the planet and ensure prosperity for all as part of the 2030 Agenda for Sustainable Development.

DSM and the DJSI

As the DJSI gained momentum, the inclination of boards was to make the C-suite more responsible for sustainability targets, for example, by adopting bonus structures that reflected these objectives. Companies such as Shell and AkzoNobel developed incentive schemes that explicitly incorporated DJSI scores. DSM, however, elected to develop a more refined remuneration policy that included both short-term and long-term incentives based on measurable sustainability targets such as the share of business of sustainable products, the employee engagement index, and the safety performance and efficiency improvements in energy and greenhouse-gas emissions.

While performance in the DJSI was not explicitly part of the management incentive targets for DSM, continued recognition as part of RobecoSAM's Gold Class[5] was one of the company's overall sustainability targets for 2020 [16]. Since 2004, DSM had been among the global leaders, and the company was recognized as number one in the sector seven times. On the occasion of achieving the position of Industry Group Leader in 2016, Feike Sijbesma, CEO and chairman of the DSM Managing Board, said [17]:

> We are very proud to again be named the global leader in the Dow Jones Sustainability World Index. For DSM, sustainability is more than a responsibility; it is our company's core value and an important business driver. Business has an invaluable role to play in achieving the Sustainable Development Goals and the COP21 climate deal. Our skills and competencies to address the global challenges allow DSM to make a real difference, creating brighter lives for people today and generations to come.

Managing Sustainability for Recognition and Valuation

Since its start in 1902 as a coal mining company, DSM has made several major transitions to ensure the sustainability of the company. The biggest challenge facing DSM is no longer to simply contribute to the world people aspired to but to take responsibility for creating and (re)shaping it. With DSM's 2018 strategy update, appropriately entitled "Growth & Value—Purpose led, Performance driven," CEO Sijbesma formulated it as:

---

[5] Within each industry, companies with a minimum total score of 60 and whose score is within 1% of the top-performing company's score receive the RobecoSAM Gold Class Award.

DSM will evolve further towards a purpose-led, science-based company in Nutrition, Health and Sustainable Living. We have created a strong platform for growth, centered on developing innovative solutions addressing Nutrition & Health, Climate & Energy and Resources & Circularity. [18]

The company's strategy clearly recognizes the fact that operating as a good corporate citizen is the foundation of its license to operate. This means furthering sustainability thinking, from a tool for adapting to the changing environment to the natural next stage where people and planet metrics will become accepted tools for company valuation, contributing visibly to profits—and attracting and retaining happy shareholders. The continued recognition by investor benchmarks such as the DJSI is therefore a mark of confidence for the company's future.

Tips, Traps and Takeaways

♨ Tips

- Develop a vectoring approach to present your sustainability strategy to investors and rating agencies based on ESG factors with a focus on links to your core business.
- Determine the sandbox in which you want to play: which ESG ratings are relevant enough for your company to allocate resources to?
- Use the feedback from ESG ratings not just to iterate your questionnaire answers but also to help improve your sustainability program in a structural manner, for instance, by organizing feedback cycles with topic owners.

💣 Traps

- A check-box approach to ESG issues. Do not delegate the intelligence of your sustainability program to the questionnaire of the ESG ratings.
- Answering all ESG rating requests without prioritizing resources is likely to lead to mediocre results.
- ESG ratings are evolving. Too little resource spending on the updates and changes to the ESG questionnaires will hamper the scores. For instance, the inclusion of the new dimension of SDGs should not be overlooked as this is a new area of interest to ESG analysts.

🖋 Takeaways

This chapter on ESG ratings and their assessment by investors illustrated the mounting awareness and engagement from institutional investors, asset managers and financial institutions. The ESG ratings market is a booming industry that is developing ever more sophisticated tools and procedures to assess companies. These tools are continuously updated to reflect new areas of concern, as illustrated, for example, by the response of the DJSI composer to the Volkswagen *Dieselgate* scandal. In the two years following the scandal, the average score of the automotive industry dropped almost 14%, partially because of new metrics introduced in the methodology. Moreover, as the example of the APG/PPGM partnership in this chapter illustrated, inclusion of SDGs as relevant factors in ESG assessment methodologies is an emerging field of interest that is conducive to more business-aligned SDG approaches.

The field of ESG ratings is clearly becoming more competitive: the methodologies are progressively being refined, the availability of data is improving and, consequently, the thresholds for receiving high ESG marks are on the rise. For participating companies looking to inform potential and current investors, this increased complexity results in an expanding reporting burden. The latter supports the case for a lean approach to sustainability reporting and the careful pruning of material sustainability topics. In particular, it becomes essential to select the best-fitting ESG ratings agencies, using the suggested reach-richness mapping, to balance the influence potential of the individual ESG ratings with their learning potential. To jump-start this mapping exercise, an overview of the most relevant ESG ratings together with their properties was provided as a basis for further in-house analysis.

Last but not least, for an enhanced leverage of ESG scores, the chapter suggested applying the ESG Program Canvas tool by connecting the sustainability strategy checklist to the biggest gaps on sustainability topics. Application of the ESG Program Canvas tool should eventually lead to the development of a fact-based action plan in line with the corporate objective on ESG ratings.

References

1. Thompson, J. (2018, May 28) UN responsible investing body threatens to kick out laggards. *Financial Times*. Retrieved from https://www.ft.com/content/794219c0-6002-11e8-ad91-e01af256df68

2. Robeco (2017) *2017 Active ownership report*. Retrieved from https://www.robeco.com/docm/docu-2017-active-ownership-report.pdf

3. This case is an abridged and edited version of the eMBA case assignment by Claudio Mellace, Etienne Zeller and Laurent Gaye (IMD eMBA June 2018) conducted with CADMOS and its engagements funds under the supervision of Professor Benoit Leleux. Copyright © 2018 by IMD—International Institute for Management Development, Lausanne, Switzerland (www.imd.org). No part of this publication may be reproduced, stored in a retrieval system or transmitted in any form or by any means without the prior written permission of IMD.

4. De Pury Pictet Turretini & Cie S.A. (2018) Cadmos Engagement Funds. https://www.ppt.ch/en/cadmos/. Accessed 18 April 2018.

5. Interviews with Melchior de Muralt, Managing Partner at De Pury Pictet Turretini & Cie S.A. (2018).

6. BlackRock Inc. (2018) Larry Fink's annual letter to CEOs. https://www.blackrock.com/corporate/investor-relations/larry-fink-ceo-letter. Accessed 7 April 2018.

7. Grewal, P. (2018, March 16) Suspending Cambridge Analytica and SCL Group from Facebook. Retrieved from https://newsroom.fb.com/news/2018/03/suspending-cambridge-analytica/

8. Shen, L. (2018, March 26) Facebook Stock Is in the Red for the Year After the FTC Confirms Investigation. *Fortune*. Retrieved from http://fortune.com/2018/03/26/facebook-stock-ftc-investigation-cambridge-analytica/

9. Van der Kaaij, J. et al. (2015) Avoiding the Reporting Trap, A Frontrunner Approach for Building "Investor Proof" Sustainability Strategies [PowerPoint slides]. Retrieved from https://www.slideshare.net/finch-beak/avoiding-the-reporting-trap-a-frontrunner-approach-for-building-investor-proof-sustainability-strategies-52488721

10. European Union, European Parliament and Council (2014, October 22) EU Directive 2014/95/EU amending Directive 2013/34/EU as regards disclosure of non-financial and diversity information by certain large undertakings and groups. Retrieved from https://eur-lex.europa.eu/legal-content/EN/TXT/?uri=CELEX%3A32014L0095

11. Wong, C. (2018, March) *Rate the Raters 2018: Ratings Revisited*. Retrieved from http://s10458.pcdn.co/wp-content/uploads/2017/12/SA-RateTheRaters_Ratings-Revisited_March18.pdf

12. APG Group (2017, May) *Sustainable Development Investments (SDIs) Taxonomies*. Retrieved from https://www.apg.nl/pdfs/SDI%20Taxonomies%20website.pdf

13. This case is an abridged version of DARWINIANS AT THE GATE: SUSTAINABILITY, INNOVATION AND GROWTH AT DSM (IMD-3-2355). Copyright © 2018 by IMD—International Institute for Management Development, Lausanne, Switzerland (www.imd.org). No part of this publication may be reproduced, stored in a retrieval system or transmitted in any form or by any means without the prior written permission of IMD.

14. DSM (2018) *Royal DSM Integrated Annual Report 2017*. Retrieved from https:// annualreport.dsm.com/content/dam/annualreport/ar2017/en_US/documents/ DSM-Annual-Report-2017.pdf

15. DSM (2018) DSM's 5 Key SDG's. https://www.dsm.com/corporate/sustainabil- ity/vision-and-strategy/five-sdgs-where-dsm-most-influential.html. Accessed 20 June 2018

16. DSM (2017) *DSM Sustainability Introduction*. Retrieved from https://www.dsm. com/content/dam/dsm/cworld/en_US/documents/dsm-sustainability-introduc- tion.pdf

17. DSM (2016, September 8). DSM named leader in Dow Jones Sustainability World Index [Press release]. Retrieved from https://www.dsm.com/corporate/ media/informationcenter-news/2016/09/37-16-dsm-named-leader-in- dow-jones-sustainability-world-index.html

18. DSM (2018, June 20) DSM strategy update [Press release]. Retrieved from https://www.dsm.com/corporate/media/informationcenter-news/2018/06/19- 18-dsm-strategy-update.html

7

Investors' Perspectives on Sustainability

In the previous chapters, we noted how the financial industry in general, and institutional investors in particular, have started to imbed environmental, social and governance (ESG) factors and UN Sustainable Development Goals (SDGs) into their valuation and portfolio management methodologies. In effect, the industry is acknowledging the fact that companies actively managing relevant ESG parameters are not only controlling their risk exposure better but also constructing more sustainable futures, with both dimensions leveraging each other to increase valuations. In this chapter, we elaborate on this rationale by looking at how major financial investors have adopted sustainability, either by incorporating the principles in their practices or by developing investment schemes around it. For this, we have sequentially reviewed the worlds of venture capital, private equity, hedge fund and mutual fund managers, with examples in each.

We successively document how the various investor classes incorporated ESG metrics into their value creation arsenals, dedicating investments and personnel to the pursuit of higher goals. We start the journey with venture capitalists and the startups they support, which play a fundamental role in sustainability innovation. Venture capitalists not only seed the most promising, impactful technology ventures but are key actors in their scaling up and playing a key role in the rapid deployment of some of the most life-changing technologies. Venture capitalists have long viewed sustainability as not only an essential business attribute but also a powerful investment theme, piling capital into and constructing elaborate portfolios of technology companies at the forefront of environmental and social transformations. After looking at venture capitalists, we proceed to discuss sustainability efforts in later-stage

© The Author(s) 2019
B. Leleux, J. van der Kaaij, *Winning Sustainability Strategies*,
https://doi.org/10.1007/978-3-319-97445-3_7

investors, such as expansion capital and buyout specialists. Hedge fund specialists will then be investigated, before moving on to mutual fund investors and their stable of original sustainability-based products.

Sustainability in the World of Money

The money world is never late to catch on a new value creation opportunity, green or not so green. But the conversion to sustainability has been not only remarkable but also quite profitable. Venture capitalists in particular have been quick to develop investment vehicles targeting the technologies required to create a more sustainable future. These *green, impact* or simply *responsible* funds have raised tens of billions of dollars to seed the technological revolutions required to transform the planet. Private equity managers, some of the most active shareholders, have been in a position to influence the adoption of sustainability standards in their portfolio companies, much more so than the simple board activism of large institutional investors. These buyout and expansion capital specialists long ago discovered the value enhancement potential of CSR and established clear guidelines for their portfolio companies to provide not only incentives but also support for the implementation of leading-edge sustainability programs. Close on their heels, hedge fund managers also initiated efforts to adopt improved practices. Finally, mutual fund managers, like venture capitalists, also realized that sustainability and impact were investment themes of great interest to a large population of retail investors and responded by putting a collection of retail vehicles with clear sustainability credentials on the market.

These various professional investor groups offer a beautiful opportunity to test the premises of the vectoring approach promoted by the book, that is, the need to clearly identify a select set of relevant materialities and then to align resources in the pursuit of superior performance.

Venture capital and private equity investors share a *buy-and-sell* attitude, born out of the preference expressed by their investors (also known in the trade as limited partners because of their limited personal responsibility) for the use of limited lifetime vehicles. This implies that VCs and buyout specialists have to go back to their investors regularly and raise the subsequent funds, which only happens when the prior vehicle has performed. This regular *return to funders* creates an obligation for the general partners (the managers of the funds) to create and realize value rapidly, within the eight- to ten-year typical timeframe of such vehicles. This naturally focuses their attention on measures and interventions that will rapidly impact value in portfolio companies. As such, the vectoring concept *per se* is not new to the industry, except it was generically focused on value creation activities, not specifically ESG related ones. As will be shown, these investors often *discovered* the potential value impact of CSR activities before companies themselves, and with their usual efficiency, elaborated various schemes to benefit from them. Hedge fund investors, for their part, were, until recently, relatively immune to the sustainability calling. Their business models, focused on various arbitrage strategies, were more short term and, for the most part, focused on relatively liquid (and leveraged) instruments. The short, liquid interventions were not seen as very amenable to CSR benefits, but even there, things have changed, and many hedge fund houses have found ways to incorporate ESG ideals into their ways and means, if not necessarily as investment strategies. Finally, mutual fund managers, also relatively longer-term managers, have incorporated ESG principles in new classes of vehicles, offering managed funds with clear sustainability profiles to the general public.

Startups and Sustainability

At the base of the innovation pyramid are a myriad of new ventures concocting solutions to today's critical pain points. It is interesting to point out that both innovation and corporate sustainability research have focused mostly on large companies. Clearly, large firms have the administrative systems and corporate reputation motives for more extensive sustainability reporting [1]. Smaller companies often lack the resources, the structures, the visibility and the reporting capabilities to engage in extensive sustainability publications; hence, they do not generate the information needed for researchers to generate extensive publications. On the other hand, startups are often characterized by an entrepreneurial style of management, with founders who are close to their customers and life's realities. It is thus perfectly accurate to view startups as offering the answers to many social and environmental problems [2]. Startups have a key role to play in the emergence of sustainable businesses, innovations and business models:

> … SMEs, and especially startups, can be the ideal incubators for eco-innovation, and can bring to market new, less environmentally damaging products, services and processes. [3]

Startups are a rich source of sustainability innovation, not only in products but also in services and business models. One needs look no further than some of the most recent "sharing economy" examples such as BlaBlaCar (car sharing), Uber (ride hailing) and Airbnb (home and room rental) to realize the life-changing potential of these new ventures. Airbnb has grown to become larger than many established hotel groups, claiming a large part of the market for short-term business and holiday stays. As an anecdote, on August 5, 2017, Airbnb's biggest night to date, some 2.5 million people stayed in accommodation listed on the platform [4]. On any given night, some 2 million people are staying in other people's homes around the world thanks to Airbnb. With over 4 million listings in 191+ countries, the platform has registered 200 million+ arrivals since its founding in 2008.

These business models that encourage the sharing of space or equipment (cars, houses, tools, etc.) are claimed to be more sustainable than the incumbents' business models. Zipcar claims every one of its cars takes six privately owned vehicles off the road, and 60% of its members drive less than 1000 miles per year saving 829 liters of petrol per Zipcar member [5]. Moreover, car-sharing models may encourage the right behaviors from the car operators, which have a vested interest in ensuring reparability, fuel efficiency and durability. A study commissioned by Airbnb [6] also found that in Europe, Airbnb guests use 78% less energy than hotel guests.

Of course, not all sustainability initiatives have been equally successful. One of the pioneers of the sharing economy, car battery swapper Better Place, is on record as one of the biggest busts in history. With almost $1 billion in funding and the ambition to replace petroleum-based cars with a network of cheap electrics, Shai Agassi's Better Place was remarkable even by the standards of world-changing startups. So was its epic failure [7].

A whole new generation of sustainable entrepreneurs has appeared, who seek to manage the *triple bottom line*, balancing economic health (economy), social equity (people) and environmental resilience (planet) through their entrepreneurial behavior. Sustainable entrepreneurs operate with an organizational purpose focused on maximizing human and natural resources, synergies and *benefits stacking* (rather than pure profit maximization), a focus on satisfying multiple stakeholder needs, on quality of outcomes (rather than quantity) and allocation of benefits across those who contributed positively to the enterprise (not just to those with power, money or control).

Accelerating Sustainability: Seed Funding Green Initiatives

The adoption of the SDGs encouraged innovation from the private sector as companies were tasked with the responsibility of becoming the engine for innovation and technological development. This new mission bred fantastic opportunities for entrepreneurs around the globe, and of course generated the birth of new types of accelerators, dedicated to the pursuit and support of green ventures. An example of one such instrument is the Katapult Accelerator [8], a Norwegian initiative with a global reach aiming to fast-track solutions to global problems within the environmental and societal domains, such as clean energy, the circular economy, food and water and education. Of particular interest to the accelerator are companies that address these problems with exponential technologies such as artificial intelligence, blockchain, virtual reality and applications of the Internet of things. The Katapult Accelerator Fund invests up to US$150,000 in each startup. To support them, on top of providing access to 120+ international mentors, it provides a network of global investors and partnerships that potentially boosts the startups in their next phase of development. Its partner network includes corporate leaders such as PwC, Amazon Web Services, IBM and Microsoft, just to name some of the most visible.

Venture Capital: Sustainability as a Theme

Venture capital, a relatively new field of activity that appeared in the mid-1960s, invests in early stage, mostly technology-based companies and capitalizes on their successes. Business models evolved over the years, starting with relatively small, diversified bets. Kleiner Perkins Caufield & Byers (KPCB), a pioneer and leader in the industry, launched its first fund in 1972 at about $40 million, investing in a total of 17 ventures over its investment period, including home runs such as Genentech and Tandem Computers. Over time, deals grew much larger and portfolios became more focused, making significantly larger investments later in the life of new ventures. In the first quarter of 2018, Norwest Venture Partners fund XIV closed on a respectable $1.5 billion, way behind industry powerhouses such as New Enterprise Associates (NEA) whose fund XV closed in 2015 at $2.8 billion and fund XIV closed in 2012 at $2.6 billion. As a point of reference, NEA raised some $10.7 billion from 2005 to 2015, compared to $9 billion for Sequoia Capital and

$6.5 billion for Kleiner Perkins Caufield & Byers (KPCB) [9]. With this kind of money to put to use, venture capitalists have naturally drifted toward larger deals, meaning later investment stages in the development of technology companies. With a focus on risk investments and the consequent need to generate large returns on their positions, venture capitalists are always searching for the *next big thing*, so it is no surprise they were pioneer investors in many *green* technology leaders, in areas such as renewable energy (windmills, fuel cells, etc.), smart grids, intelligent homes and electric cars.

Over the last decade, a new breed of venture capitalists has also emerged, dubbing itself sustainable venture capitalists, dedicated to investments that have the potential to generate large economic returns, while creating positive environmental and social impacts. Rather than maximizing only economic returns, these venture capitalists seek to optimize the triple bottom line, an obvious managerial challenge. Sustainable venture capitalists use an original investment thesis as a guideline for creating a more balanced sustainable investment portfolio.

A first example of this new breed is Aster [10], a multi-corporate VC financed by Alstom, Schneider Electric, Solvay and the European Investment Fund. Aster, which finances startups globally, recently launched six funds and now has €620 million in assets under management (AUM), with a mix of 40% in seed investments, 40% in startups and 20% for growth projects. It declares its belief in entrepreneurs applying innovative technology and business models to solve pressing problems, particularly in the energy, industrial and mobility sectors. Since 2000, it has invested in more than 50 projects, building fast-growing companies and transforming industries.

Breakthrough Energy Ventures [11] is the new $1 billion fund initiated by Bill Gates and a few of his billionaire friends around the world. The strategy of the fund is to invest in early stage, disruptive technologies that can make the world a better place and accelerate the global energy transition to a 100% renewable energy system. To provide reliable and affordable power without contributing to climate change, the fund focuses on five key areas: electricity, transportation, agriculture, manufacturing and buildings. Investment managers and scientific advisors come primarily from ARPA-E and MIT. Breakthrough declares it provides patient, risk-tolerant capital badly needed by capital-intensive hardware startups.

Chrysalix [12] is a reputed cleantech VC active in North America with a motto that does a good job of summarizing its objective: "We build innovation companies that make a better future possible. #futurepossible." It invests in breakthrough technologies like 3D printing of steel, fast-charging electric vehicle infrastructure, emissions-free solar steam, smart mining and nuclear fusion. It also claims to have a strong industrial network and processes to successfully accelerate and commercialize technologies to make a better future possible.

Demeter [13] is a French cleantech VC (merged into Emertec in November 2016) that managed over €1 billion in AUM, focusing on early stage and infrastructure investments for energy and ecological transitions. They typically invest from €500,000 to €30 million to support companies in their development.

The list of venture capitalists with sustainability credentials is now very long, including specialists like Ecapital [14] (Germany), Ecomachines Ventures [15] (UK) and a roster of other specialist investors.

Private Equity and the Value Creation Potential of Sustainability

Private equity is often described, tongue in cheek, as capitalism on steroids. By that, observers mean that private equity investors have a keen eye for fast value-creation opportunities, on which they unleash the most effective tools management and financial theory have to offer. Strategically, their game plans are usually very simple and very focused, because focus ensures precision in the interventions. Leaving some value creation opportunities on the table at the end of the intervention period is seen as a pre-requisite for ensuring, with a solid degree of probability, the required exit after three to five years of investment.

McKinsey research revealed that approximately 50% of private equity firms were still "sitting on the fence" with regard to sustainability as an investment driver. European asset managers were found to have the highest proportion of sustainable investments (52.6% at the beginning of 2016), followed by Australia and New Zealand (50.6%) and Canada (37.8%) [16]. With the average private equity holding period for US-based companies increasing to 6.17 years by late 2017 [17], while the average holding period for stocks listed on the New York Stock Exchange (NYSE) declined to 8.3 months [18], the relative conservatism of private equity players seemed a bit odd. Sustainability benefits take notoriously long to materialize, but private equity investors seem perfectly suited to take a more pro-active stand on sustainability issues, and they have.

The evolution began in 2006, when the United Nations Principles of Responsible Investment (PRI) released a framework for how private equity firms should incorporate environmental, social and governance criteria into their investments. According to John Hodges, managing director of Business for Social Responsibility (BSR™)[1]:

> The industry overall is lagging other parts of the financial services industry. Nonetheless, there has definitely been an upswing in the past couple years. [19]

Initially, six private equity firms signed on to the framework in 2006, but six years later, in 2012, there were over 1000 signatories from firms managing $30 trillion+ in assets. The jump in signatories came about as investors increasingly started recognizing sustainability and environmental issues as real financial risks and began demanding more ESG information from private equity firms. Interestingly, the former *Barbarians at the Gate* central character, Kohlberg Kravis Roberts (KKR), was one of the leaders in that evolution. Forty years after its well-documented creation, KKR has become one of the largest private equity players in the market with $168 billion in AUM and a total global workforce of approximately 695,000 people employed in their portfolio companies [20]. Starting in 2008, KKR intensified its efforts to include ESG issues in its investment and post-investment management decisions. Ten years on, the firm has adopted three different approaches to ESG inclusion in its investment portfolio:

- **ESG Integrated** The most basic approach, where KKR integrates ESG considerations into pre-investment due diligence and post-investment management.
- **ESG Targeted** Those include investments where an improved performance on material ESG issues helps create value or mitigate risks. The firm is supporting its portfolio companies with its global green solutions platform across three major areas: eco-efficiency, eco-innovation and/or eco-solutions. Other initiatives include a global sourcing initiative and worker safety program.
- **Solutions Focused** Those include investments in real estate, energy and infrastructure that provide solutions for sustainability issues, such as healthcare and climate change. An example of this is KKR's investment in

---

[1] BSR™ is a global non-profit organization working with a network of 250+ member companies and partners to build a just and sustainable world. With offices in Asia, Europe and North America, BSR™ develops sustainable business strategies and solutions through consulting, research and cross-sector collaborations.

X-ELIO, a company dedicated to the development, construction and operation of photovoltaic plants.

Another interesting KKR portfolio investment is PortAventura, a family-oriented theme park and destination resort near Barcelona, Spain, renowned for its Ferrari Land partnership with the legendary Italian car manufacturer. With the tourism industry accounting for approximately 5% of global greenhouse gas (GHG) emissions, which are expected to more than double by 2035 under a business-as-usual scenario, tourism companies such as PortAventura were on the lookout for opportunities to reduce their environmental footprint. Internal analyses at PortAventura World showed that 68% of the company's GHG emissions were the indirect consequence of their electricity consumption, electricity which was produced in the most non-ecological manner. As part of its commitment to sustainability, the company implemented a large renewable energy sourcing project and one year later, PortAventura World had eliminated all GHG emissions from its electricity consumption. The company's overall equivalent tons of CO_2 generated tumbled from 16,350 to 5565 in 2016.

📂 Tumi and the Doughty Hanson Value Enhancement Group (VEG) [21]

In early 2012, Doughty Hanson's (DH) investment committee met to discuss the future of the firm's investment in Tumi, a high-end luggage company DH had acquired in 2004 in a hotly contested secondary buyout. At stake was the definition of the proper exit strategy from Tumi, which now generated some US$330 million in sales. Was this the right time to sell or should DH continue to build the company? During the eight years since it acquired the firm, DH and the Tumi management team had achieved a three-fold growth in sales and close to a four-fold increase in earnings before interest, taxes, depreciation and amortization (EBITDA), an effort that was strongly supported by the DH Value Enhancement Group (VEG), a team of five internal operational experts. Tumi was now an established global brand, with a broad portfolio of products, extensive distribution channels and a true global reach with key logistics facilities in the US, Europe and Asia. Its products were available in over 65 countries through more than 1600 points of sale. But how did that happen, and what role did sustainability play in this successful global rollout?

Tumi's Development Into a Super Premium Brand

Tumi was founded in 1975 by Charlie Clifford, a young Peace Corps volunteer who had served in Peru, and his partner Seth McQuillan. The company started as an importer of Colombian leather travel bags and totes. From the beginning, Tumi's number one priority was to develop top-quality products for discerning customers. Sales steadily grew in the late 1970s and early 1980s, until the company started to feel the signs of the US economy's impending slowdown. Clifford was forced to reconsider Tumi's whole business strategy. After buying out his partner, he launched a significant effort to build Tumi as a real brand. Many key concepts of Tumi[2] were created during that period, such as the black-on-black look and unique technical features such as the use of high-grade ballistic nylon and the "wheel away" steel bearings. What came out of the exercise was one of the more creative luggage brands for the professional road warrior. By concentrating exclusively on professional travelers, Tumi's sales soared, reaching $4 million in 1985, $16 million by 1990 and $42 million by 1995.

Innovation and Excellence Leading to Global Success

To achieve and maintain a high level of technical excellence, Tumi invested heavily in research and development (R&D) to enhance its products with hundreds of custom-designed and engineered parts.[3] As the company expanded quickly, its founder hired an experienced CEO in 1999, Laurence Franklin, a former CEO of Coach, a leading leather goods brand. Tumi continued to expand its reach in terms of products, introducing women's and business casual categories in 2000, and distribution channels. Building on its existing multi-channel strategy to distribute products through wholesale and retail channels, Tumi also initiated a company-owned full-price retail format in 2000, and Internet and catalogue channels in 2002 to sell its products online. By 2000, annual sales had topped $100 million, with Tumi products being sold in the US and internationally through department stores such as Harrod's, Neiman Marcus, Saks Fifth Avenue and specialty stores. Tumi positioned itself in the *super premium* segment of the global luggage market—

---

[2] A classic Tumi characteristic was its upside-down U-shaped pockets that provided real compartments and a convenient alternative for zipping and unzipping the luggage.

[3] The company owned 25 design and mechanical patents and controlled all intellectual property associated with the design, production and distribution of its products worldwide.

operating between the *premium* category with brands such as Samsonite, TravelPro and Victorinox, and the *luxury* segment occupied by the likes of LVMH and Hermes.

The Pains of Fast Growth

Clifford and his management team relied on a dual strategy for growth: internationalization and a rollout of full-price domestic retail stores. To implement it, Tumi realized it needed an equity partner. The search for a growth equity partner was cut short by the recession that hit the world in early 2001, combined with the profound impact of 9/11 on the travel industry. Many of Tumi's major specialty store accounts soon went bankrupt, leading to the closure of hundreds of Tumi-carrying stores in 2002.

With an unsuccessful fundraising effort, a nervous bank and declining profitability, cash generation and sales, Tumi turned to Oaktree Capital Management for financing, a California-based specialist in distressed investments. Under Oaktree's new stewardship, Tumi accomplished a complete turnaround. EBITDA more than doubled after the first year of new leadership, and then doubled again the following year to reach $22 million and a 17% EBITDA margin in 2004. By then, Oaktree decided that it was time for a new *pair of hands* at Tumi—industry parlance to indicate they were keen to realize the value that had been created and find an exit for their investment.

Doughty Hanson's Acquisition of Tumi and the New Game Plan

Doughty Hanson (DH), one of leading and most established European private equity firms, emerged as the winning bidder for Tumi and closed the deal for a reported $276 million. DH focused on the majority ownership and control of businesses at the upper end of the European middle market with enterprise values of between €250 million and €1 billion. As an active owner, DH took a guiding role by working in close partnership with the management teams of its portfolio companies. It even went one step further by creating an in-house value enhancement group that provided ongoing support to portfolio companies. As DH co-head John Leahy explained:

> At Doughty Hanson, our value enhancement approach is constantly evolving, and we are increasingly getting more involved on the pre-deal phase so that we

can develop a better understanding of value enhancement opportunities. In the case of Tumi, we stepped in immediately after we bought the company.

Core to DH's philosophy was the inclusion of environmental, social and governance (ESG) components in its strategy, initially as a way of mitigating financial and reputational risks, but increasingly to generate new growth opportunities in its portfolio companies.[4]

The Doughty Hanson Value Enhancement Group

DH had a total of 30 in-house executives dedicated to private equity, including a team of five individuals who actively supported portfolio companies. Led by John Leahy, the VEG was responsible for identifying, implementing and managing strategic processes that enhanced value and for promoting value-creating sustainable business practices across portfolio companies. John worked with four other executives who all focused on specific value enhancement areas, ranging from business strategy and product portfolio optimization to supply chain, production, sustainability and ESG competencies.

The VEG worked across all of DH's portfolio companies, typically establishing a steering committee with a mixture of the operating top management and VEG executives or parachuting in VEG executives on an as-needed basis. When DH acquired a company, the investment team updated the VEG team on the due diligence findings and informed it about the first set of actions. The VEG team then performed a joint review with the management team to identify and define potential areas that could benefit from enhancing strategies aimed at, for instance, sales growth, supply chain management, sustainability and procurement cost optimization.

A Vision for Tumi's Future

Having finalized its acquisition of Tumi, DH proceeded with a full review of operations in early 2005. Management planned to grow organically by rolling out the direct retail channel, strengthening the brand and developing category extensions. DH believed the plan could be much more ambitious given the brand's reputation. However, before implementing an ambitious retail

---

[4] In June 2007, the firm actually became one of the first private equity signatories of the United Nations Principles for Responsible Investment (PRI).

expansion plan, the VEG needed to remove significant roadblocks to improve efficiency. As a result, supplier lead times were almost cut in half, while quality was reinforced through the review of all suppliers, causing many of them to be replaced.

The financial crisis of 2008 deeply affected Tumi, which was still exposed with more than 70% of its sales to the domestic US market. Depressed sales combined with a high-operating leverage significantly reduced EBITDA in 2008 to $26 million below budget, $14 million lower than the previous year. While DH was impressed by the management team's capabilities, it became clear that rolling out a network of retail stores required different skills. Jerome Griffith, who had enjoyed a successful career in retail with leadership positions at Esprit and the Gap, was selected as the new CEO of Tumi.

By the time Griffith joined Tumi in April 2009, the company was in a more challenging financial situation. He spent the first nine months focusing on cash management, carefully planning with DH's VEG team where to allocate the company's cash. This resulted in significant cash-saving initiatives, a focus on improving retail productivity and a redesign of the product development process to speed up market launches, which were especially important for products with more fashionable attributes.

The New Growth Strategy: 2009–2012

The efforts paid off; by 2010 the company was fully back on track, with sales exceeding $250 million for the first time and an EBITDA margin exceeding 20%. Management and DH had clear, agreed priorities for further growth: accelerate retail expansion (with a focus on Asia), diversify distribution channels (particularly online) and launch new product extensions (such as iPad covers and sunglasses).

Sustainability and CSR always stood at the core of DH's philosophy. VEG's sustainability champion, Adam Black, conducted a full review with local management and identified opportunities to improve its CSR profile with respect to suppliers, products, employees, carbon footprint and regulatory authorities. Adam mentioned:

> All of Tumi's factories signed a code of conduct and, under DH's stewardship, participated in the Fair Labor Association [FLA], a non-profit initiative dedicated to ending sweatshop labor and improving working conditions in factories worldwide. Suppliers were also audited for environmental sustainability and workplace health and safety and given training when needed.

The company also joined the Leather Working Group, subjecting itself to higher standards of manufacturing policies and procedures. Tumi also reinforced its commitment to product safety legislation and, when viable, elected to master pack[5] products for shipping to reduce freight costs and the use of cardboard and other shipping materials as well as to reduce carbon emissions.

No stone was left unturned in the CSR landscape. In an interview with the authors, Jerome Griffith recollected one of his *eureka* moments when visiting a Tumi store in New York City soon after his arrival as CEO:

> I was having a conversation with the store manager. He raised a small issue that bothered him. We used to supply the stores with special bags to pack the customers' purchases. These bags were really fancy and brand enhancing, shiny and opulent. Then, a few months earlier, we had introduced new bag models he found less exciting, less rich. What had happened is that our CSR specialist, Adam Black, had discovered that the old bags were probably the worst we could have found in terms of their environmental footprint. The raw materials used were not renewable, the processes used to manufacture them were wasteful, the chemicals applied to give the shine were harmful to the environment, etc. So he worked with suppliers to develop and source a new type of bag for Tumi, manufactured from recycled materials and processed ecologically. The new bags were less shiny, less brand-enhancing. And at Tumi we used some 2 million bags a year ... I explained that to the store manager and he was astounded and delighted to hear the story behind the bag. That moment really stuck with me: I realized how good we were with ESG issues ... and how pathetic we were at communicating these elements, even to our own people! From there on, we made sure to explain our actions and make them visible to everyone, within Tumi and outside Tumi. Because they matter a lot to employees and customers ...

In explaining DH's sustainable investment practices, Stephen Marquardt, the company's joint chief operating officer said:

> We believe companies that engage in sustainable investment practices not only de-risk their business models, but can achieve greater cost efficiencies and profitability, resulting in higher valuations in the capital markets. [22]

---

[5] A master pack is a large box used to pack many smaller boxes or containers. The box assists in protecting the smaller cartons or packages and reduces the number of cartons to be handled during the material handling process.

The Exit

Exits were often tricky moments in the private equity investment cycle. If not managed properly, they could potentially damage the whole performance of investments. The strong CSR profile again facilitated the access to multiple exit channels, in effect contributing to the realization of the value created during the DH holding period.

Ultimately, DH decided to go with an initial public offering (IPO). Griffith rang the opening bell in celebration of the company's IPO at the New York Stock Exchange on April 19, 2012 [23]. With 18.8 million shares at $18 per share, the company raised US$338.4 million, allowing DH to reduce its stake in Tumi to just over 60%. Four years later, DH sold its remaining shares to Samsonite, a company strategically focused on the design, manufacture, sourcing and distribution of luggage, business and computer bags, outdoor and casual bags and other travel accessories throughout the world. Known mostly for brands such as Samsonite, American Tourister and Hartmann, the company was the undisputable market leader in its segment. Samsonite acquired Tumi at a total equity value of US$1.8 billion [24]. Subsequently, DH reported a projection for the total return to a multiple of 7.1x for the fund's investors [25].

ESG Interventions at Doughty Hanson

In an article published in 2015 in the journal *Private Equity International*, Black elaborated on the Doughty Hanson philosophy for ESG interventions with portfolio companies, saying that the firm was able to "drill right down" into the supply chain and make it fit for purpose [26]. The investment pre-dated his arrival at Doughty Hanson but when he started to investigate the Tumi supply chain, he understood the level of exposure for the firm. Asian suppliers were often non-compliant in terms of staff safety and worker welfare, leathers were not always sourced ethically and the traceability was at best incomplete. Black endeavored to control the reputational risks as quickly as possible:

> We asked ourselves, if we didn't do this what would happen during an IPO process if it transpired the company was exposed through the supply chain because of child labour concerns, unacceptable safety practices or through the procurement of raw materials from disreputable or unsustainable sources.

Black argued in the interview that it was essential to identify and address the ESG *elephant(s) in the room* as early as possible to give the private equity investor, as a temporary owner, time to address the issues. With 20+ years of experience in the sector, Black pointed out that it became relatively easy to spot potential ESG challenges, but it remained essential to intervene rapidly. Quoting again from the interview:

> No-one in the firm has any doubt that doing this work and getting it right isn't just a nice-to-have; they know it's commercial.
>
> It's still the case that often the environmental due diligence is thought about late on in the process, which isn't smart given that a material issue absolutely can disrupt or delay a transaction. And when people start late, often the due diligence becomes more about box-ticking and remains limited in scope, focusing mainly on compliance. That almost always results in missed opportunities in terms of identifying risks and value creation potential.

This should thus start during the pre-acquisition due diligence work and continue throughout the firm's holding period, all the way to the critical exit phase, during which the potential new owner would normally also conduct its acquisition due diligence, including ESG risk exposure.

Black also recalled a similar case he encountered earlier with a company called Norit, a water and air purification technologies producer with manufacturing capabilities spread around the world.

> When I joined and found out what some of the raw materials were, I knew the company was exposed; a well-informed trade buyer would almost certainly have asked about them. This was an issue that was buried deep in the technical details of how they made their products and shows how in-house expertise allows you to ask more focused questions and enhance the external due diligence, providing the general partners with some competitive advantage.

Hedge Funds' Conversion to Sustainable Investing

A recent development is how hedge fund investors have jumped on the ESG bandwagon, as outlined in a cnbc.com article [27]. These Wall Street activist investors, once known for pushing for extreme cost-cutting measures, have emerged as active promoters of a different kind of corporate action, namely social and environmental change. It is of course questionable whether they are acting out of moral responsibility or simply as part of their business objective, that is, to generate outsized returns for clients. Socially responsible investing, long the bastion of faith-based activists and civic do-gooders, now counts in its ranks some high-profile hedge fund investors, such as Clifton Robbins of Blue Harbour Group and Barry Rosenstein of Jana Partners.

Assets under management in US-based socially responsible investment strategies climbed to $8.72 trillion at the start of 2016, roughly 20% of all investments under professional management and an increase of 33% from the start of 2014 [28]. In an annual speech to hedge fund leaders, Robbins, Blue Harbour's chief executive, said that social and environmental considerations have become integral to how the fund's partners decide where to invest its $3 billion in assets. As he told the crowd at the 13D Monitor Active-Passive Summit:

> This is hugely important—I think this is a new paradigm for smart investing. Now when I'm calling up a CEO three months after we make an investment, in addition to saying: "Where are we on the spin-out? Where are we on the balance sheet? Where are we on the margins?" I'm saying, "Where are we on that commitment you made to me to make the board more diverse?"

The Greenwich, Connecticut-based hedge fund prides itself on meticulous work with company management, a process Robbins considers "one of the most important" in determining whether to invest. That simultaneous focus on both management and ESG was put to the test on its minority stake in software company OpenText. In an industry infamous for its lack of gender diversity, OpenText's decision to appoint Madhu Ranganathan as chief financial officer came as welcome news to the Blue Harbour team. As Silverman, Blue Harbour's managing director in charge of ESG issues, told CNBC:

> OpenText just added a new CFO who happens to be a woman of diverse background … we think she's going to be a great CFO. That's important at a tech company, as more broadly in the industry there have been issues of diversity and inclusion.

Silverman reiterated that Blue Harbour's focus on ESG stemmed from financial interest. Company-specific ESG concerns, he said, could help activists unlock previously hidden value. Rosenstein, a Partner at Jana Partners, would not disagree. A *Reuters* reports [29] said she was heavily recruiting social activists for a new fund targeting companies on issues like climate change and wage inequality. Those activists, including rock star Sting, were to pool cash for the fund—expected to be called Jana Impact Capital—in an effort to put pressure on companies they feel can be better corporate citizens.

In kicking off its latest push into socially responsible investing, the $4 billion hedge fund teamed up with the California State Teachers' Retirement System (or CalSTRS), which controls roughly $2 billion in Apple equity, to urge the iPhone maker to develop new settings to help parents control children's time on mobile devices. Jana believes Apple could easily fix what the firm sees as the pernicious problem of young people getting addicted to the tech giant's phones. As Rosenstein told CNBC:

> This should be an easy fix for Apple. There's no question that it needs to be more responsive to children's needs and children's activities.

For Jana, it was its forceful foray into pushing for social issues after it had long been successful in prodding corporations to improve their governance. The new fund will look to target other companies on issues like climate change or wage inequality and will likely target as many as ten companies, according to people familiar with Jana's plans.

📁 CADMOS and Socially Responsible Investment Vehicles [30]

In 2006, Pury Pictet Turrettini & Cie S.A. (PPT) the Geneva-based wealth management company, launched the Cadmos European Engagement Fund, aimed at going beyond what the general socially responsible investments (SRIs) were offering by promoting active engagement between shareholders and companies. Over the following three years, the company fine-tuned its investment strategies, launching more initiatives to support its commitment to sustainable investments. The Cadmos Emerging Markets Engagement Fund was launched in 2009, followed by a Cadmos Swiss Engagement Fund in 2014, with the firm managing some CHF 3.8 billion in assets by Q1 2018 on behalf of institutional and individual clients. While these ESG-driven funds have established themselves, they have also generated new concerns, demands and questions, some of which are delegitimizing ESG as an investment principle.

The Genesis of CADMOS Funds

When I joined PPT in 2001, the whole PPT team was already actively working on a new concept of portfolio construction that would address not only the financial interests of investors but also have a socially responsible impact on society through the actions of companies they invested in. At that time, we were persuaded that taking companies' ESG practices into account would really offer investment benefits, including an enhanced risk-return balance, and that sustainable funds would have the potential of outperforming traditional funds.

Melchior de Muralt, Managing Partner at PPT (interview with the authors)

Five years later, the Cadmos European Engagement Fund was created. Between its inception in October 2006 and late 2008, the results were promising but mitigated (refer to Fig. 7.1). The fund's portfolio was beating expectations but not the performance of a passive index such as MSCI Europe NR.

The international financial crisis that happened at the end of 2008 eroded the trust in business and in markets. Our fund was not spared. However, I recall UN Secretary-General Ban Ki-moon's plenary speech in Davos in 2009 refueling the enthusiasm and the commitment for a better world.

From then on, PPT pursued even more direct engagement with the company management teams, helping companies create value and positive social impact. This became Cadmos's unique value proposition. Through dialogue, portfolio managers obtained deeper insights into the sustainability profiles of

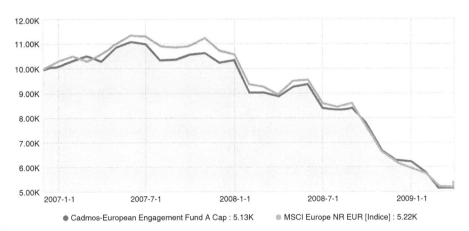

Fig. 7.1 Comparative performance of Cadmos European Engagement fund vs. MSCI EU NR

the companies and were able to better incorporate these characteristics into their financial analyses. More important, the fund offered investors a convenient means to align personal values with financial goals.

ESG Principles and Financial Performance

As Melchior explained:

> I have been working on providing wealth management services with a focus on funds that observe ESG standards for over 17 years. Since the Cadmos inception, PPT succeeded in engaging with more than 120 companies, simultaneously delivering financial performance and tangible sustainability impacts. Today, the interest for ESG-oriented investments is mainstream. However, I acknowledge that their capability to effectively deliver higher returns is still extremely controversial. [30]

Melchior was convinced that funds observing ESG standards outperformed those that did not, by a significant margin. Since the beginning of 2009, for instance, the Cadmos European Engagement fund consistently outperformed the STOXX 50 benchmark (refer to Fig. 7.2).

Additional evidence he found in the fact that the MSCI Emerging Markets Leaders Index (an index of 417 companies with high ESG scores) had outperformed the classic MSCI Emerging Markets benchmark since the 2008–2009 financial crisis (refer to Fig. 7.3). Responsible funds seemed less likely to experience unforeseen losses and more likely to outperform their benchmarks.

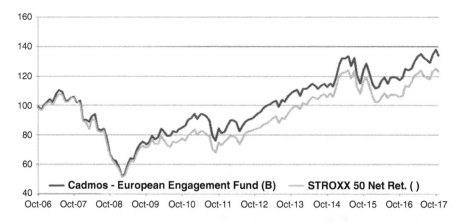

Fig. 7.2 Performance since inception, Cadmos European Engagement Fund

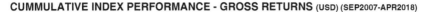

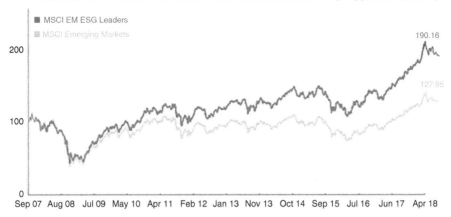

CUMMULATIVE INDEX PERFORMANCE - GROSS RETURNS (USD) (SEP2007-APR2018)

Fig. 7.3 MSCI emerging markets ESG leaders vs. MSCI emerging markets (2007–2018)

According to Fiona Reynolds, managing director of the UN's responsible investment initiative, the UNPRI:

> If we look at the news over the past few weeks, we see prime examples of what happens to established names such as Bell Pottinger, KPMG and Miramax when ESG issues are ignored.

New investments into ESG index-tracking funds on BlackRock's iShares platform reached a record US$390 million in July 2017, bringing total inflows since December 2009 to US$5.7 billion.

An analysis conducted by the Boston Consulting Group [31] on more than 300 of the world's largest companies in five industries (consumer packaged goods, biopharmaceuticals, oil and gas, retail and business banking) claimed to have found a clear link between the total societal impact and the total return for stakeholders, in a way that impacted the ability of ESG-conscious firms to deliver attractive returns.

Tips, Traps and Takeaways

♦ Tips

- Sustainability provides a rich investment theme for technology-driven investors, such as venture capitalists. The size of the markets, their growth rates and their needs for new, original technologies and business models are the fuel that drives VC investments.

- Private equity investors, because of their short buy-and-sell strategies, are naturally focused on what can create value rapidly for their investee firms. It is no surprise then that they pay significant attention to ESG factors, not only in the investment phase but also during their active involvement period.
- Many private equity firms have turned CSR into a competitive advantage when negotiating purchases with sustainability- sensitive sellers, such as family-owned firms.
- Private equity firms are very competitive against each other. CSR has become an effective weapon in the negotiating wars with sellers, for example, those owned by institutional owners with their own pro-active ESG agenda.
- Mutual funds have developed sophisticated ESG-driven investment strategies, actively engaging companies on behalf of ever-more sophisticated and demanding customers.

💣 Traps

- Sustainability needs to be considered as a source of value creation opportunities, not simply as a risk exposure. With holding periods increasing in private equity, this mindset shift from a defensive to offensive approach to CSR is fundamental in generating the impact from sustainability activities.
- Beware of the reporting purpose only sustainability programs. No private equity firm today will unleash a website that does not explicitly mention sustainability concerns. That said, there is a lot of variability in their actual commitment to it in their actions.
- Do not underestimate the incentive and motivational potential of an active CSR agenda in the war for talent.
- Avoid the less material issues. With their strong focus on quick value impact, private equity firms prioritize performance on material issues and discard activities on less material issues.

✍ Takeaways

In this chapter, we highlighted how some of the most sophisticated investors have taken notice of sustainability in their lines of business, not only incorporating some of the principles in their wealth management firms but also turning sustainability into a sustainable investment theme. Venture capitalists were quick to spot the potential of new technologies required to create a greener, more responsible future, backing leading-edge entrepreneurs in alternative energies, smart grids, the sharing economy and other world-changing applications. Funds were launched with pure or mixed sustainability strategies to pursue emerging technologies with the potential to create new industries.

Private equity investors were hot on their heels, first paying lip-service to the cause in their annual reports to limited partners but then realizing the potential of sustainability for their portfolio companies. Interventions have taken various forms, from simply adding sustainability as an item on the due diligence list as a way to manage reputational risk to actively pursuing sustainability initiatives in each portfolio company through a dedicated cadre of ESG specialists. Hedge fund investors, without the luxury of the relatively long investment horizon of private equity investors, jumped on the bandwagon as well, ensuring that their arbitrage strategies would also be supported by strong compliance policies. Finally, we visited some of the novel mutual fund managers with strong ESG credentials and investigated the performance of ESG-driven mutual fund products.

A practical conclusion of the chapter is that even the most financially savvy investors have not only accepted but incorporated sustainability into their products and strategies. Those are not philanthropists but hard-core capitalists with a clear focus on the bottom line. If they found reasons to pay attention, then there is little space for others to question the validity of the theme.

References

1. Bocken, N.M.P. (2005) Sustainable venture capital: Catalyst for sustainable start-up success? *Journal of Cleaner Production*.
2. Hall, J., Daneke, J., Lenox, M. (2010) Sustainable development and entrepreneurship: past contributions and future directions. *Journal of Business Venturing*.
3. European Commission (2012, October 29) Small Companies, Big Ideas. Retrieved from https://ec.europa.eu/environment/ecoap/about-eco-innovation/policies-matters/eu/20121029-small-companies-big-ideas_en

4. Airbnb (2017) *Airbnb fast facts*. Retrieved from https://press.atairbnb.com/app/uploads/2017/08/4-Million-Listings-Announcement-1.pd
5. Zipcar (2014) Who Exactly Is the Car Club Type? http://www.zipcar.co.uk/is-it. Accessed May 2018.
6. Airbnb (2014) New Study Reveals a Greener Way to Travel: Airbnb Community Shows Environmental Benefits of Home Sharing [Press release]. Retrieved from https://de.airbnb.com/press/news/new-study-reveals-a-greener-way-to-travel-airbnb-community-shows-environmental-benefits-of-home-sharing
7. Chafkin, M. (2014, July 4) A Broken Place: The Spectacular Failure of The Startup That Was Going to Change the World. *Fast Company*. Retrieved from https://www.fastcompany.com/3028159/a-broken-place-better-place
8. Katapult Accelerator (2017) Katapult Accelerator details. http://katapultaccelerator.com/. Accessed 17 May 2018.
9. Preqin (2015) *2015 Preqin Global Private Equity & Venture Capital Report*. Retrieved from http://docs.preqin.com/reports/2015-Preqin-Global-Private-Equity-and-Venture-Capital-Report-Sample-Pages.pdf
10. Aster Capital (2018) Aster hub. http://aster.com/hub-2/. Accessed 17 May 2018.
11. Breakthrough Energy (2018) Breakthrough Energy Ventures. http://www.b-t.energy/ventures/. Accessed 16 May 2018.
12. Chrysalix Venture Capital (2018) Our methodology. http://www.chrysalix.com/methodology/. Accessed 8 May 2018.
13. Demeter (2017) *2017 ESG report*. Retrieved from http://demeter-im.com/wp-content/uploads/2018/06/2017-ESG-Report.pdf
14. eCAPITAL (2018) About eCAPITAL. https://ecapital.de/en/. Accessed 4 May 2018.
15. EcoMachines ventures (2017) About EcoMachines Ventures. http://ecomachinesventures.com/. Accessed 5 May 2018.
16. Bernow, S., Klempner, B., Magnin, C. (2017, October) From 'why' to 'why not': Sustainable investing as the new normal. *McKinsey & Company*. Retrieved from https://www.mckinsey.com/industries/private-equity-and-principal-investors/our-insights/from-why-to-why-not-sustainable-investing-as-the-new-normal
17. Lewis, A. (2017, November 15) PE hold times keep going on. *PitchBook*. Retrieved from https://pitchbook.com/news/articles/pe-hold-times-keep-going-up
18. Roberge, M.W., Flaherty, J.C., Almeida, R.M. et al. (2017, July) Lengthening the investment time horizon. https://www.mfs.com/content/en_us/mfs-insights/lengthening-the-investment-time-horizon.html. Accessed 25 March 2018.
19. Larsen, K. (2016, May 10) KKR, Carlyle Group and private equity's sustainability evolution. *Greenbiz*. Retrieved from https://www.greenbiz.com/article/kkr-carlyle-group-and-private-equitys-sustainability-evolution
20. Kohlberg Kravis Roberts (2018) KKR Today. http://www.kkr.com/kkr-today. Accessed 19 April 2018.

21. This case is an abridged version of TUMI and the Doughty Hanson Value Enhancement Group (IMD-3-2299) Copyright © 2018 by IMD—International Institute for Management Development, Lausanne, Switzerland (www.imd.org). No part of this publication may be reproduced, stored in a retrieval system or transmitted in any form or by any means without the prior written permission of IMD.

22. PricewaterhouseCoopers (2014) *Why Sustainability is essential for Private Equity Houses?* Retrieved from https://www.pwc.lu/en/sustainability/docs/pwc-pe.pdf

23. Agrawal, T. & Pandey, A. (2012, April 20) Luxury bag maker Tumi surges in market debut. *Reuters*. Retrieved from https://www.reuters.com/article/us-tumi-ipo/luxury-bag-maker-tumi-surges-in-market-debut-idUSBRE-83I1DJ20120420

24. Wei, D. & Chang, R. (2016, March 3) Samsonite to buy Tumi for about $1.8 billion in biggest deal. *Bloomberg*. Retrieved from https://www.bloomberg.com/news/articles/2016-03-03/samsonite-nears-deal-to-buy-luggage-maker-tumi-wsj-reports

25. DH Private Equity Partners (2016, March 8) Doughty Hanson to sell remaining Tumi shares [Press release]. Retrieved from http://www.dhpep.com/news-and-notices/news/2016/08-03-2016

26. Private Equity International (2015) Dealing with the elephant. *The Responsible Investment Special 2015*. Retrieved from https://www.act.is/media/1318/private-equity-international_the-responsible-investment-special-2015.pdf

27. Franck, T. (2018, April 27) Social and sustainable investing gets a boost from an unlikely source: Wall Street activists. *CNBC*. https://www.cnbc.com/2018/04/27/social-investing-gets-a-boost-from-an-unlikely-source-activists.html

28. The Forum for Sustainable and Responsible Investment (2017) SIR Basics. https://www.ussif.org/sribasics. Accessed May 26, 2018.

29. Herbst-Bayliss, S. (2018, April 17) Activist investor Jana hired staff for socially responsible fund. *Reuters*. Retrieved from https://www.reuters.com/article/us-hedgefunds-jana/activist-investor-jana-hired-staff-for-new-socially-responsible-fund-idUSKBN1HO200

30. This case is an abridged and edited version of the eMBA case assignment by Claudio Mellace, Etienne Zeller and Laurent Gaye (IMD eMBA June 2018) conducted with CADMOS and its engagements funds under the supervision of Professor Benoit Leleux. Copyright © 2018 by IMD—International Institute for Management Development, Lausanne, Switzerland (www.imd.org). No part of this publication may be reproduced, stored in a retrieval system or transmitted in any form or by any means without the prior written permission of IMD.

31. The Boston Consulting Group (2017) *Total Societal Impact: A new lens for Strategy*. Retrieved from https://www.bcg.com/Images/BCG-Total-Societal-Impact-Oct-2017-R_tcm36-174019.pdf

8

Encouraging a Culture of Sustainability

In the previous chapters, we have illustrated the importance of companies developing a clear sense of direction through the formulation of a clear statement of purpose. Based upon case studies, industry data and best practices from top decile sustainability leaders, we have uncovered different ways in which purpose statements can become effective drivers of sustainability programs, building on examples from adidas and Interface. The relevance of establishing a sustainability strategy based on carefully selected material issues for ESG ratings was highlighted. More importantly, we have portrayed the tendency of organizations to address too many sustainability topics that bear little to no relevance to their core businesses, which results in reducing the impact of the programs. In the following sections, we underline the significance of the leadership's effort to embed sustainability into the core business strategy, the importance of harnessing a culture of sustainability and the impact of corporate behavior on performance. In the later sections, we suggest a tool for measuring corporate culture and stress the benefits of the systematic measurement of sustainability performance on culture, talent attraction and retention.

Leadership in Sustainability

As Simon Sinek pointed out in his famous TED Talk, now seen by over 39 million people, most organizations still think in term of what—how—why. In contrast, great leaders and great organizations are putting the why first, bringing innovation to those audiences who believe what the companies believe. For

© The Author(s) 2019
B. Leleux, J. van der Kaaij, *Winning Sustainability Strategies*,
https://doi.org/10.1007/978-3-319-97445-3_8

sustainable development, that same mantra applies. Those who lead sustainability transitions inspire the people around them, sparking a culture of sustainability in the company that leads to changes in behaviors and attitudes.

In the sustainability literature, iconoclastic leadership is often touted as a crucial driver of outstanding sustainability programs [1]. Fueled by inspiring stories from sustainability pioneers such as Anita Roddick (the Body Shop), Yvon Chouinard (Patagonia) and Ray Anderson (Interface), sustainability initiatives seem to always be on the lookout for directional guidance from the top-seat. In this section, we underline the importance of leadership in turning purpose into actions. At the same time, leadership should not be regarded as *haarlemmerolie*—Dutch for *Haarlem oil*, a potent mixture of sulfur, herbs and terebinth oil. The oil was invented around 1696, and it was marketed as a cure for many, if not all, ailments. Its fame was such that nowadays the term "haarlemmerolie" is still used by the Dutch to indicate a fix for all problems [2]. To successfully develop a culture of sustainability, the C-level requires help from middle management, a certain level of maturity in the industry and some closeness to consumers' needs.

In the 2017 version of the GlobeScan—SustainAbility Survey, a 20-year running study based on the opinions of over 1000 sustainability experts, sustainability leaders scored noticeably higher on their ability to articulate a vision and define ambitious goals [3]. The experts surveyed also expressed the belief that an integrated sustainability strategy, a clear vision, innovation and transparency were prevailing qualities required for leading organizations in the decade to come. According to the same survey, leadership in sustainability has evolved from a *do-less-harm* era (up until about 2006), when pioneering entrepreneurs were miles ahead of all others, to a more broadly embraced *sustainable growth* era, when sustainability issues are embedded into the core business of companies.

If the experts are right and the "ability to articulate a vision and define ambitious goals" sets leading companies apart, having a closer look at two high-flying companies should provide some interesting insights. In the following sections, Unilever, ranked first for the seventh year running as a global sustainability leader, and Interface, ranked third and the only company to be included in the leadership category ever since the establishment of the survey 20 years ago, are discussed in more detail.

Unilever

Soon after taking the helm as CEO of Unilever in 2009, Paul Polman made some courageous decisions to get the maker of Dove soap, Hellmann's mayonnaise and Magnum ice cream back on track. He vowed to cut Unilever's environmental footprint in half by 2020, while doubling its turnover. Under Polman's predecessor, Unilever was far from passive on the sustainability front, but by developing the Unilever Sustainable Living Plan (USLP) in 2010, Polman and his team set new standards for corporate sustainability programs. The Sustainable Living Plan was designed not as an isolated strategy with many individual sustainability initiatives but as an integrated, themed program to fundamentally change the way Unilever conducted business, including the required management structures fully integrated into the organizational framework of the company. The company publicly committed to helping more than a billion people take action to improve their health and well-being and to source all agricultural raw materials sustainably by 2020. In its target setting, the plan decoupled the company's intended growth from its environmental impact [4].

> When I came here, this company had done everything you can think of. Created sustainable initiatives, sustainable fishery, sustainable agriculture. Round tables. But we were only 10 per cent sustainable. Now we're 65 per cent sustainable.
> Paul Polman, CEO Unilever [5]

The business was impacted, but so were shareholders. The emphasis on sustainability was not to every shareholder's taste, with many electing to "vote with their feet," but others, with more favorable views on the new approach, were quick to replace them. A significant change of guards but without additional volatility: before Polman took the CEO position, 60% of Unilever's top 10 shareholders had been there for five years or more; by 2016, 70% of the top 10 had held their shares for more than seven years [5].

Interface

Interface's story began in 1973, when Ray Anderson discovered a market for flexible flooring. With its focus on the production and marketing of modular carpet tiles, Interface catered to the quickly rising needs of the office building boom of the mid-1970s. After a stellar entry into the market, the company grew from strength to strength. Over the past decades, Interface has acquired more than 50 companies, become a $1 billion business, and cemented its position as a leader in sustainable business. Founder Anderson wanted his firm to lead by example; by 2020, this self-described "radical industrialist" wanted Interface to become the first company with zero environmental impact. With that inspiring purpose, suitably labeled Mission Zero®, the company adopted a sustainability culture that outlived even its CEO. The company's focused commitment to eliminating any negative impact it may have on the environment instilled a strong and lasting culture of change that resulted in several breakthrough innovations in the carpet industry. As the targets of Mission Zero® came within sight, the company embarked on a new, even more ambitious mission. With *Climate Take Back*, Interface hoped to shift from restorative to regenerative, striving to restore nature.

Both company stories emphasize the role of a strong, iconoclastic leadership. In turn, the leadership at both Unilever and Interface provided the *stickiness* required to progress from a powerful purpose statement to a culture rooted in sustainability. In the sections below, the impact of a strong corporate sustainability culture is underlined with research that is more quantitative in nature.

Culture and Impact

Besides signposting qualities for future sustainability leadership, the GlobeScan—SustainAbility survey also uncovered a rapid rise in the sustainability ranking of consumer-facing brands between 2007 and 2017. Surprisingly, during that period, the head start enjoyed by the top performers grew wider, instead of narrower. In other words, the accomplishments of sustainability leaders such as Unilever, Natura (Brazil's number one cosmetics manufacturer, ranked sixth in the expert ranking), and Nestlé (ranked eighth) outshone other players within the industry. The perception of the experts was that the performance gap was sizable and more worryingly, increasing. This disparity was more than just perception. The Unilever sustainable living brands were applauded by Unilever CEO Polman for their performance in the marketplace when he declared:

> Brands that help solve problems are relevant and accepted. Not surprisingly, the stronger this purpose, the better the brands do. Our sustainable living brands are delivering more than 60% of Unilever's growth and growing over 50% faster than the rest of the business.
> Paul Polman [6]

The results from the 2017 survey also showed a strong consistency with the results of the 2012 Harvard Business School study on the impact of a culture of sustainability [7] on behaviors and performance. In their attempt to capture the elusive value of culture, HBS researchers started from the premise that the level of integration of social and environmental policies within companies was a good proxy for a firm's culture of sustainability. Companies that had many social and environmental policies were deemed to have a stronger culture of sustainability. Comparing a sample of 90 companies that demonstrated superior adoption of sustainability policies (referred to as *high-sustainability firms*) with a matching sample of 90 similar firms with little or no adoption of sustainability policies (referred to as *low-sustainability firms*), researchers uncovered differences in performance and behaviors between the two groups over the period 1993–2011.

The research also analyzed the impact of that culture of sustainability on stock market performance by tracking 18 years of total shareholder returns (TSR) for both sub-groups. The results were intriguing: high-sustainability firms outperformed low-sustainability firms on TSR by about 4.8% annually, after taking into consideration the usual control variables! These implications were confirmed by comparing the two sub-groups on other financial performance metrics, such as return on assets and return on equity. Investing $1 in a portfolio of high-sustainability firms in 1993 would have returned $22.60 by the end of 2010. In comparison, the same $1 investment in a comparable portfolio of low-sustainability firms would have yielded only $15.40.

When analyzing the drivers of the outperformance, the authors identified governance-related factors as the main determinants; high-sustainability firms were better at involving their boards of directors and made more use of dedicated sustainability board committees. The incentive methodology of senior executives was also found to be better aligned with environmental, social and client metrics. In other words, high-sustainability companies were better at embedding sustainability into their senior management structures.

Obviously, much has evolved since the 2012 study and laggards have been making efforts to catch up, at least in certain areas (refer to Fig. 8.1). When taking a closer look at the more recent data from the Dow Jones Sustainability Index (DJSI) scores from all participating companies from 2015 to 2017 in ten different industries, the gap on governance-related factors appears to have closed almost entirely. During this period, the separation between the top decile and the industry average on *governance* issues was reduced to less than 9%.

But the sustainability leaders were not sitting still; over the same period, the overall gap between the identified sustainability leaders and their industry peers widened significantly. This was in large part due to top decile performers further developing their abilities to capture value from sustainability as illustrated by their *operational eco-efficiency* score. Sustainability leaders have turned their earlier advantage on governance into hard cash by further embedding sustainability into their business.

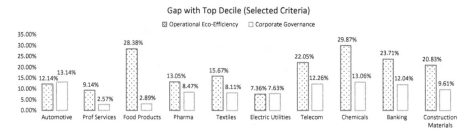

Fig. 8.1 Gap between top decile and industry average on selected criteria (operational eco-efficiency and corporate governance)

Measuring Culture

The previous sections highlighted the positive impact of a culture of sustainability on performance. Principally, the board of directors is charged with safeguarding the firm's competitive advantage, ensuring that the firm is talent rich, and building a winning, ethical strategy supported by deep-operating excellence that drives long-term shareholder value. From that perspective, managing and measuring culture seems an obvious choice. Unfortunately, many directors are more attentive to key financial metrics and strategic priorities and consequently fail to recognize that their mission cannot be fulfilled without the appropriate corporate culture. An undermanaged culture can backfire badly, as exemplified by Uber, the ride-hailing company that chalked up losses of $4.5 billion in 2017 alone [8].

> Uber's aggressive workplace culture spilled out at a global all-hands meeting in late 2015 in Las Vegas, where the company hired Beyoncé to perform at the rooftop bar of the Palms Hotel. Between bouts of drinking and gambling, Uber employees used cocaine in the bathrooms at private parties, said three attendees, and a manager groped several female employees. [9]

This incident, and a number of similar ones, triggered a change of CEO later in the year. Under founder Kalanick's leadership, the company faced allegations of a culture of sexism and sexual harassment, including a memo in which Kalanick detailed ground rules for consensual sex practices between employees. After an internal investigation, the board decided to replace Kalanick. The firm's new CEO, Dara Khosrowshahi, stated shortly after his installation that Uber's *moral compass* had been off under co-founder Kalanick [10]. Without the presence of balanced directional leadership from the C-suite and the absence of measurement of the actual state of the company culture, even one of the most successful startups in the world slipped out of control quickly.

The embarrassing example of Uber's undermanaged corporate culture is unfortunately not an isolated case. In 2016, Wells Fargo bank fired 5300 employees involved in a widespread illegal practice. To meet the performance targets of their *cross-selling* strategy, employees secretly created millions of unauthorized bank and credit card accounts, without clients' knowledge [11]! The mere scale of the scandal makes it unmistakably clear that the issue was not 5300 individual *bad apples*, but the *bad orchard* that created them [12]. It was a failure of corporate culture. In recognition of its bad orchard, the bank agreed to pay a fine of $185 million, along with a $5 million refund for customers. Both Uber and Wells Fargo exemplify how flaws in corporate culture can lead to damaging business failures.

To define and measure culture, several tools are available. In addition to in-house scorecards and surveys, standardized organizational culture measurement models have been developed. The Denison Organizational Culture Model, for example, is based on over two decades of research linking culture to bottom-line performance, such as profitability, growth, quality, innovation, customer and employee satisfaction. The Denison Model identifies and assesses four key traits of cultural strength: mission, consistency, adaptability and involvement (refer to Fig. 8.2). Two of these traits, involvement and adaptability, are indicators of flexibility, openness and responsiveness; they were also found to be strong predictors of growth. The other two traits, consistency and mission, are indicators of integration, direction and vision; hence, they are better predictors of profitability [13]. Using a survey-based approach, the Denison Model benchmarks the organization's performance against a large, diverse global database of over 1000 companies.

From its four-legged structure alone, the Denison Organizational Culture Model accentuates the importance of culture for the development and implementation of a sustainability strategy. As advocated, the definition of a meaningful long-term direction that is backed by values and systems (consistency) is essential for the development of a vectoring approach to sustainability. Moreover, listening to the marketplace (adaptability) is indispensable for staying informed on material sustainability topics. And lastly, the alignment and engagement of employees (involvement) need to be first-rate for a company to become a sustainability leader [14].

Building a Culture of Sustainability: The Power of Coalitions

After addressing the importance of sustainability leadership and the value of a strong company culture, this section concentrates on the role of coalitions to make things happen. The essential proposition is that a culture of change can

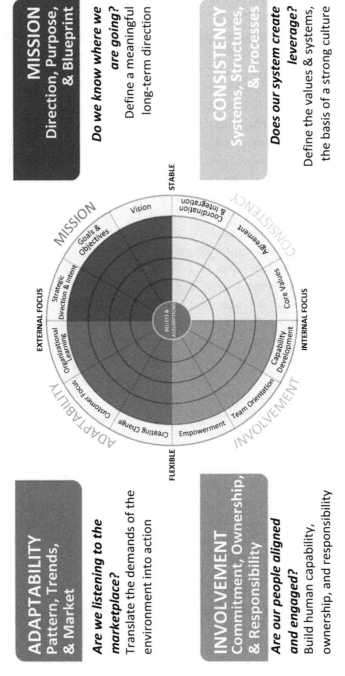

MISSION
Direction, Purpose, & Blueprint

Do we know where we are going?
Define a meaningful long-term direction

CONSISTENCY
Systems, Structures, & Processes

Does our system create leverage?
Define the values & systems, the basis of a strong culture

ADAPTABILITY
Pattern, Trends, & Market

Are we listening to the marketplace?
Translate the demands of the environment into action

INVOLVEMENT
Commitment, Ownership, & Responsibility

Are our people aligned and engaged?
Build human capability, ownership, and responsibility

Fig. 8.2 The Denison organizational culture model

be strengthened by groups of like-minded companies forming *coalitions of the willing* that share a common culture.

Going back 15 years, the World Business Council for Sustainable Development (WBCSD) founder Stephan Schmidheiny and his co-authors in their 2002 book *Walking the Talk: The Business Case for Sustainable Development* explained a telling vision on coalitions and partnerships.

> Business has much experience with stakeholder dialogue, but still too little with the next step: practical partnerships composed of players in different sectors. Not only do such partnerships combine skills and provide access to constituencies that one partner might not have, but they also enhance the credibility of results—results that might be less effective and believable if they only come from business, civil society, or government. [15]

A point that was definitely true then, and one that is likely still true today.

Going even further back in history, a famous example of a coalition with a shared culture can be found in the Hanseatic League, also known as Hansa. The league was a commercial confederation of merchants that initially united the Northern German towns of Lübeck, Hamburg and Bremen in the second half of the 1100s, subsequently spreading across the Baltic and the North Sea to dominate maritime trade for over three centuries. The word "Hansa" originates from Hanse, the Middle Low German word for a convoy, referring to bands of merchants traveling between the Hanseatic cities whether by land or sea [16]. The league was created to protect the guilds' economic interests and diplomatic privileges in their affiliated cities and countries, as well as along the trade routes. The Hanseatic cities had their own legal system and furnished their own armies for mutual protection and aid. The Hanseatic cities regularly came to the aid of one another, jointly trained pilots, erected lighthouses along the strategic routes and opened offices (Kontors) in their member cities. Despite this, the organization was not a state or a confederation of city-states as only a few cities in the league were entirely autonomous.

At its peak, the League stretched from Novgorod in the East to London in the West, with an impressive list of cities, such as Tallinn, Riga, Gdańsk, Berlin, Groningen, Cologne, Antwerp, Brugge, Stockholm, Bergen, Kiel, Rostock, Turku, Wroclaw and Kaliningrad, all becoming members of the League at some point in time. The guilds traded many commodities, such as fur, wool, wood, silver, cod and salt with little formal structure in the arrangement. In fact, the absence of an organizational superstructure was key to the working of the Hansa: it was the coalition of the willing that created a great cultural and architectural heritage. Hanseatic merchants were known for the high-ethical standards they held in business, virtues that continued to be cultivated by the Honourable Society of Hamburg Merchants well into the twenty-first century.

Nowadays, with what could be regarded as a modernized version of guilds, similar partnerships are established. Companies with strong sustainability cultures are forming coalitions with like-minded companies to advance knowledge, create momentum and engage partners in developing value chains that possess a higher level of sustainability.

In Chap. 3, we introduced Tony's Chocolonely, the child-labor-free chocolate pioneer. The NGO-turned-company elected to be accredited as a B Corp, a certification available to companies certified by an independent body, the B Lab [17]. To obtain the B Corp certification, the companies must pass rigorous standards of social and environmental performance, accountability and transparency. Started in the US in 2006 as a tool for impact assessment, B Corps have become a lively community of more than 2100 companies endeavoring to become a force for good [17]. All members, from 50 countries and representing over 130 industries, are obliged to use the power of the markets to solve social and environmental problems and to create benefits for stakeholders at large, not just shareholders. With leading member companies such as Ben & Jerry's and Ecover, the certification label became more than a status symbol; it helped secure the culture and company values from farmer to end consumers in a holistic way, providing tangible stimulus to all stakeholders to keep raising the sustainability bar.

Patagonia, another early B Corp member, was an iconic role model. Founded by rock-climbing aficionado Yvon Chouinard in 1973, the firm became one of the most admired outdoor apparel brands in the world. Its company mission was simple: build the best product, cause no unnecessary harm, use business to inspire and implement solutions to the environmental crisis. That mission helped Patagonia develop a sustainability culture from day one and, for instance, change to 100% organic cotton sportswear as early as 1996. While growing awareness on environmental issues and climate change, the company was continuously on the lookout for new ways to make its supply chain more sustainable, inspired by the leadership of Chouinard.

Creating Your Own Coalition

A possible alternative to becoming a member of an existing movement is to create a coalition of your own. This is what wine company CEO Miguel Torres elected to do in a pioneering effort to protect the Torres heritage and

Table 8.1 The primum familiae vini charter [18]

As custodians of national heritage, the members uphold regional winemaking traditions and:
• They share the challenges of running independent family businesses and passing them from one generation to the next
• They exchange viticultural/oenological information and promote the traditional methods that underpin the quality of their wines and respect for terroir
• They foster environmental and social responsibility in family winemaking businesses
• They increase awareness of the benefits of moderation in the consumption of fine wines, essential for their appreciation, and for a healthy lifestyle

culture. Obviously, the Torres family was not alone in its endeavor to maintain family values and company culture. The highly fragmented wine industry is, almost by default, a family business with a strong sense of tradition. The culture of the vine and the slow, meticulous creation of the best wines, require a long-term perspective and a great sense of respect for nature and the company's impact on it.

So, when Miguel Torres was looking for ways to harness his company culture and heritage, he launched an association called the "Primum Familiae Vini" (first families of wine). As the association's charter (outlined if Table 8.1) details, members of the Primum Familiae Vini concentrate on ensuring their legacies with a strong sense for environmental and social responsibility, while jointly improving their businesses.

Besides representing a successful vehicle for harnessing family values and exchanging knowledge, the Primum Familiae Vini turned out to be a powerful marketing instrument for its members. As some of the most admired wine brands in the world and their family owners joined the club, including the Antinori, Vega-Sicilia, Torres, Joseph Drouhin and Mouton Rothschild families, the Primum Familiae Vini started to yield significant influence within the world of wine and beyond. The shared family values brought together a coalition that was making an effort to protect its heritage, in business and in nature.

Coalitions can also be forged around sustainability issues, as the previously mentioned initiative of the Champions 12.3 illustrates (see Chap. 5). This coalition of almost 40 leading CEOs, ministers and other global leaders is dedicated to achieving the Sustainable Development Goals (SDGs) on food loss and waste. The Champions regularly get together to assess progress on achieving the SDG target 12.3, sharing best practices and analyses on food loss and waste reduction and how to overcome barriers to the application of those best practices. The results of the initiative are openly shared with internal and external stakeholders.

🗀 GMA Garnet and the Hanseatic Culture [19]

Nowhere is the Hanseatic culture better illustrated than in the experience of GMA Garnet, a world leader in the production, distribution and recycling of garnet, one of the Earth's most resistant minerals. In this abridged case, we investigate the contribution made by culture and values to the creation of the long-term partnerships.

GMA Garnet and Jebsen & Jessen Family Enterprise

Torsten Ketelsen discovered the fledgling West Australian mining operation of Garnet Millers Associates (later renamed GMA Garnet) in the late 1980s and, as GMA Garnet's agent, he started to develop a market for garnet in the Arabian Gulf ship-building/repair and oil industries from his newly established Ketelsen Enterprise, based in Perth. At the time, garnet was still a largely unknown industrial commodity. A natural mineral belonging to a group of silicates used since the Bronze Age, principally as gemstones, garnet was known not only for its hardness but also for its toughness and density—which made it exceptionally effective as an industrial abrasive with excellent cutting capabilities.

In the late 1980s, GMA Garnet started developing a market for garnet by creating a series of differentiated products with clever marketing and branding, ultimately establishing itself as a market leader with a 40% global market share, by replacing traditional abrasives and opening new applications. By 2016, there were over 40 garnet applications in the waterjet-cutting and abrasive blasting industries, including steel and marble cutting in shipyards and aircraft production facilities, and new applications were being developed regularly. Torsten recalled:

> The first 20 years of my journey were the toughest: I kept bringing samples of garnet to a region where traditional abrasives such as sand were well established, very cheap and easily available. You can imagine there is no shortage of sand in the Middle East ... From the beginning we realized the only way forward was to offer a superior value proposition, including supreme efficiency and environmental safety. Initially, our customers were too busy sandblasting to even try our product: it was more expensive up-front, and profits only showed up later. But when they tried it, they usually fell for it quickly. They would often say, "Why didn't you come to me 10 years ago?"

When the first Gulf War broke out, Torsten looked to distribute the abrasive in Europe, starting first at Jebsen & Jessen Hamburg, the European trading house of the Jebsen & Jessen Family Enterprise (JJFE). At the time, Jebsen

& Jessen Hamburg was trading mainly chemicals and textiles between Asia and Europe, and garnet would be a complete novelty for the firm. However, the firm's familiarity with shipyards (garnet's first application area) and its openness to diversification helped.

In 1991, Torsten Ketelsen and Wolfhart Putzier—CEO of Jebsen & Jessen Hamburg and a non-family shareholder in JJFE—established a joint venture between Ketelsen Enterprise Pty Ltd and Jebsen & Jessen Hamburg and named it GMA Garnet (Europe) GmbH. The new entity was fully embedded in Jebsen & Jessen Hamburg's offices with the purpose of distributing and selling garnet in Europe.

Full Integration and Moving Up the Value Chain

Ten years later, in 2001, GMA Garnet (Europe) and Torsten's Middle East & South-East Asia distribution networks accounted for almost the entire production offtake of GMA Garnet, but they still did not actually own the mining operation. To secure uninterrupted product supply, Torsten, together with the two principal family shareholders of JJFE (Hans Michael Jebsen and Heinrich Jessen) and Wolfhart Putzier, established Garnet International Resources Ltd (GIRL), a vehicle that then purchased a 50% share in the GMA Garnet mining and processing operation in Western Australia.

GIRL was integrated into JJFE on terms similar to its other operating entities. GIRL's board included the two Jebsen & Jessen principal shareholders, two non-family shareholders—Torsten Ketelsen and Wolfhart Putzier—and a fifth director nominated by Hans Michael Jebsen and Heinrich Jessen to reflect their controlling stake. The two non-family shareholders remained operationally involved and enjoyed a great deal of latitude to develop the business.

GIRL's single purpose was to acquire the West Australian mining & processing operations of GMA Garnet, but the journey to full vertical integration in the garnet business was only beginning. After protracted negotiations and a convoluted acquisition process, GIRL took full ownership of GMA's West Australian mining and production assets in 2005. As a result, GIRL became the largest producer and distributor of industrial garnet in the world, with the distribution assets of Ketelsen Enterprise in the Middle East and Southeast Asia as well as the joint European distribution of GMA Garnet Europe JV. GIRL then bought a second mine in Montana, which processed a hard-rock garnet using a very different manufacturing process. This secured GMA Garnet a presence in the biggest garnet market worldwide—the US.

The Quest for Environmental Mining

GMA Garnet moved down the value chain by adding garnet recycling capabilities to its portfolio. With its extraordinary hardness and toughness, garnet retained most of its abrasive characteristics after use and could be recycled up to seven times. Large industrial-scale recycling plants were established close to major customer centers, that is, Dubai, Saudi Arabia, Italy, Philadelphia and New Orleans.

This recycling capability completed the company's control over the entire production and distribution value chain, from mining through processing, logistics and shipping to distribution to the final users worldwide as well as reprocessing and recycling. The GMA Garnet vertical integration/circular economy model was progressively adopted in other parts of the Jebsen & Jessen Family Enterprise; the traditional trading model was no longer able to safeguard the existence of the firm.

Even though Australia had very high mining, waste and land management standards, GMA Garnet went way beyond environmental compliance. Before starting mining operations, it first collected plant seeds and only then removed the top soil. After extracting the garnet, it completely rehabilitated the grounds with the original seeds and top soil.

Additionally, GMA Garnet relied on gravity and centrifugal processing and used only water to clean the extractions, a much safer approach than the traditional chemical processing. Finally, garnet itself was a much safer abrasive than silica sand, which was banned in most countries because the dust it created is linked to silicosis—a fatal lung disease. Garnet was preferable to other alternative abrasives such as coal and copper slags, which are also associated with environmental and health hazards.

A Front-Door Exit for a Successful Endeavour

Torsten Ketelsen could look back at the last 15 years with great pride. Under his leadership, the company had grown tremendously, increasing its value more than 15 times, all without new external financing. It was now time for him to consider the well-deserved next step—retirement.

In terms of ownership, GMA Garnet started negotiations with a reputed private equity firm. A thorough due diligence was performed over eight months, concluding with a strong valuation proposal. It quickly became clear, however, that the buyer and seller were not aligned in their views of the future of the company. The private equity firm was focused on an accelerated value creation game plan, leading to a fast exit in the form of an IPO or a trade sale, putting the long-term sustainability of the business into question.

The tipping point came when the full purchase offer showed figures on critical key performance indicators (KPIs) that were quite different from the originally negotiated numbers. An emergency meeting of the board in Hong Kong was arranged, and within a day they had worked out an alternative ownership exit—an internal one. The internal exit price ended up being based on the external valuation and the due diligence. Two successive buyouts of shares from both Torsten and Wolfhart would result in them completely exiting their ownership of GMA Garnet.

With the ownership exit engineered, it was now time to consider the management exit. Torsten was fully aware that GMA Garnet in 2015 was very different from the original company, with a dominant global market share and a fairly flat corporate structure. Suitable successors were found in Stephen Gobby, taking over as CEO, and Keith Gordon, as non-executive chairman of the board of directors. Having finalized the exit, Torsten Ketelsen retired from the CEO function in June 2015, fully confident the company was in the hands of a formidable management team, and caring owners.

New Management: Renewed Energy

GMA Garnet's new management team established lofty goals for the company, striving to double the value of the business again within the next five-year period by finding new applications for garnet and expanding the market for GMA Garnet worldwide. Time would tell if the top management team, major shareholders for the first time, would still prioritize the firm's long-term sustainability over its quest to achieve this growth, and whether the full integration of GMA Garnet into the Jebsen & Jessen Family Enterprise would effectively support or hamper the company along the way.

In true Hanseatic style, the new management team carried forward the existing sustainability principles. One of the signs of the company's focus on sustainability and eagerness to partner was indeed visible when, in October 2017, GMA Garnet signed a long-term agreement with Advanced Energy Resources (AER) to construct a three-megawatt wind and solar farm in Western Australia. This collaboration would eventually result in 100% renewable energy for the mine's electricity requirements [20].

Tips, Traps and Takeaways

☝ Tips

- Involve the middle management early to help turn the firm's statement of purpose into an effective culture of sustainability.
- Check for coalitions that are compatible with the company culture on the topic of sustainability for knowledge exchange and gaining momentum.
- Measure, and keep measuring, the current state of corporate culture and respond to the outcomes of these surveys.

💣 Traps

- Although buy-in from the top is an essential component for success, it is not enough. Be careful not to focus on the boardroom only.
- Avoid launching a spree of well-intended sustainability initiatives from the top, especially without an appropriate unifying theme and/or overarching target.
- Compliance on governance issues is just a starting point. Once the governance within the organization has been covered, redirect the sustainability efforts toward value capture from innovation and operational eco-efficiencies.

☝ Takeaways

This chapter highlighted the positive impact a culture of sustainability has on corporate performance and on corporate behavior. Firms with high-sustainability cultures deliver significantly better stock market performance than those with low-sustainability cultures. Developing a potent sustainability culture requires leadership qualities very similar to those required to lead major change processes. Best-in-class examples from Unilever and Interface illustrated the fact that outstanding leaders are able to develop cutting-edge sustainability programs. The business performance of these two sustainability leaders confirmed the positive impact of a sustainability culture. Unilever has claimed its sustainable living brands are responsible for more than 60% of its growth and are growing 50% faster than the rest of the business; Interfaces' breakthrough innovations turned the company from a startup into a global $1 billion carpet tile business with a sustainability reputation second to none.

Laggards have taken notice and are not sitting on their hands. The divide on the performance of governance-related factors between decile extremes has been decreasing, even though sustainability pioneers seem to continue to harvest the fruits of their early starts. Experts predict that sustainability leaders will have to excel at integrated sustainability strategies, vision, innovation and transparency in the future to maintain their prime positions.

Examples from the ride-hailing company Uber and Wells Fargo bank provides empirical evidence that measuring a company culture is essential, and that failures in corporate culture can lead to major shortcomings in the business. To help prevent such failures, the Denison Organizational Culture Model was introduced as a possible culture measurement and management instrument.

Coalitions are shown to be powerful vehicles for exchanging information on sustainability programs, jointly raising awareness and gaining momentum for cultural change with internal and external stakeholders. In the absence of a suitable established coalition, companies have at times resorted to creating their own, as was shown with Champions 12.3 on food waste and the Torres wine company on ensuring its legacy regarding environmental and social responsibility.

References

1. Freya Williams, E. (2015) *Green Giants: How Smart Companies Turn Sustainability into Billion-Dollar Businesses*. LLC Gildan Media.
2. Wikipedia contributors (2016, October 28) Haarlem oil. *Wikipedia, The Free Encyclopedia*. https://en.wikipedia.org/w/index.php?title=Haarlem_oil&oldid=746575116. Accessed 4 May 2018.
3. GlobeScan SustainAbility Survey (2016) *The 2017 Sustainability Leaders: Celebrating 20 Years of Leadership*. Accessed 15 March 2018.
4. Unilever (2018) Sustainable Living. https://www.unilever.com/sustainable-living/. Accessed 17 April 2018.
5. Skapinker, M., Daneshkhu, S. (2016, September 29) Can Unilever's Paul Polman change the way we do business? *Financial Times*. Retrieved from https://www.ft.com/content/e6696b4a-8505-11e6-8897-2359a58ac7a5
6. Ignatius, A. (2017, November 14) The Opportunity of Sustainability. *Harvard Business Review*. Retrieved from https://hbr.org/2017/11/the-future-economy-project-qa-with-paul-polman
7. Eccles, G., Ioannou, I., Serafeim, G. (2012, May 9) The Impact of a Corporate Culture of Sustainability on Corporate Behaviour and Performance. Working Paper 12-035, Harvard Business School. Retrieved from https://hbswk.hbs.edu/item/the-impact-of-corporate-sustainability-on-organizational-process-and-performance

8. Aiello, C. (2018, February 13) Uber's loss jumped 61 percent to $4.5 billion in 2017. *CNBC.* Retrieved from https://www.cnbc.com/2018/02/13/ubers-loss-jumped-61-percent-to-4-point-5-billion-in-2017.html

9. Isaac, M. (2017, February 22) Inside Uber's Aggressive, Unrestrained Workplace Culture. *The New York Times.* Retrieved from https://www.nytimes.com/2017/02/22/technology/uber-workplace-culture.html

10. Belvedere, M. (2018, January 23) 'Moral compass' was off at Uber under co-founder Kalanick, says new CEO Dara Khosrowshahi. *CNBC.* Retrieved from https://www.cnbc.com/2018/01/23/uber-moral-compass-under-co-founder-kalanick-was-off-new-ceo-says.html

11. Egan, M. (2016, September 9) 5,300 Wells Fargo employees fired over 2 million phony accounts. *CNN Money.* Retrieved from http://money.cnn.com/2016/09/08/investing/wells-fargo-created-phony-accounts-bank-fees/index.html

12. Denison, D.R., Halligan, R., Ferry, K. (2017, March) The Board Perspective: Does Corporate Culture Matter? *Denison Consulting.* Retrieved from https://www.denisonconsulting.com/transform/article-corporate-culture-matter/

13. Denison, D.R., Mishra, A.K. (1995, April 1) Toward a Theory of Organizational Culture and Effectiveness. *Organization Science,* Pages 204–223.

14. Denison, D., Hooijberg, R., Lane, N., Lief, C. (2012, June 26) *Leading culture change in global organisations: Aligning culture and strategy.* San Francisco, CA: Jossey-Bass.

15. Holliday, C., Schmidheiny, S., Watts, P. (2002, August 16) *Walking the Talk: The Business Case for Sustainable Development.* Berrett-Koehler Publishers, Inc.

16. Wikipedia contributors. (2018, June 27). Hanseatic League. *Wikipedia, The Free Encyclopedia.* Accessed 17 April 2018, from https://en.wikipedia.org/w/index.php?title=Hanseatic_League&oldid=847706943

17. B Lab (2018) B Lab homepage. https://www.bcorporation.net/. Accessed 30 April 2018.

18. Primum Familiae Vini website, A Charter of Excellence, http://www.pfv.org/en/#/en/philosophy. Accessed 17 April 2018.

19. This case is an abridged version of GMA GARNET: JEBSEN & JESSEN'S ENVIRONMENTAL MINING (IMD-7-1860) Copyright © 2018 by IMD—International Institute for Management Development, Lausanne, Switzerland (www.imd.org). No part of this publication may be reproduced, stored in a retrieval system or transmitted in any form or by any means without the prior written permission of IMD.

20. GMA Garnet (2017, October 20) GMA Garnet to Deploy A 3 MW Solar, Wind and Battery System in West Australia [Press release]. Retrieved from http://www.gmagarnet.com/en-au/info-hub/news-events/gma-garnet-to-deploy-a-3-mw-solar,-wind-and-batter/

Part III

Acceleration

9

Partnering as Strategy

Part II of the book addressed the directional elements of the vectoring model, starting with the statement of purpose then proceeding to discuss materialities, environmental, social and governance (ESG) ratings and professional investors' attitudes toward sustainability efforts. Part III proceeds to uncover and harness the power of various accelerators of the sustainability efforts. In other words, once you have determined a potent direction for your sustainability program, how do you provide the maximum impetus for the program, particularly in a business environment that might not welcome it with open arms? What are the secret drivers for effective execution? In this part of the book, we investigate concepts such as partnering (often one of the most underrated drivers of impact), the concept of the circular economy,[1] innovation and finally team-building. In Chap. 9, we illustrate the importance of human capital development for generating productive relationships with various stakeholders and discuss examples of creative sustainability partnerships. We present and discuss an original checklist to help you structure potential strategic partnerships, based on the concept of MASS development, where MASS stands for more alternative sustainable solutions. To illustrate the concepts in action, we conduct an in-depth analysis of the programs initiated by Novozymes, a Danish biotechnology company that turned partnering for sustainability into a core component of its corporate strategy.

---

[1] In a circular economy, the value of products and materials is maintained for as long as possible. Waste and resource use are minimized, and when a product reaches the end of its life, it is used again to create further value. This can bring major economic benefits, contributing to innovation, growth and job creation. Source: ec.europa.eu.

© The Author(s) 2019
B. Leleux, J. van der Kaaij, *Winning Sustainability Strategies*,
https://doi.org/10.1007/978-3-319-97445-3_9

Partnering for Sustainability

As highlighted earlier, collaboration between companies and external stake-holders is a prerequisite for achieving the ambitious Sustainable Development Goals (SDGs), particularly for the development and delivery of innovation for sustainability. However, many companies struggle with the development and implementation of such partnerships. According to MIT Sloan's research [1], less than half (47%) of all of businesses are actively engaged in sustainability-related partnerships, while the majority (61%) of those companies assesses their collaborations as "quite" or "very" successful. Those partner-ships were said to be essentially strategic and transformational, with nearly three-quarters (74%) of them addressing a strategic challenge and more than half (54%) changing the rules and transforming the market in which they operate.

The adoption of the SDGs supported the development of new partnerships for sustainability as well as their increasing sophistication, with an ever more varied set of objectives, such as jointly setting standards, exchanging best prac-tices, developing sustainable innovations or impacting mindsets and effecting behavioral changes. Consider as a first example what happened to the world of corrective lenses. To set the stage, remember that impaired vision is one of the most common disabilities in the world. Some 2.5 billion low-income con-sumers require lenses and may not get proper access to them, due to difficulty reaching them, economic constraints and/or ideological isolation. Without proper correction, bad eyesight has a crippling impact on education and job perspectives.

Essilor, the world market leader in corrective lenses and a recognized pio-neer in the industry, decided to take decisive steps to address the pressing issue by launching a business unit entirely dedicated to serving those 2.5 bil-lion consumers [2]. This inclusive, for-profit division was named the *2.5 New Vision Generation*, and was given responsibility for deploying and scal-ing up the most viable inclusive business models to provide access to vision care for low-income consumers in underserved regions. Adapted products were developed in collaboration with Essilor's BoP (bottom-of-the pyramid)[2] Innovation Lab, which were then distributed in 25-plus countries across all continents through strategic partnerships with the public, private and non-profit sectors.

---

[2] The BoP, bottom of the pyramid, is the largest, but poorest socio-economic group in existence. In global terms, this is the 2.7 billion people who live on less than $2.50 a day. Source: Wikipedia, adapted.

In India, Essilor's 2.5 New Vision Generation division launched its Eye Mitra (Friend of the Eyes) program in the middle of 2013 as part of a strategy to improve awareness and access to vision care for underserved communities. The program educated young micro-entrepreneurs as opticians, so they could earn a living while helping the visually impaired in their local communities. Five years later, the number of young people trained as Eye Mitra had grown to an estimated 2600 [3]. By partnering with several strategic stakeholders with an interest in improving the lives of the underserved, Essilor established an effective network of local distributors.

Management specialists often refer to the current business environment as VUCA, that is, volatile, uncertain, complex and ambiguous. As companies' roles in society are more largely acknowledged, so is their dependency on employees, customers and other stakeholders to simply behave as good citizens. A poor track record creates a substantial risk of impairing a company's value. Conversely, regular engagement and partnering with stakeholders on sustainability topics such as climate change, data security and diversity, and acting upon the outcomes of those interactions, can generate benefits in employee satisfaction, customer loyalty and new growth opportunities.

The 2018 Deloitte Global Human Capital Trends Report [4] provides interesting insights on the changing landscape of partnering for sustainability. In an earlier version, the report observed that many firms were evolving toward a "network of teams" model to reach a higher level of collaboration and internal agility. In the 2018 edition, aptly named "The Rise of the Social Enterprise," the authors capitalized on the survey of some 11,000 businesses and human resource leaders to highlight some interesting new trends. One of the most noticeable was a growing shift from an internal focus to an external one, which includes the entire ecosystem outside of the company. The trend is still in its infancy though and would need confirmation in the years to come. While over three-quarters (77%) of the respondents stated that citizenship was important, only 18% put it as a top priority on their strategic agenda. More worrisome is the fact that nearly one-third (34%) of the respondents reported few or poorly funded citizenship programs, and as much as 22% stated they were not focused on the theme at all.

> Integrating the C-suite to build a more social enterprise will be a differentiator for businesses to attract the right talent, drive customer loyalty and sustain long-term growth. [5]
>
> Erica Volini, Principal, Deloitte Consulting LLP, U.S. Human Capital Leader

📁 Partnering Takes Center Stage

Solving complex societal issues such as climate change, ocean plastics and child labor is unthinkable without collaborative efforts between organizations working closely together to find scalable solutions. More and more examples have emerged of sustainability programs leaning heavily on partnering as a key operational feature. In 2017, Danish brewer Carlsberg devised its ambitious new sustainability program that was entirely centered around collaboration. The program—*Together Towards ZERO*—was built on four fundamental ambitions: zero carbon footprints, zero water waste, zero irresponsible drinking and a zero-accident culture (refer to Table 9.1). Each of the four ambitions was underlined by intermediate targets for 2022 and final 2030 targets connected to Carlsberg's most material SDGs [6].

As the program name suggests, Carlsberg was betting on innovative partnerships to make its sustainability strategy work. Since much of Carlsberg's impact occurred in other stages of the product life cycle, the company had to deliver innovation within the entire value chain, which meant working hand in hand with suppliers and business partners. For instance, only 14% of the brewer's greenhouse gasses were emitted during the brewing process, while 17% could be attributed to agriculture and as much as 40% to packaging [7]. To reach its ambitious goals, the company was targeting 30 active partnerships by 2022 to reduce the total carbon footprint in the value chain.

> Partnership is very, very important for us … we can learn from other industries; we would like to collaborate with others.
>
> Professor Flemming Besenbacher, Chairman of the Supervisory Board at Carlsberg A/S[3]

📁 SEAChange and Design Criteria for a New Partnership Model [8]

With sustainability partnerships clearly on the rise, companies do acknowledge facing challenges in making those larger ecosystems work for them. In this section, a set of criteria is developed for effective ecosystem collaboration. In particular, three criteria are shown to shape modern multi-stakeholder partnerships for sustainability: flexibility, customer focus and multiple

---

[3] Collaboration is key to success, says Carlsberg Group during climate week NYC, the Climategroup.org.

Table 9.1 Carlberg's together toward zero program

Ambition	Target by 2022	Target by 2030	Most material SDGs
Zero carbon footprint	• 50% reduction in carbon emissions at our breweries • 100% electricity from renewable sources at our breweries • Zero coal at our breweries • 15% reduction in beer-in-hand carbon footprint • 100% low climate impact cooling • 30 partnerships to reduce shared carbon footprint	• Zero carbon emissions at our breweries • 30% reduction in beer-in-hand carbon footprint	• 7.2 By 2030, substantially increase the share of renewable energy in the global energy mix • 7.3 By 2030, double the global rate of improvement in energy efficiency • 13.1 Strengthen resilience and adaptive capacity to climate-related hazards and natural disasters • 13.3 Improve education, awareness-raising and capacity on climate change mitigation, adaptation, impact reduction and early warning
Zero waste water	• 25% reduction in water usage at our breweries • Explore going below 2.0 hectoliters per hectoliter at all high-risk breweries	• 50% reduction in water usage at our breweries • Partner to safeguard shared water resources in high-risk areas	• 6.4 By 2030, substantially increase water-use efficiency and ensure sustainable withdrawals and supply of freshwater to address water scarcity • 6.5 By 2030, implement integrated water resource management at all levels
Zero irresponsible drinking	• 100% availability of alcohol-free brews (AFB) • 100% responsible drinking messaging through packaging and brand activations • 100% of our markets run partnerships to support responsible consumption	• 100% of our markets improve on responsible drinking year on year	• 3.5 Strengthen the prevention and treatment of substance abuse, including harmful use of alcohol • 3.6 By 2020, halve the number of global deaths and injuries from road traffic accidents
Zero accidents culture	• Reduction in accident rate year on year	• Zero lost-time accidents	• 8.8 Protect labor rights and promote safe and secure working environments for all workers

solutions. These criteria will be investigated in the context of an existing multi-stakeholder environment in Asia Pacific, the SEAChange partnership.

Quality nutrition is a basic human right, represented as Sustainable Development Goal 2—Zero Hunger. Across Southeast Asia alone, though, an estimated 60 million children under the age of five are under-nourished. Even as the child mortality rate per thousand live births has fallen by 62%, from 125 per thousand live births in 1990 to 47 in 2015 [9], one in five children in India is still improperly fed. In Indonesia, one of the world's fastest-growing countries, approximately one in ten children are improperly nourished, resulting in them being either under- or overweight. This polarized outcome is dubbed the double burden of malnutrition because both situations are equally dangerous and damaging. Working as a coalition of cross-sector partners, SEAChange, an initiative launched and supported by DSM, the Dutch health, nutrition and materials science company, has sought to address the issue by jointly developing effective, affordable and nutritious products aimed at low- to middle-income consumers for Asian markets.

SEAChange was launched at a regional multi-stakeholder meeting, with government representatives, industry professionals, academia and civil society, to address the need for more local partnerships, relevant innovation and to clear paths for adoption. DSM, with fellow sponsors such as Danone, Unilever, Indofood, Tata Trusts and the World Food Programme, agreed that a new model for partnerships was needed—one that eliminated existing barriers to success and prevented new ones from surfacing. In the post-meeting declaration, three design criteria for successful partnering models were highlighted:

- **Flexibility** In a culture of speed, time is of the essence; successful collaborations need to be flexible and responsive to rapid market changes. Traditional rules, embodied in long-term memorandums of understandings, are obsolete and inappropriate. This does not antagonize the need for long-term partnerships but stresses the importance of setting them up with embedded flexibility, that is, the ability to evolve with the industry they serve, around shared values and concrete projects, rather than with rigid key performance indicators (KPIs) and immovable goal posts. Flexibility should also extend to the time horizons of the partnerships, with shorter-term ones complementing the longer-term projects.
- **Customer Focus** Low-income groups are also potential consumers, with specific needs and desires, capable of their own purchasing decisions, particularly when it comes to nutrition and health. Thus, it is

essential to make them responsible, not just rescue them. While social safety nets have a role to play at the bottom of the pyramid, it is also critical to understand the market's role to offer commercially viable nutritious and affordable products. These products must speak directly to Asia's unique consumption and purchasing needs and preferences. Leveraging the availability of such products with better education on nutrition empowers this new group of consumers to make the right nutrition choices.

• **Multiple Solutions** Nutrition solutions have to be conceived as part of a holistic approach, not as single products in isolation. In fact, many past initiatives have failed because a single-solution approach cannot tackle the full size of the problem. Cross-sector collaboration is fundamental in addressing the large-scale challenges of the SDGs.

Besides the three design criteria cited above, communication was also found to be wanting, creating considerable information gaps between the public and private sectors.

☞ MASS and Strategic Partnering

In a rapidly changing world in dire need of creative sustainability initiatives, focusing sequentially on one initiative after the other does not ensure that the required impact is happening fast enough. Rapid impact requires action on two fronts: partnering and/or launching more initiatives simultaneously.

Partnering along the value chain has been discussed previously as a way to augment the number of sustainability solutions, as illustrated with Essilor and its BoP Innovation Lab and the SEAChange multi-stakeholder partnership. The second approach involves the adoption of a "Fail early, fail often, fail forward" [10] culture. This evidence led to the development of MASS, a learning journey based on the continuous improvement of various resources such as materials supply, support, natural sources as well as information and expertise. With a high diversity of required solutions, each having a relatively low chance for success, carefully selecting suitable, equally motivated partner(s) becomes ever more critical.

Pragmatically, to make those two dimensions work for you (MASS and partnering), a three-step process is recommended, from identifying issues that matter to prioritizing the improvement strategies and finally targeting the appropriate strategic partners.

Identifying the Hotspots

The actual issues, materials or processes that stand to be improved—the *hotspots*—can be identified using data from a products' life cycle assessment (LCA). An LCA is a methodology used to assess the environmental and/or social impacts associated with all stages of a product's life cycle, from start to end. By merging the results from the LCA with the outcomes of the corporate materiality analysis, hotspots can be identified in a combined bottom-up/top-down analysis.

To achieve optimal comparability between the candidates for improvement, the results can be stated based on standardized KPIs. This mapping classically includes information on a broad range of environmental impact areas, such as raw material acquisition, energy use and efficiency, content of materials and chemical substances, emissions to air, soil and water and waste generation.

As seen earlier, materiality assessments are a powerful means for singling out corporate sustainability issues that resonate with stakeholders. Fusing life cycle data with the material sustainability issues provides the essential ingredients to identify and rank the hotspots [11]. Once the hotspots have been identified, then various solutions and improvement strategies can be examined.

Prioritizing Improvement Strategies

To prioritize improvement strategies, a simple framework has prospered since the end of the 1970s—*the waste hierarchy*. This hierarchy, also known as Lansink's Ladder after Dutch member of parliament Ad Lansink who introduced the ladder to prioritize government waste policies. The waste hierarchy proposed an explicit order of preference in which to rank solutions to reduce the impact of waste.

•	Prevention	– Avoid the resource altogether, use less material or extend life cycle
•	Reuse	– Return the resource, check, clean, refurbish and use it again
•	Recycling	– Take back the resource and reuse its raw material
•	Energy recovery	– Incinerate the resource for energy recovery
•	Landfill	– Dispose of the resource in landfill

Over the years, the ladder has been refined. The original 3Rs—reduce, reuse and recycle—have been expanded to 5Rs—reduce, reuse, recycle, rethink, replace—and even 10Rs (refer to Table 9.2). Originally, Lansink's ladder helped move away from the standard default choice (landfilling) and helped create a structured, holistic approach to waste management policies. The ladder is still topical, albeit in a somewhat altered form, for ranking solutions to environmental challenges in the circular economy and measuring their progress.

In a 2017 policy report, the Netherlands Environmental Assessment Agency upgraded further Lansink's ladder by redesigning it for circular economy progress measurement [12]. The list of solution strategies was increased to 10 and each strategy could be categorized into one of three stages: (1) useful application of materials, (2) extended lifespan and (3) eco-efficiency.

Developing MASS requires a mixture of circular strategies selected from Table 9.2. The more circularity in a product chain, the lower the environmental impact because fewer resources are consumed. At the same time, more circularity also implies the involvement of a broader, more complex range of players from different parts of the ecosystem.

The method of identifying target hotspots and prioritizing improvement strategies is again well illustrated with another example from the beer industry—*The 100+ Sustainability Accelerator* [13]. The vehicle was launched in 2018 by market leader AB InBev to solve four sustainability challenges aligned with the brewers' overall 2025 sustainability goals:

- **Smart Agriculture** 100% of direct farmers will be skilled, connected and financially empowered.
- **Water Stewardship** 100% of communities in high stress areas will have measurably improved water availability and quality.
- **Circular Packaging** 100% of products will be in packaging that is returnable or made mostly from recycled content.
- **Climate Action**
  - 100% of purchased electricity will be from renewable sources.
  - 25% reduction in CO_2 emissions across the value chain.

Looking at the biggest greenhouse gas emitting stage within the beer value chain, namely packaging, it is possible to identify potential improvement strategies. In its quest for circular packaging, the Belgium-based brewer could, for example, increase the return rate of its glass bottles. This would involve a return–logistics process. Alternatively, together with associates, AB InBev could develop bottles made from renewable sources similar to developments at fellow beer maker Carlsberg. Together with a packaging partner, the Danish

Table 9.2 Circular strategies within the product chain, in order of priority

Category	Circularity strategy	Description	Example of cable company services (set-top boxes)
Eco-efficiency	Refuse	Make product function redundant or offer the same function in a radically different product	Smart TVs that have built-in Internet connectivity
	Rethink	Make product use more intensive (e.g. through sharing products or by putting multi-functional products on the market)	Deliver more services via the set-top box such as internet, telephony and Netflix
	Reduce	Increase manufacturing efficiency of the product or consume fewer natural resources and materials	Reduce energy consumption of set-top boxes; optimized packaging with lower paper use
Extend lifespan	Reuse	Reuse, by another consumer, the discarded product which is still in good condition and fulfills its original function	After lease expires or customer ends the contract, reapply the decommissioned set-top boxes in the same market
	Repair	Repair and maintain defective product so it can be used for its original function	Fix technical problems after swapping the malfunctioning box; reapply the decommissioned set-top boxes in the same market
	Refurbish	Refurbish an old product to bring it up to date	Update the set-top box with new software; apply decommissioned boxes in less developed markets
	Re-manufacture	Use parts of discarded products in a new product with the same function	Strip malfunctioning set-top boxes for (repair) parts
	Repurpose	Use discarded products or its parts in a new product with a different function	Apply components of the set-top box to different solutions
Materials application	Recycle	Process materials to obtain the same or lower quality	Process materials to obtain the same or lower quality
	Recover	Incineration of materials with energy recovery	Burn non-recyclable (packaging) materials for energy recovery

Source: PBL, 2016, adapted

brewer developed a beer bottle made from sustainably sourced wood fiber as part of the Carlsberg Circular Community efforts. There are two different approaches to the problem then—returning versus refusing. Both strategies for glass bottles address the same issue—circular packaging—but they employ different levels of the waste ladder and require entirely different skills from their partners to come to life.

Profiling Partners

With hotspots identified and possible solutions prioritized using a version of the waste hierarchy, the identification of potential partners becomes the next natural step. To make things happen requires bringing together various stakeholders and enabling them to collaborate effectively. The implementation of circular sustainable solutions relies to a large extent on logistics and supply chain issues, in which training and fine-tuning of processes are fundamental. To make this possible the proper partners need to be identified and selected. Partners can be evaluated by looking for alignment on three distinctive levels: (1) the market fit, that is, addressing the relative positions of the partners in the value chain, (2) the resource fit, that is, tackling the required capabilities, and (3) the organizational fit, that is, the cultural alignment between them

Table 9.3 Sample of fundamental questions for evaluating partners

Level	Sample questions
Market fit	• How would the economic model of the partnership work? How would you share future revenues with your partner? What about costs? • How would you staff the partnership opportunity you are evaluating?
Resource fit	• How vulnerable is the market for the material or process you intend to address through the partnership? Are there many alternatives on the market? • Does the potential partner possess the right expertise to jointly develop MASS? How broad is their knowledge? • Is the partnership opportunity satisfying the practices of flexibility, client focus and working on multiple solutions as brought forward in the SEAChange example?
Organizational fit	• Does the potential partner share the same level of engagement for addressing the sustainability issue(s)? • What type of governance mechanisms do you think will be most appropriate for the partnership opportunity you are evaluating? If you are re-examining an existing partnership, do you see any areas for improvement in the governance of this partnership?

[14]. This three-legged approach helps identify the fundamental questions, synthesized in Table 9.3, that need to be addressed.

For example, on the issue of resource fit, how vulnerable is the market for the material or process we intend to address through partnering? Are there many alternatives on the market? Does the partner possess the right expertise to jointly develop MASS? Is the partnership opportunity satisfying the practices of flexibility, client focus and working on multiple solutions as brought forward in the SEAChange example?

In the next section, the story of industrial enzyme specialist Novozymes illustrates how such questions can be answered in practice. Novozymes takes partnering to an even higher level than fellow Danish company Carlsberg; collaboration is not just a component of their sustainability strategy but a shining center piece of their business strategy.

🗁 Novozymes: Partnering for Impact

Since demerging from Novo Nordisk in 2000, Danish biotechnology company Novozymes had grown at lightning speed, resulting in a global market share of 48% in industrial enzymes. Flourishing financial results translated into a price/earnings ratio unparalleled in its industry, outperforming peers by an estimated 25%. At the same time Novozymes has been widely applauded for its sustainable innovation efforts that brought enzymes to the market, replacing chemical solutions by, for instance, enabling low temperature washing and developing first-, second- and third-generation biofuels.

The company was praised for excellence, not only financially, but also on the sustainability front. With 4% organic sales growth, 27.9% earnings before interest and taxes (EBIT) margin and 2% net profit growth, 2017 was a good year, in line with analysts' expectations. The company also managed to reduce its carbon footprint by 76 million tons of CO_2, use 24% renewable energy and have 26% women in senior management [15].

A New Millennium Business: Building on a 70-Year Legacy

Although Novozymes was created in 2000, its history started much earlier, with the foundation of two Danish companies, Nordisk Insulinlaboratorium (1923) and Novo Terapeutisk Laboratorium (1925), which were focused on biotechnological innovation to produce and improve insulin, a revolutionary drug recently discovered. Progressively enzymes became an integral part of

Novo's portfolio and, to attract more external capital, both Novo and Nordisk ultimately became publicly listed companies.

In January 1989, after competing with each other for more than 60 years, the two companies joined forces under the name of Novo Nordisk A/S, creating the world's leading manufacturer of insulin in the process. The new scale of Novo Nordisk improved its competitiveness and margins in its major international markets through synergies in research and distribution. In 2000, Novo elected to pivot again, splitting into three separate organizations:

- Novo Nordisk A/S—continuing the business of the former Health Care Division
- Novozymes A/S—handling the enzyme business
- Novo A/S—the holding vehicle of the Novo Nordisk Foundation.

While both Novo Nordisk A/S and Novozymes A/S remain publicly traded, the Novo Nordisk Foundation maintains a controlling interest in both companies through Novo A/S.

Unlocking the Magic of Nature (2000–2007)

After the re-organization, Novozymes was ordered to stand on its own feet in a rapidly evolving, highly fragmented marketplace. This forced the company to adopt a new mindset and sharpen its strategic direction. Steen Riisgaard, Novozymes' first president and CEO, was a seasoned enzymes veteran who joined the company as early as 1979. For Steen, safeguarding nature and the environment was a business priority. After the demerger, Steen redirected the research and development (R&D) efforts toward specialty bioengineered enzymes but also toward addressing the customers' needs for new solutions. Novozymes' innovation-based strategy aimed at growing its market for industrial enzymes and optimizing what the company calls the "enzyme window."[4]

One of Novozymes' most rapidly growing global market segments was biofuels, which mainly consisted of bioethanol. Unfortunately, the first generation of biofuels had a serious Achilles heel; the feedstock for production was often edible cereals such as corn. As the world food prices increased dramatically in 2007 and 2008, the *food-for-fuel* discussion became increasingly tense with biofuels being touted as the perpetrator—even though sev-

---

[4] The enzyme window is the price range where an enzyme solution can displace the existing (typically chemical) solution.

eral studies confirmed that biofuel production was not at the expense of food production. Novozymes was taken off guard by the severity of the dispute, and an important lesson was learned; for its breakthrough bio-innovations, the company had to ensure adequate stakeholder support from the general public and governments to preserve its license-to-operate and increase its license-to-grow.

Sustainability-Driven Innovation

To maintain its leading position and to further integrate sustainability into its core business, Novozymes established ambitious targets for its sustainability program, including ensuring 100% supplier adherence to supply chain standards and improving water, energy and CO_2 efficiency by 40%, 50%, and 50% respectively, compared to a 2005 baseline.

In addition to these internal objectives, Novozymes had an even larger opportunity for positive environmental and social impact with its customers. The company's objective was to enable a 75-million-ton reduction in CO_2 emissions in 2015 through the application of Novozymes products. This would be obtained, for example, by supplying enzymes that lowered temperatures in washing machines compared to conventional laundry detergents. Lowering the temperature not only reduces CO_2 emissions, an environmental benefit, but also lowers the overall energy cost of laundry, a clear economic benefit to the consumer and the enzymes manufacturer.

> **Low temperature detergents: A Belgian calculation example.** The average Belgian household operates a washing machine 4.5 times a week, or approximately 250 times a year. The average washing temperature is about 48°C. If all households were to do the laundry at 30°C, the carbon dioxide reduction potential would be as big as the emission of 100,000 cars. If all households were to lower the washing temperature by one standard temperature increment (60°C instead of 90°C, or 30°C instead of 40°C) the carbon dioxide reduction potential would be as big as the emission of 30,000 cars.
> Source: BewarE, Ecolife, Leuven, Belgium

Novozymes partner Procter & Gamble (P&G) was also looking for opportunities to promote environmental sustainability. When the company started working on the revitalization of its Ariel brand, it conducted a comprehensive life cycle assessment, measuring Ariel's environmental impact from raw materials extraction up to disposal or recycling. The effort demonstrated that the highest amount of energy was consumed at the end customer's home during the heating of the water in the washing machine. As a result, P&G launched its Ariel *Turn to 30°* campaign in 2006. It turned out to be the first global brand to promote washing at 30 degrees rather, than the previous standard of 40 or even 60 degrees.

This initiative was soon followed by competitors. At the end of 2014, 95% of detergents in Europe contained enzymes, 70% in Latin America and in the US, 60% in Asia Pacific and 55% in the Middle East and Africa. Novozymes was responsible for providing about 300 customers with different types of enzymes. Its household care division ended up representing 36% of its 2013 sales. In recognition of its services to industry, the company received numerous innovation awards from its key clients, such as P&G, Unilever and Henkel.

Partnering for Impact

Between 2007 and 2013, Novozymes started to spread its bets by developing *business platforms*, that is, knowledge and sectors in the value chains in which Novozymes could construct solid ecosystems with strategic partners, for instance, bio-agriculture and biomass conversion.

To Novozymes, partnerships, alliances and networks of the willing were the backbone of a "Partnering for Impact" strategy aimed at making a measurable difference for customers, partners and the world (refer to Table 9.4). Revenue growth was not just about competing but also about converting customers and expanding the market as a whole.

One of the foundations of the company's success is its application-based market segmentation, with a strong emphasis on strategic value chain partnerships with companies such as Monsanto and Poet. Partnering for Impact has become a central theme of the corporate strategy, incorporating explicitly the role that sustainability should play in it. The strategy contains four focus areas for execution:

- **Rally for Change** Form partnerships and networks with customers, organizations and governments to make a sustainable difference.
- **Lead Innovation** Excite our customers by delivering more significant innovation, tailored to their local markets.
- **Focus on Opportunities** Prioritize the customers, markets and activities that hold the biggest opportunity for creating impact.

Table 9.4 Partnering for impact

	Percentage of business (2017)	Competition	Application	Example partners
Household care	32%	Genencor	Low temperature detergents	Henkel, P&G
Food & beverages	28%	DSM, Genencor, AB Enzymes	Baking, starch conversion, brewing	Unilever
Bioenergy	18%	Genencor, Captive Producers	Corn ethanol, biomass conversion	Poet
Agriculture & feed	15%	Genencor, BASF, Bayer, CropScience	Monogastric animals, maximizing protein utilization, substituting phosphate, aquaculture	Monsanto
Technical & pharma	7%	Genencor	Textiles, leather treatment, biocatalysis	Merck

- **Grow People** Support Novozymes' employees and people around us in unfolding their full potential.

Selling or Selling Out? The BioAg Partnership with Monsanto

With its focus on value chain partnerships, Novozymes stood ahead of its competitors in terms of sustainable innovation. With experience, it developed the skills required to select and implement better alliances. But as the saying goes, while good decisions are usually based on experience, experience is mostly developed by making many bad decisions. And Novozymes had to contend with its fair share of unsuccessful co-ventures. In December 2013, it established a major partnership with Monsanto called BioAg, with the aim of becoming a global leader in sustainable microbial technology that could help farmers increase productivity of the world's crops.

In the alliance structure, both Monsanto and Novozymes maintained independent research programs; Novozymes was responsible for producing the microbial products and Monsanto served as the lead for field testing, registration and commercialization of the alliance products, including Novozymes' existing product portfolio in agricultural biologicals. The alliance was jointly managed, and profits were to be shared.

The public outcry against genetically modified organisms (GMOs) and other restrictions on biodiversity resulted in Monsanto's public image being tarnished. Some external stakeholders saw the partnership as a potential reputational risk to Novozymes' immaculate sustainability profile. As a result, the controversial partnership required serious internal and external communication efforts by senior management to obtain full internal support. Despite the controversy, the BioAg Alliance helped Novozymes access new R&D talent pools in a sector in which the company was not well known.

Strengthening Partnering for Impact: The Next Phase

Supported by early successes from products such as biological insecticides for the control of pests, the partnership with Monsanto grew over time. But at the start of 2018, Bayer's pending acquisition of Monsanto [16] brought new uncertainty about the ability and willingness to continue the BioAg Alliance, and the conditions for doing so. For Monsanto, the image problem never went away. It ultimately merged with Bayer in 2018, with Bayer announcing a few days later that the name Monsanto would simply be erased from the combined entity in the future because it was just too heavily tainted.

Tips, Traps and Takeaways

👍 Tips

- Develop partnerships that are in line with the strategic reasoning and ensure they are properly supported financially and strategically.
- Apply the three criteria that are vital for developing multi-stakeholder partnerships:
  - Flexibility
  - Customer focus
  - Multiple solutions
- Beware of "The Rise of the Social Enterprise" and leverage the *network of teams* in collaboration with partners.
- Remove the word "waste" from the corporate vocabulary.

☀ Traps

- Avoid getting stuck on a single solution. Instead, develop many alternative sustainable solutions (MASS).
- Do not underestimate the importance of developing your company's partnering capabilities.
- Not all solutions deserve the same credit and attention. Prioritize the solutions to environmental issues by applying a useful framework such as the waste hierarchy ladder.
- Avoid partnerships with insufficient fit in terms of market, resources and organization.

⚓ Takeaways

This part of the book addressed how to accelerate sustainability programs during execution. A first powerful angle of attack is partnering and developing broad alliances for impact. Companies and entire value chains are now competing with each other on sustainability performance; accordingly, the ability to build and maintain partnership is an important and growing field of competence.

While a minority of firms are actively engaged in partnerships for sustainability, those who are report an overwhelming sense of success from their efforts. The majority of these alliances were forged on a strategic and transformational level, vying to change the rules of business and transform the market in which the companies operate. The Essilor example illustrated how such transformational partnerships can lead to the development of a distribution network of micro-entrepreneurs reaching some of the 2.5 billion visually impaired consumers in difficult-to-reach areas.

Clearly, companies are still learning by doing but the number of partnerships for sustainability is rising, in part due to the adoption of the SDGs. With that increase, alliances among organizations are becoming more forward-thinking, as a recent example from Southeast Asia demonstrated—SEAChange, the coalition of cross-sector partners whose objective is to develop effective, affordable and nutritious products in Asia. The alliance introduced three criteria essential to fruitful multi-stakeholder partnerships: flexibility, customer focus and working on multiple solutions. With the ambition of creating MASS, the case for strategic partnering was clearly stated, with an equally strong claim for a hands-on approach for partner selection and management.

Finally, we delivered additional insights and requirements in selecting suitable strategic partners for MASS development. First, the importance of clearly identifying the resource, product or service up for improvement was highlighted. Next, the concept of waste hierarchy was introduced, initially as prevention, reuse, recycle, energy recovery and landfill. The tool, and its later improvements, helped determine priorities. Finally, a checklist was provided to assess the actual fit with potential partners in terms of market, resources and organization.

To illustrate the concepts, the Novozymes case was introduced. A sustainability leader and stock market favorite, Novozymes delivers biological, enzyme-based solutions to replace products that generate more pollution and enables, for example, lower temperature detergents. Novozymes incorporated partnering into its core strategy, which illustrates how a company with a broad range of applications has accelerated growth through strategic partnering and developed as one of the most sustainable companies within its industry.

References

1. Kiron, D., Kruschwitz, N., Reeves, M., et al. (2015) *Joining forces: collaboration and leadership for sustainability.* Cambridge, MA: Sloan Management Review Association, MIT Sloan School of Management.
2. Essilor (2015, December) *See Change Our Contribution to Sustainable Development.* Retrieved from https://www.essilor.com/essilor-content/uploads/2016/10/Essilor_See_Change_05_03_2015_DOUBLES-EN.pdf
3. Essilor (2017, July 4) Creating successful primary vision care providers in rural India. https://www.essilorseechange.com/website/creating-successful-primary-vision-care-providers-rural-india. Accessed 6 May 2018.
4. Abbatiello, A., Agarwal, D., Bersin, J., et al. (2018) The rise of the social enterprise, 2018 Deloitte Global Human Capital Trends. *Deloitte.* Retrieved from https://www2.deloitte.com/content/dam/Deloitte/be/Documents/human-capital/0000_HC%20Trends_2018_BE.PDF
5. Deloitte (2018, April 3) Deloitte Study: 73 Percent Report C-Suite Isn't Working Together Despite Need for Increased Collaboration on Human Capital Challenges [Press release]. *PR Newswire.* Retrieved from https://www.prnewswire.com/news-releases/deloitte-study-73-percent-report-c-suite-isnt-working-together-despite-need-for-increased-collaboration-on-human-capital-challenges-300622910.html
6. Andersen, E. (2018) Beer's untapped potential: the growing consumer appetite for environmentally-friendly products. Presentation at the Brewers of Europe Forum, 7–8 June 2019.
7. Carlsberg (2018) Zero carbon footprint. https://carlsberggroup.com/sustainability/our-ambitions/zero-carbon-footprint/. Accessed 19 March 2018.

8. Foing, Y. (2018, February 27) Feeding Asia: Collaboration is key to combating malnutrition. *Asian Correspondent.* Retrieved from https://asiancorrespondent.com/2018/02/feeding-asia-collaboration-key-combating-malnutrition/#TAqy5FbYwEiz0cRx.97

9. Fadel, S.A., Rasaily, R., Awasthi, S., et al. (2017, September 19) Changes in cause-specific neonatal and 1–59-month child mortality in India from 2000 to 2015: a nationally representative survey. *The Lancet Global Health*, Vol. 390, No. 10106, pp. 1972–1980.

10. Economy, P. (2018, February 6) How to Live at the Edge of Your Capabilities, According to Will Smith. *Inc.* Retrieved from https://www.inc.com/peter-economy/how-to-live-at-edge-of-your-capabilities-according-to-will-smith.html

11. Mieras, E. (2014, August 11) Business Decision Making | Materiality Assessment vs. Hotspot Analysis. PRé Sustainability. Retrieved from https://www.pre-sustainability.com/news/business-decision-making-materiality-assessment-vs.-hotspot-analysis

12. Potting, J., Hekkert, M., Worrell, E. et al. (2017, January) *Circular economy: measuring innovation in the product chain.* The Hague: PBL Netherlands Environmental Assessment Agency. Retrieved from http://www.pbl.nl/sites/default/files/cms/publicaties/pbl-2016-circular-economy-measuring-innovation-in-product-chains-2544.pdf

13. AB InBev (2018, March 21) AB InBev launches 2025 Sustainability Goals and 100+ Accelerator to advance local innovations for pressing global challenges [Press release]. Retrieved from http://www.ab-inbev.com/content/dam/universal-template/ab-inbev/News/press-releases/public/2018/03/20180321_EN.pdf

14. Henderson, J. (IMD) (2015) Leveraging Strategic Partnerships program [Open edX]. Retrieved from https://onlinecourses.imd.org/courses/Strategy/LSP/2015_1/about

15. Novozymes (2018) *The Novozymes Report 2017.* Retrieved from https://report2017.novozymes.com

16. Bayer (2018, June 7) Bayer closes Monsanto acquisition [Press release]. Retrieved from https://media.bayer.com/baynews/baynews.nsf/id/Bayer-closes-Monsanto-acquisition

10

Toward a Circular Economy

So far, the book has introduced vectoring as an effective model for architecting corporate sustainability efforts. By focusing on a limited number of material sustainability issues and developing the appropriate leadership, culture, and environmental, social and governance (ESG) profile, vectoring provides sound foundations for purposeful contributions to society at large. With the moral compass heading in a few selected, impactful directions, the book then proceeded to elaborate on the most effective execution strategies—that is, sustainability acceleration. The previous chapter highlighted the contributions from broad-based value chain collaborations and partnership arrangements. A method for selecting suitable strategic partners for innovation was proposed and the concept of many alternative sustainable solutions (MASS) was introduced to support the acceleration of sustainability innovation.

These topics are extended here by developing the concept of circular economy, a radical departure from the more traditional linear way of thinking, that is, take–make–dispose. After introducing the potential impact of the transition to circular economy thinking, the chapter provides several examples of different forms of circular economy improvement strategies. As usual, the chapter concludes by offering a collection of practical tools, illustrated by the use of the Business Model Canvas in a team-training exercise aimed at developing circular economy solutions based on the value proposition of the BMW i3.

© The Author(s) 2019
B. Leleux, J. van der Kaaij, *Winning Sustainability Strategies*,
https://doi.org/10.1007/978-3-319-97445-3_10

The Circular Economy

One of the world's biggest challenges is to find ways to decouple economic growth from increasing resource constraints. In the fall of 2015, the European Commission adopted an ambitious Circular Economy Package with the aim of helping European businesses and consumers make the transition to a stronger and more circular economy, in which resources are used in a more sustainable way. Factors such as natural resource constraints, population growth and climate change are gradually forcing corporations to move from a traditional linear approach toward a circular one. The ultimate circular economy, in which all product chains are closed loop ecosystems where materials are applied over and over again, might prove to be elusive in practice. Nevertheless, this is exactly the predicament that circular economy transitions aspire to resolve [1].

Sizing the opportunity provided by the circular economy is an interesting task. According to a 2015 McKinsey study, adopting circular economy principles would net Europe benefits of €1.8 trillion by 2030 [2]. The adoption would also foster better societal outcomes and halve carbon dioxide emissions compared with current levels. A 2016 extension to the study provided even more explicit accounts of these benefits. Currently, plastics production relies almost entirely on feedstocks of non-renewable resources. Some 95% of the value of plastic packaging, an estimated €67 billion to €100 billion per year, is lost after a single use, with the plastics ending up in landfills, oceans or as litter [3]. Undoubtedly, this poses a massive challenge for the entire industry. The UN Environment Programme estimates the environmental costs of plastic packaging at €34 billion each year, more than the whole industry's profits! The same institution assesses the financial damage caused by plastic waste to marine ecosystems alone at €11 billion each year. It is hardly surprising then that at the 2018 World Economic Forum in Davos, leading brands, retailers and packaging companies—including Amcor, L'Oréal, Mars, M&S, Walmart and the Coca-Cola Company—announced their pledge to use 100% reusable, recyclable or compostable packaging by 2025 [4]. This is potentially a coalition with impact: together the signatories represent more than 6 million tons of plastic packaging per year!

Some are taking impact improvement a step further by viewing carbon dioxide as a valuable raw material that can be harnessed, resulting in *carbon positive* products. Interface, with its purpose statement of "climate takeback," is investigating biomimicry[1] innovations that outshine the sustainability performance of its existing, already low impact, carpet tiles. The company combines natural photosynthesis with industrial chemistry to bind carbon in its carbon-capture tiles, which are still at the prototype stage.

In assessing the impact of the *paradigmatic shift* caused by circular economy thinking, real-life examples are helpful. In the following sections, several such examples are discussed and brought into perspective with the help of a framework for selecting circular economy strategies based upon the waste hierarchy ladder.

The Circular Economy in Practice

As noted in Chap. 9 on partnering, the waste hierarchy ladder is a practical framework for selecting strategies for the circular economy. It can help find the most relevant product impact in the value chain as well as to select specific targets for improvement. Once the projected impact and the associated targets have been defined, the process of (re-)designing the value proposition can commence in earnest.

To illustrate the process, let us examine Sea2see, a startup launched to contribute to alleviating the estimated €11 billion in damages caused to marine ecosystems each year by ocean plastics. The recent UN resolution on marine litter and micro-plastics and new studies claiming that the oceans will contain more plastics than fish by 2050 [5] have made the problem of ocean plastics a top environmental priority.

Roughly 13% of all ocean plastics come from abandoned fishing nets. Not only do these nets contaminate the water before disintegrating but they also lead to deadly "ghost fishing," as hundreds of thousands of sea creatures become entangled and die. Fishermen are obvious key stakeholders in this global challenge. Based on this notion, the Barcelona-based entrepreneur François van den Abeele initiated a creative solution: making stylish sunglasses from ocean plastic waste, such as that from retrieved fishing nets.

As a keen sailor, François was very aware of the threat caused by ocean plastics, so he started Sea2see as a social enterprise in 2016.

---

[1] Biomimicry is an approach to innovation that seeks sustainable solutions to human challenges by emulating nature's time-tested patterns and strategies. Source: Biomimicry.org.

After closing down a less successful venture, I was looking for high value consumer goods that could be produced from ocean plastics—glasses were the perfect answer! With the help of €45,000 of crowd funding, I was able to kick-off
Sea2see, and as I have been living in Barcelona for many years, engaging local
fishermen for me was a no-brainer.

Sea2see's product development involved a lot of trial and error, as the raw
material proved to be difficult to gather and of mixed quality. For its purposes,
only high-quality waste could be used. After a series of iterations, Sea2see succeeded in producing glasses that met its technical specifications. It then scaled
up by entering into agreements with 22 port authorities throughout Catalonia.
With the help of private waste management companies, waste was collected,
cleaned and sorted in a central location. The usable material was upcycled into
pellets, shipped to Italy, molded into frames and tainted in the desired colors.
The frames were then sold in optical stores across Europe, with markets such
as Australia and the US already on the radar for the future. The refuse, that is,
material that did not meet Sea2see's stringent requirements, was sold to third
parties for reuse in other applications.

Going back to the suggested waste hierarchy ladder, François identified the
impact he wanted to achieve (reduce ocean plastics), his target for improvement (upcycle the material into high-value consumer goods), his value proposition (cool sunglasses) and the required partners. Success quickly followed
the market introduction: actress Penélope Cruz, celebrated for her Oscar-
winning performance in the movie *Vicky Cristina Barcelona*, was spotted at
the 2018 Cannes Film Festival wearing a pair of Sea2see shades—saving the
ocean in style.

Although rather unusual, Sea2see is not an exception in looking for circular economy solutions. Many companies have turned to circular economy
thinking to leverage their sustainability efforts. In the following sections, we
review six very different efforts, each with a clear circular economy driver.
As Table 10.1 shows, the examples are divided into three categories, namely
eco-efficiency, extend lifespan and materials application. The examples illustrate the dos and don'ts of developing circular economy strategies. Consistent
with the waste hierarchy, the cases are prioritized by their place in the ladder, with the higher rungs associated with higher potential for value
adding.

Table 10.1 Overview of circularity strategies

Category	Circularity strategy	Description	Example cases in this chapter
Eco-efficiency	Refuse	Make product redundant by its function or by offering the same function with a radically different product	Coco-Mat
	Rethink	Make product use more intensive (e.g. by sharing products or putting multifunctional products on the market)	
	Reduce	Increase efficiency in product manufacture or use by consuming fewer natural resources and materials	Happy Shrimp Farm
Extend lifespan	Reuse	Reuse by another consumer of discarded product that is still in good condition and fulfills its original function	
	Repair	Repair and maintenance of defective product so it can be used with its original function	
	Refurbish	Restore an old product and bring it up to date	Patagonia
	Re-manufacture	Use parts of discarded products in a new product with the same function	Renault/Volvo Trucks
	Repurpose	Use discarded product or its parts in a new product with a different function	Rodenburg Polymers
Materials application	Recycle	Process materials to obtain the same or lower quality	DSM-Niaga
	Recover	Incinerate materials and recover energy	

🗁 Recycle: Capturing the Value of Polyurethane Mattresses

The mattress market worldwide was estimated at about €23 billion in 2017. In line with population growth, it was predicted to increase by about 6.5% between 2017 and 2024 [6]. Nearly 90% of all mattresses produced in the EU contained between 2 kg and 15 kg of polyurethane foam, and over 90% of furniture upholstery also contained polyurethane foam [7]. The prime challenge with polyurethane foam is its limited recyclability. Unlike most plastics, polyurethane foam decomposes rather than melts at elevated temperatures, making it difficult to reuse. As a consequence, too many mattresses end up on street curbs, destined for landfills.

As governments became increasingly aware of circular economy challenges, and with mattresses featuring in the top 5 landfill material around the globe, the European bedding industry was quick to assess the impact of the European Commission's 2015 Circular Economy Package. The predicted industry change offered an opportunity for producers to tackle the recycling challenge quickly with a viable business model. In turn, the mattress producers encouraged the chemical industry to look for solutions, and several alternatives quickly emerged.

Royal DSM, a global Dutch company active in health, nutrition and materials, for example, cemented a joint venture with startup Niaga. Niaga, a wordplay on spelling *again* backwards, was started by a team of redesigners focused on making products healthier and fully recyclable. With the inception of the joint venture with DSM, the startup first tackled the challenge of creating a new type of glue that delaminated carpets on command when exposed to a signal. Using this reversible glue to bond the two basic layers of most carpets—a polyurethane foam and a polyester fiber top layer—it was possible to recycle the carpets more completely, a major challenge for the carpet industry. The reversible glue was composed of polyester, the same material as the top layer, so it did not stand in the way of the polyester recycling process.

With this first success under its belt, the joint venture moved on to address an even bigger challenge, that faced by the mattress market. Similar techniques were developed, with the ambition to develop a 100% recyclable mattress by 2020. To this end, a long-term partnership was forged with bedding specialist Royal Auping to increase the use of renewable materials in mattresses [8].

DSM-Niaga was not alone in recognizing the massive circular economy opportunities presented by the vast amount of non-recyclable polyurethane mattresses. Dow Polyurethanes announced a collaboration with Germany-based manufacturer H&S Anlagentechnik to jointly develop recycled polyols from end-of-life mattresses [9]. The polyols were to be recycled through a specially developed process and could be applied to a variety of polyurethane applications. Not to be outdone, Bayer spin-off Covestro developed a process that used carbon dioxide to manufacture the polyols used in mattress foams, thus replacing up to 20% of the crude oil traditionally used in their production [10].

These three companies independently delivered three improvement strategies to address the challenge of dealing with vast amounts of non-recyclable polyurethane. The different choices of circular strategies by DSM, Dow and Covestro resulted in differentiated value propositions, with distinctive strategic partnerships.

🗁 Repurpose: From Pig Feed to Polymers

In the past, industrial waste derived from the French fries' industry, such as potato slivers and peels, was collected and disposed of as pig feed. One of the pioneer waste collection companies in the Netherlands was Rodenburg, entering the market in the mid-twentieth century. In 1998, after observing a steady decline in the agricultural sector in general and in the cattle feed industry in particular, the Rodenburg family decided to build a bioplastics pilot plant to investigate the potential for waste stream valorization. After initial tests proved successful, a large-scale production site followed, leading to the creation of Rodenburg Polymers in 2001.

The earliest development efforts resulted in a low-grade thermoplastic starch material with little added value and few applications, but the company persevered. After many trials and quite a few dead ends, the company succeeded in developing innovative extrusion production processes that allowed it to create and produce biodegradable compounds. It was a forerunner in its market, with an operating model primarily centered on co-creation and partnerships as its main success factors.

After a decade of pioneering, Rodenburg was approached by global confectionery company Mars with a specific challenge: Could Rodenburg develop a bio-based wrapper for the company's candy bars that was just as good as the current one? [11] In a five-year co-creation effort, Rodenburg partnered not only with Mars but also with Italian film specialist Taghleef and Mondi to manufacture the packaging. The collaboration resulted in a food grade polymer film compound that was compostable, biodegradable and took only one-third of the energy to produce compared with oil-based alternatives such as polypropylene. The innovation essentially repurposed pig feed into high-tech packaging.

Mars's bioplastics wrapper paved the way for innovations in packaging, developments that were required by mounting stakeholder pressure in response to issues such as ocean plastics and food waste. At the 2018 World Economic Forum in Davos, a broad coalition of companies, including Mars, announced their pledge to use 100% reusable, recyclable or compostable packaging by 2025, a massive boost to the biopolymers market.

If we are to help deliver on the targets agreed in Paris and the UN Sustainable Development Goals, there has to be a huge step change. While many companies have been working on being more sustainable, the current level of progress is nowhere near enough.

Grant F. Reid, CEO Mars [12]

The company's accomplishments give rise to an intriguing question: Does waste still exist? When concentrating on solving environmental issues, reducing flows of discarded materials is a natural starting point. Historically, the valorization of these streams was an underdeveloped area, as confirmed by the use of the term "waste" for them. The term originates from the Anglo-French and Old North French *waster*, "to waste, squander, spoil, ruin." Via the Old French word *gaster*, it can be traced back further to the Latin word *vastare*, "lay waste," from *vastus*, "empty, desolate" [13]. But in an environment in which new applications for waste materials are highly sought after and increasingly being found, waste simply ceases to exist, suggesting the need to remove the word from the corporate vocabulary!

🗁 Remanufacture: Renault Trucks and Its Vehicle Components [14]

In 2001, Volvo Trucks acquired Renault Trucks to form the largest truck manufacturer in Europe. Within the industry, remanufacturing was rapidly growing in popularity: it encompassed all the activities involved in rebuilding used spare parts to achieve a performance level on a par with or just below that of new parts. Remanufactured parts provided price-sensitive truck owners with a low cost, like-new alternative to the original equipment manufacturer replacements, with the added benefit of environmental awareness.

The Vehicle Components Aftermarket

The automotive and truck industry required a wide variety of components to ensure vehicle safety, reliability, convenience and comfort. The aftermarket dealt with components used for regular servicing and maintenance or to repair accident damage. In 2001, industry experts estimated total revenues in the vehicle components aftermarket to be more than €46 billion in the US and €25 billion in Europe. The so-called slow-moving components segment incorporated engine blocks, cylinder heads, gear boxes and other components that typically did not fail during a vehicle's regular life but that might be required in case of occasional failures. Most slow-moving components were high-value items that had to be fitted by professionally trained labor. As a result, vehicle owners often concluded that the vehicle's age or condition did not warrant the expense of replacing the part: they would rather buy a second-hand or new vehicle. When vehicle owners *did* decide to replace a slow-moving part, they could choose between original equipment designed by the manufacturer or substitutes with the same characteristics. Substitutes could be either second-hand components or remanufactured parts, both of which offered a significant price advantage over the new part.

Advantages of Remanufactured Parts: Price, Quality, Time

Remanufacturing a component, such as a complete engine block, meant removing it from the vehicle, discarding worn parts, reassembling the engine and testing it. To minimize downtime, another engine that had already been remanufactured was installed in the vehicle as soon as the original one was removed. This operation was slightly different from rebuilding, in which worn parts were replaced in an engine without removing it from the vehicle. Remanufacturing was therefore quicker than rebuilding, which translated into a quicker turnaround and less downtime. Added to the cost savings of 30% to 50% for most components compared with new parts, remanufactured versions were cheaper, enabling companies with large fleets to significantly reduce their servicing and maintenance costs.

This price difference was particularly interesting because remanufactured components were of only slightly lower quality than completely new components. Remanufactured engines, for example, went through a process that included a thorough cleaning and pre-inspection of all parts to ascertain whether they met original standards, ensuring that the component was brought back to the same specifications as a new one. Because remanufacturers knew the quality of each component, they were also able to offer warranties of 12 to 24 months or 150,000 km for an engine. Remanufactured components, especially engines, also often benefited from recent technology upgrades, which sometimes made them more efficient than the original component in terms of performance and emission regulations.

Remanufactured parts thus provided vehicle owners with a low cost, like-new replacement component with the added environmental benefit of managing their equipment on a *cradle-to-cradle* versus a *cradle-to-grave* life cycle. In 2001, remanufactured parts accounted for 16% of Renault Trucks' parts revenues, and the company was developing its strategic rationale to move more aggressively into the remanufacturing business.

Fast Forward: Reuse as a Competitive Value Driver

A decade and a half later, the topic of remanufacturing still features high on the agenda of vehicle makers. Volvo Group included reuse as one of its drivers for long-term competitiveness by maximizing value creation across the value chain. In the product development phase, resource efficiency and recycling potential were designed into the products: 85% of a truck produced by Volvo Group was recyclable. In 2017, Volvo Group's total sales of remanufactured components amounted to more than €0.9 billion, about 3% of the company's total net sales [15].

Renault Trucks' former owner, Groupe Renault, also doubled down on the topic. The company joined the Ellen MacArthur Foundation as a founding Global Partner when it launched in 2010 and has since renewed its commitment until 2020 [16]. The renewal was accompanied by new commitments to transition from a linear to a circular economy model, which the company regards as essential for securing the group's long-term future. Projects include extending its European remanufacturing model to other regions such as India, Brazil, Morocco and China.

🗁 Refurbishment in Fashion: Patagonia and Its Worn Wear Program

Although expensive assets such as truck engines are obvious candidates for remanufacturing and recycling, consumer gear such as fast fashion items might seem less likely to adopt circular economy practices. Well, not anymore. The resale market for fashion is reportedly growing 24 times faster than the traditional apparel retail market, from $20 billion today to $41 billion by 2022 in the US alone [17].

When Yvon Chouinard decided to create his sportswear brand in California in 1973, alongside his small company that made tools for climbers, he dreamed of a business that would have a minimal impact on the environment. Naming his company Patagonia, after the sparsely populated region at the southern tip of South America, he always vowed to stay true to that dream. His initial desire was reflected in the firm's mission: "Build the best product, cause no unnecessary harm, use business to inspire and implement solutions to the environmental crisis," [18] and it inspired Patagonia to become one of the most admired companies in the world. The admiration came not only from consumers but also from sustainability experts, over 1000 of whom ranked Patagonia as the second-best brand in the world in a well-known 2017 survey [19].

> Fixing something we might otherwise throw away is almost inconceivable to many in the heyday of fast fashion and rapidly advancing technology, but the impact is enormous.
>   Rose Marcario, CEO Patagonia [20]

Chouinard and his management team believed that one of the most responsible things a company could do was to make high-quality gear that lasted for years and could be repaired. Before circular economy thinking had moved into the mainstream, the company famously took out an advertisement in the *New York Times* in 2011 that read, "Don't buy this jacket." The ad explained the impact of one of the company's bestselling items, the R2® Jacket, to generate more awareness of consumerism and to promote Patagonia's reduce, repair, reuse, recycle and reimagine program and the associated Common Threads Initiative pledge.

A few years later, Patagonia introduced its Worn Wear program as part of its ongoing repair and recycle efforts. The objective was to extend the lifespan of its gear and provide a simpler logistics system to recycle Patagonia garments that were beyond repair. A partnership with eBay was forged to set up an online marketplace for used apparel. The same channel was used to raise awareness and encourage more Patagonia clients to pledge to keep Patagonia products from becoming landfill or fuel.

The company operated the largest garment repair facility in North America, with more than 40,000 individual repairs in 2016 alone. To avoid unnecessary logistics and service requests, the company published more than 40 free repair guides for Patagonia products on its website, so consumers could perform easy repairs themselves. Patagonia Worn Wear repair patches were made available to support self-repair efforts, and local retail staff were trained to handle simple repair jobs.

Since it began, Patagonia's products had come with a life-long guarantee. This sales argument gained even more credibility with the introduction of the Worn Wear program, as the repair efforts substantially added to the company's already outstanding reputation. An additional benefit of the program was the market intelligence repair centers collected. Seeing what parts of their gear were most vulnerable, enabled product designers to improve clothing and equipment in the areas where this was most needed.

Patagonia became a beautiful example of how sustainability could be a great source of brand value, loyalty and customer experience. At the same time, the company became a champion and ambassador of the circular economy, helping raise awareness about the challenges that are cross-linked with the fast fashion phenomenon. Design for longevity and refurbishment in fashion are more than just marketing speak: they are essential in a world where the list of finite resources is becoming increasingly longer.

🗁 Reduce: Pioneering Circular Crustaceans at the Happy Shrimp Farm [21]

In the late 1990s, shrimp farms of all types, from extensive to super-intensive, caused severe ecological problems in large parts of the world. For extensive farms, huge areas of mangroves had to be cleared, reducing biodiversity and increasing sea erosion. During the 1980s and 1990s, about 35% of the world's mangrove forests vanished, with shrimp farming one of the major offenders, reportedly accounting for about one-third of that destruction. Intensive farms, while reducing the direct impact on the mangroves, caused other problems. Such farms generated a lot of toxic pollution, for instance, from antibiotics, and exhausted fertile ponds within extremely short periods of time, leaving them unusable for any other purposes and with rehabilitation times of multiple decades. Clearly, shrimp farming needed sustainable alternatives.

In September 2007 such an alternative came to market. With only two months to go before their first product shipments, Bas Greiner and Gilbert Curtessi were on a high. Ivo Opstelten, the mayor of Rotterdam, had just auctioned the "first catch" of Happy Shrimp with record-breaking prices for these crustaceans in the Netherlands. For the founding fathers of the Happy Shrimp Farm, it had been a hectic three years. What started out as unpretentious market research for the Rotterdam Port Authority (RPA) rapidly developed into an international multi-million euro business that literally took over their lives and even featured on Dutch national television.

Bas and Gilbert had both been working for the RPA as researchers in the industrial development department. They had been commissioned to carry out research on potential ways to use the residual energy in the port through "co-siting," a concept whereby complementary businesses are located close to one another so that waste from one can become the input for another. They also received a mandate to investigate the possibility of an agro-industrial concept in the port based on sustainability principles.

One of the first and most obvious sets of opportunities emerged from the extensive power stations (oil, gas and coal-fired) based in Rotterdam harbor. These electricity-generating stations all faced challenges with their cooling systems, which were required to handle the surplus residual heat. Bas and Gilbert soon spotted a new opportunity for recycling the heated waters: farmed tropical shrimp. The RPA, however, was reluctant to take things forward; it was not its mandate to get involved with startups. Bas and Gilbert decided to quit their jobs and set up their own company called Bass+Gill to pursue the opportunities they had identified.

From Idea to Reality: Disrupting the Business System

With the results of the initial research performed for the RPA, Bass+Gill developed a comprehensive feasibility study and business plan for Happy Shrimp, an in-land, fresh shrimp production facility based upon the use of residual energy. As Gilbert recalled:

> There were many more opportunities, but the shrimp farm had the advantage of being located very close to the power plant and hence required smaller capital outlays.

As a first step, Bas and Gilbert had to secure the residual energy contracts with the producers. E.ON was prepared to sign a 15-year contract on favorable terms, as long as Happy Shrimp would take care of the whole heat extraction process, including the construction and financing of the 3-kilometer-long heat pipeline to the shrimp facilities. Also, Bass + Gill had to secure long-term financing for the project. With the help of a specialized consultant, it was able to access various grants totaling some €900,000. Furthermore, to gain access to a shrimp distribution channel, the entrepreneurs sealed an exclusive deal with Schmidt Zeevis, arguably the most reputed and best-known fishmonger in the Netherlands.

Based on what had been accomplished, the business was valued at €1.5 million. With this valuation in hand, the company was able to attract several business angels to co-finance the construction of the first Happy Shrimp Farm. Together with an €800,000 bank loan, Bass+Gill had assembled the €2.3 million that was needed to set up the first farm. The Happy Shrimp Farm would be the first in Europe to use residual energy to heat its basins. It capitalized on the eco-cycle concept, providing new meaning to the "waste is food" idea. With 24 basins, the farm was laid out to provide a peak capacity of about 50 tons of fresh, highly prized shrimp per year. Considering the sales price of about €25 per kilogram, the farm was expected to generate an annual revenue of around €1.25 million, with a comfortable net income margin in the high teens.

Happy Shrimp Value Proposition: Focusing on Simplicity and Responsibility

The value proposition of Happy Shrimp was simple to state and clearly capitalized on major trends of the day, such as social and environmental responsibility, as well as the "back to nature" movement.

- **Environmentally Friendly** Traditional shrimp farming involved extensive destruction of prime, very sensitive biotopes. The shrimp farm in Rotterdam was land-based and had controlled exchanges with the exterior environment.
- **Socially Responsible** Oxygen and other utilities for the shrimp-farming process were available at low cost in the port area because of existing infrastructure and economies of scale. Co-siting enhanced spatial and environmental efficiency in the port area.
- **Superfresh and Safe** One of the most potent selling points was that the shrimp would be offered as "never frozen." This would enhance the perceived food quality (freshness) and provide better traceability. Happy Shrimp facilities and processes were designed by food safety specialists from the outset to meet the highest food safety standards.

Happy Shrimp products would be distributed to exclusive restaurants and seafood bars through Schmidt Zeevis and directly to customers through farm gate sales and contracts for high-end catering at festivals and conferences.

Starting Operations

After beginning construction, Bas and Gilbert faced the challenge of maintaining the initial market interest while building the site. During the construction phase, they discovered how complex shrimp farming was. Since neither entrepreneur had ever worked in the agribusiness before, they hired a specialist to help engineer and fine-tune the conditions for growing the shrimp. Laying the energy pipeline from E.ON to the farm was delayed due to technical difficulties, and the necessary construction permits took longer than anticipated to obtain. As a result, the planned launch had to be postponed by six months.

Bas and Gilbert had the ambition to create the most complete and efficient eco-cycle of clustered products in the business. So, with construction of the farm and tasting pavilion progressing, the company developed several other product concepts based on the same principles. The conditions developed at the Happy Shrimp Farm for producing shrimp were, for instance, ideal for cultivating *Salicornia*, a type of edible seaweed. *Salicornia* could be grown in containers hanging over the shrimp basins. A new company was created to exploit the *Salicornia* opportunity, which would pay Happy Shrimp Farm to rent the production space. The clustering of the two concepts would be very cost effective, with sustainability credentials as well.

> But using the algae only for Happy Shrimp is too limited. Furthermore, algae biomass can be used as a source for bio diesel, food supplements, natural colorants, cosmetics and even pharmaceutical applications.
> Gilbert Curtessi, Managing Director of Happy Shrimp [22]

Unsurprisingly, some stakeholders grew concerned by the endless creativity of the project champions. It was absolutely key to deliver on the promises of the Happy Shrimp Farm before considering the rainbow of additional opportunities that were emerging. The visibility of the project was such that failure would have severe consequences for its champions.

Global Gambas: The Seduction of Growth

The public relations success of the Happy Shrimp Farm in the Netherlands brought many opportunities to take the business abroad. The European shrimp market grew rapidly, with key markets expanding by about 10% per annum. The arrival of competitors, such as the German aquaculture specialist Ecomares, added to the pressure to move forward quickly. To capture the international opportunities and leverage the experience of the Rotterdam pilot project, Bas and Gilbert started to work on the incubation of Happy Shrimp Farm International, forcing them to spread their resources very thin. Scaling proved difficult and left them facing key issues, including:

- How could they grow the business sustainably, while maintaining majority ownership and keeping their local stakeholders happy?
- Would the current ownership and governance structures sustain the hoped for global scaling?
- How could they raise the required €20 million for the 10 additional farms planned?

Epilogue: Frontrunner Failure Makes a Great Catalyst Case

The story did not end well for Happy Shrimp. In 2009, after a series of problems with suppliers and customers, the company had to shut down. Distribution partner Schmidt Zeevis attributed this mainly to Happy Shrimp prices not being competitive compared with frozen shrimp. Although high-end restaurants acknowledged the value of fresh shrimp, they still opted for the cheaper ones. In difficult economic times, restaurants were simply not able to afford the fresh crustaceans, which were on average €15 per kilogram more expensive. Scalability and the rate of mortality of baby shrimp also proved significant hurdles. In parallel, Ecomares, the German equivalent of Happy Shrimp, also fell into insolvency and ceased operations.

Over the last decade, public concern about illegal fishing has been growing as companies are challenged to bring proteins to the market at low prices. Initiatives such as the Marine Stewardship Council have gained momentum in their efforts to tackle illegal fishing and increase transparency in the sector. Way ahead of the pack, Happy Shrimp was a concept that proved to be too operationally vulnerable and too expensive in economically difficult times. The initial idea, to farm tropical shrimp in Rotterdam harbor using residual energy, had merit and made Happy Shrimp Farm a pioneer in the circular economy. The company, in its attempt to grow shrimp in a more sustainable and responsible way, while reducing the environmental impact, turned into a short-lived but valuable catalyst for the sector. Beyond the fishing industry, it proved that valuable business models can emerge from waste streams and that capturing these emerging opportunities requires top-quality operational management.

🗁 Refuse: The Greek Mattress Revolution Goes Global [23]

If the problem with mattresses stems from their extensive use of polyurethane, why not avoid the problem altogether by completely redesigning them using natural materials? That is exactly what Coco-Mat started doing back in 1989, when brothers Paul and Mike Evmorfidis embarked on a wild journey to develop an original, Greece-based bedding company. More than 25 years later, Coco-Mat was running stores in 14 countries and employed more than 250 people, most of them in Greece, and this was nowhere close to the end of the story. Paul and Mike could not stop dreaming about the next steps. They had started on a beach with virtually nothing, invented new concepts in an industry they knew little about and that could only be described as resistant to change, withstood one of the worst economic crises ever experienced by a country, and they were now discussing further international expansion and accelerating growth.

Inception: Mike, Paul and a Greek Beach

Mike and Paul Evmorfidis were born into a poor family in a small village near Sparta, Greece. Paul studied business in Athens and obtained his master's degree in Germany, while Mike earned a bachelor's degree in law from Athens School of Law, followed by a PhD from the Sorbonne in Paris. While Paul was a great storyteller, who was always trying to find solutions to make humans and nature live in harmony, Mike was very much the quiet and reflective "professor," as his doctorate implied.

One hot Peloponnesian evening in the 1980s, Paul had wanted to spend the night on the beach. Although the prospect sounded romantic, it could also be an uncomfortable experience. Paul decided to build a makeshift mattress with dried seaweed and coastal leaves. The night did indeed prove memorable and left an indelible mark on his soul. A few years later, in 1989, Paul's reconnection with local craftsman Michalis Vamvakidis set him on journey to develop better mattresses than any shop abroad. Paul's night on the beach immediately came back to mind: Could he repackage that experience in a mattress?

On the roof of his house, he started to develop a first prototype, trying to emulate the natural mattress from that memorable evening. After a disappointing quest to identify existing solutions for better sleeping, Paul and Michalis decided to reduce the problem to its core components and see if the various constituents of a mattress could individually be enhanced, in the hope that minute improvements of the parts would lead to meaningful improvement of the whole. To create the core mattress structure, it was essential to find materials that offered rigidity, but not too much. Paul remembered a fiber he had discovered during a trip to Southeast Asia that impressed him with its versatility and unique combination of lightness and stiffness: coconut fiber. These characteristics sounded perfect for a natural mattress core. To provide softness and comfort, he endeavored to cover the coconut fiber with cotton and wool. With this first mattress came the product name: Coco-Mat, for COCOnut fiber and MATtress, together with the company motto, "Sleep on Nature."

The first mattress sold immediately, validating the initial concept and possibly the business opportunity. Calling on his brother and a few friends, Paul managed to put together the launch capital to start producing more units. With no fancy business plan, a primitive proof-of-concept and a rudimentary market test, they set out to develop the best natural mattresses in the world.

The Coco-Mat Bedding System

The company's signature product was the customized mattress, the heart of a complete bedding system. Made of natural materials, it was engineered to create an elastic bed that would adapt to any shape and form to increase support and comfort. Different layers were combined to obtain just the right level of resistance for each customer, providing a new, customized sleeping experience. It usually took only one night on a Coco-Mat mattress to appreciate the validity of its claims.

The exceptional sleeping experience of a Coco-Mat bed was epitomized by the "four layer" system, with each layer contributing to the final objectives. Each bed system was customized to the final users' needs and the climate in which they lived. The company gradually introduced additional natural materials, such as horsehair, cactus fiber, seaweed and lavender, to further improve the quality of the mattress, making the bed even more special for each customer. The bedding system was soon complemented by a range of household products with the same "natural" proposition, from towels and sheets to furniture.

Initially, the mattresses were produced in a small factory in Athens, where craftsmen built them entirely by hand. As demand expanded rapidly, the founders established new production facilities in Xanthi, in the eastern part of the country, close to the Turkish and Bulgarian borders. In 1992, with no experience setting up a factory, Mike returned to Greece after his studies at age 26 and took it upon himself to turn the factory into a place to be proud of. He remained as plant manager until 2010. When it was clear that it had survived the brunt of the Greek financial crisis, Mike moved back to Athens as the company's CEO.

Coco-Mat Stores and Growth Blitz

The first Coco-Mat shop opened in Athens, followed by several others all over Greece. They were designed to personify the founders' values as well as the Greek temperament. Selling luxury mattresses was all about making the customers feel special, and Mike and Paul knew how to create a unique customer experience by fashioning beautiful stores in which people were happy to spend time. Every store had a kitchen, so customers were welcomed like guests with snacks; they were also encouraged to lie on the beds and try what it was like to sleep on a Coco-Mat bed.

Paul and Mike started small but had the ambition to take their bedding experience to the world. As early as 1997, they opened their first shop outside Greece in the Netherlands, soon followed by a store in Barcelona. These moves were in part driven by the two brothers' love for real estate, a product of their poor upbringing in Greece, where property was more valuable than cash. The international expansion continued at an accelerated pace but always on the same premise—the brothers always bought the buildings that would house their stores.

Initially, they borrowed money from friends and family, which was used as collateral to obtain larger amounts from local banks. However, the idea of having to rely on banks did not appeal to the brothers, so they repaid all the company loans by 1998 and remained debt free ever after. Financial independence and self-reliance became key principles for the company.

This absence of leverage and the business's very lean organization proved decisive in ensuring Coco-Mat's survival when the financial crisis knocked Greece off its pedestal in late 2009. The crisis even proved to be an opportunity for the Evmorfidis brothers. With no debt and some disposable capital, they invested in businesses put up for sale by desperate owners. They developed hotels and an industrial laundry business,[2] among other enterprises. Hotels proved to be rich cross-selling opportunities and great showcases for Coco-Mat mattresses and other bedding accessories.

Accelerating Growth: Structure, Finance and Business Model

Self-financing and company-owned stores constrained growth. It rapidly dawned on the family that a new expansion model was probably required, one

---

[2] The company enabled hoteliers and hospitals to lease rather than buy bed linen and towels from Coco-Mat, thus avoiding huge cash outlays.

that would not undermine what had been accomplished and would capitalize on the company's strong roots. To facilitate growth, three dimensions needed to be revisited: the management structure, the business model and the company financing.

Coco-Mat had eschewed a formal management structure for a long time: Mike was responsible for everything. That organizational model had made sense at the beginning, but its inefficiencies were becoming increasingly apparent. Several managers were hired who reported directly to the CEO; all other employees reported to the managers rather than directly to the CEO.

Self-financing meant that the family's wealth was massively invested in the company's assets. At a certain size, this created a dilemma. To foster simple risk management, the company was split into two businesses, one hosting all real assets (factories, stores, hotels) and the second responsible for the operational aspects, that is, the factory, the brand, the trademark and the profit and loss of the company under the name Coco-Mat S.A.

To finance the acceleration of the company's development, it was essential to identify an investor that shared the founders' strong values. This was when Marios Sophroniou came into the picture. Following a failed long-term negotiation with a global private equity company guided by Marios as an external advisor, a trust relationship was built. Mike asked him to join Coco-Mat's board to help them look for other investors and guide them on the company's organizational and international development. Coco-Mat would look primarily for a hands-off but value-adding investor. It did not take long for the Logothetis family—the owners of the Libra Group—to be identified as a potential candidate.

Libra Group and Cycladic Capital

Libra Group was a privately owned international business group owned by the brothers George, Constantine and Nicholas Logothetis. The family showed an immediate interest in Coco-Mat, and on March 13, 2014, Libra Group announced it had formed a joint venture with Coco-Mat S.A. The private transaction was estimated [24] at €19 million for the 50% interest acquired by Libra Holdings and London-based Cycladic Capital.[3] Emmanuel Androulakis, executive vice president of Libra Group, commented:

---

[3] Cycladic Capital was owned by Dimitris Goulandris and invested capital on behalf of his family and other investors. In its 14 years of operations, the group had invested in more than 30 businesses and founded 5 in the US, Africa, Europe, India and Latin America.

Coco-Mat is a cherished brand that we have long admired and for which we see significant international growth potential. The business has an exceptional record of product innovation and brand loyalty. We share Coco-Mat's values and vision, and these are key ingredients for a successful long-term partnership. We have great faith in the Coco-Mat philosophy and its management team. Furthermore, we believe strongly in the underlying strength of Greek businesses and of Greek human capital and expect to continue expanding our investment and operations in the country.

2016 and Beyond

For the Evmorfidis brothers, the journey was just beginning and their curiosity and thirst for discovery were barely quenched. The Coco-Mat beds proved to be a hit with major upscale hotels around the world, and highly rated airline companies such as Etihad and LATAM adopted the Coco-Mat mattresses in their first-class cabins to provide the ultimate level of comfort for passengers. Paul continued to emulate the principles and values that had made Coco-Mat successful, developing innovative products using natural materials as a substitute for synthetics or chemicals.

Within Greece, Coco-Mat worked hard to establish and maintain an image of social and environmental responsibility, treating its customers and employees with the same dedication and care. Grounded deep in Greece, it always promoted the "Greekness" of its products and gave opportunities to many young Greeks of all backgrounds.

But the future was not all about celebration: challenges still abounded. Ramping up global sales required a level of organization and management skills that were still in short supply. Producing in Greece had its challenges, in particular in terms of logistics. The country regularly flirted with bankruptcy, which triggered a backlash of strikes and disruptions to the economy, wreaking havoc with the company's operational plans. Coco-Mat continued to benefit from a cult-like following of its customers, all too eager to get their hands (or rather bodies) on the prized bedding systems.

Coco-Mat's success was empiric evidence that it was entirely possible to create a premium brand based on the premise of sustainability. Refusing existing, less sustainable solutions had brought them much success and the past had been nothing short of amazing, but where should Paul and Mike take the company next?

☞ BMW i3: A Team Exercise in Selecting Circular Economy Strategies

To help teams get more comfortable with the notion of developing MASS by identifying sustainability challenges and selecting circular economy strategies, experimentation is recommended—preferably in a safe, inspiring environment. The tried and tested workshop format for the BMW i3—the Bavarian automaker's successful all-electric car—presented here, does exactly that.

> Every once in a while, an automaker creates a car that forever changes the brand. It doesn't happen often, but when it does, it becomes a focal point for the brand's history.
>   Blogger Nico DeMattia on the BMW i3 [25]

The workshop lasts 1½ to 2 hours and starts by briefly discussing an abridged version of the BMW i3 business model visualized through the popular Business Model Canvas. Published in 2010, the Business Model Canvas [26] is a thinking tool used to design and improve business models. Introduced in Chap. 3 of this book, the canvas uses nine specific categories, referred to as the building blocks of an organization. The building blocks are key partners, key activities, key resources, the value proposition, customer relationships, channels, customer segments, cost structure and revenue streams.

As (sustainable) mobility is a topic that is close to the heart of many, workshop participants will bring plenty of knowledge, opinion and experience of the business to guarantee lively exchanges. After introducing the BMW i3 business model and the surrounding industry trends and forces in the plenary kick-off, participants are divided into groups of four to six. Each group is asked to identify circular economy strategies from the waste hierarchy ladder presented in Fig. 10.1 and to come up with at least three ideas that are contributing to "green mobility." Each group then presents to the others, outlining the recognized challenges together with the selected circular economy strategies, the types of potential partners that have been identified and the targets that are to be set for the challenges.

The full description of the BMW i3 workshop format and a proposed agenda can be downloaded from www.vectoring.online, including high-resolution files of the Business Model Canvas here.

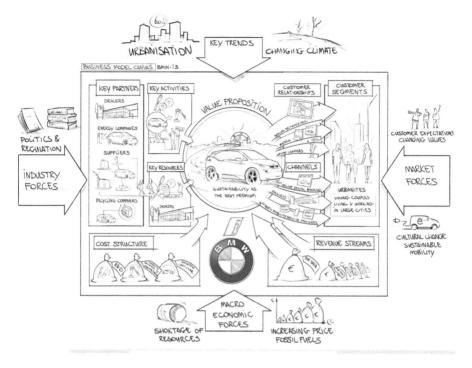

Fig. 10.1 Abridged version of the BMW i3 business model

Tips, Traps and Takeaways

👍 Tips

- Look for MASS development by applying the different circular economy strategies from the waste hierarchy ladder.
- Pay attention to the diversity of the teams that are working on circular solutions, as they require a broad variety of business angles.
- When substituting raw materials, secure the circular resource for the longer term, including scaling the business.
- Inspiration for sustainable innovation can come from others inside and outside your sector as well as from nature.
- Consider and involve value chain partners early, but only after first defining the sustainability challenge that is to be addressed.

💣 Traps

- Avoid using too much detailed data early in the value proposition design process, as it will likely over-influence your judgment.

- When thinking of asset-sharing as a potential solution, remember to factor in the changed maintenance profile of the asset. Multiple users are likely to take less care of the asset.
- Effective application of circularity strategies is not always a matter of technological innovations. Sometimes rethinking a business model with existing technologies works equally well.

⚓ Takeaways

This chapter aimed to discuss how the circular economy addresses the issue of products and services that are better aligned with an economy in which value chains become closed loop ecosystems, where materials are applied over and over again. The economic potential of these circular economy principles is substantial: Europe alone is expected to generate profits of €1.8 trillion by 2030. Six company cases are portrayed in detail, each illustrating a different circularity strategy, such as recycling, remanufacturing, refurbishing, reducing and refusing.

Turning waste material from the French fries' industry into valuable bioplastics, Rodenburg Polymers is a powerful example of repurposing raw materials. What was once sold as feed for pigs has become a desirable ingredient in packaging material for the food industry, providing a sought-after alternative to non-renewable packaging. Ten years of innovation and close collaboration with value chain partners turned the waste disposal company into a pioneer in the field of bioplastics, adding fuel to the discussion about whether waste should still exist.

Patagonia's Worn Wear initiative suggested that repairing fashion items can generate massive customer engagement, help collect customer usage data and drive the company's transition to a more circular business model. Radical marketing techniques, such as Patagonia's "Don't buy this jacket" campaign, challenge traditional growth models, but they cemented the company's reputation and advanced customer loyalty.

DSM-Niaga illustrated how a global waste problem, mattresses, quickly turned into a market for circular economy strategies, attracting different solutions in different segments of the value chain. Several options existed for recycling and reducing the use of polyurethane. And with different solutions, different models for partnerships emerged. Also in the mattress market, the success of Greek bedding systems company Coco-Mat, and its brand promise of "Sleeping on Nature," showed what can be achieved by refusing existing solutions and radically rethinking sustainable new ones. Coco-Mat illustrated the potential to create a premium brand based on the premise of sustainability. In doing so, this final company case presents a perfect bridge to Chap. 11—Capturing the Sustainability Premium—in which the topic of sustainable innovations with significant societal impact will be explored.

References

1. Potting, J., Hekkert, M., Worrell, E. et al. (2017, January) *Circular economy: measuring innovation in the product chain*. The Hague: PBL Netherlands Environmental Assessment Agency. Retrieved from http://www.pbl.nl/sites/default/files/cms/publicaties/pbl-2016-circular-economy-measuring-innovation-in-product-chains-2544.pdf
2. McKinsey & Company (2015, September) *Europe's circular-economy opportunity.* Retrieved from https://www.mckinsey.com/business-functions/sustainability-and-resource-productivity/our-insights/europes-circular-economy-opportunity
3. McKinsey & Company (2016, October) *The circular economy: Moving from theory to practice.* Retrieved from https://www.mckinsey.com/~/media/McKinsey/Business%20Functions/Sustainability%20and%20Resource%20Productivity/Our%20Insights/The%20circular%20economy%20Moving%20from%20theory%20to%20practice/The%20circular%20economy%20Moving%20from%20theory%20to%20practice.ashx
4. The New Plastics Economy (2018, January 22) Companies take major step towards a New Plastics Economy. *The New Plastics Economy.* Retrieved from https://newplasticseconomy.org/news/11-companies-commit-to-100-reusable-recyclable-or-compostable-packaging-by-2025
5. World Economic Forum (2016, January) *The New Plastics Economy: Rethinking the future of plastics.* Retrieved from http://www3.weforum.org/docs/WEF_The_New_Plastics_Economy.pdf
6. Transparency Market Research (2018, April) Global Mattress Market: Local Players Give Competition to Global Players with Competitive Prices. *Transparency Market Research.* Retrieved from https://www.transparencymarketresearch.com/pressrelease/mattress-market.htm
7. EUROPUR (2016) *Flexible polyurethane foam in mattresses and furniture, an overview of possible end of life solutions.* Retrieved from https://www.europur.org/publications/item/44-facsheet-eol-foam-from-matresses-and-furniture
8. Hoex, L. (2018, January 12) This reversible glue puts a screw in manufacturing. *GreenBiz.* Retrieved from https://www.greenbiz.com/article/reversible-glue-puts-screw-manufacturing
9. The Dow Chemical Company (2017, November 6) Dow Announces Collaboration for Breakthrough in Polyurethane Mattress Recycling [Press

release]. Retrieved from https://www.dow.com/en-us/polyurethanes/news/dow-announces-collaboration-for-breakthrough-in-polyurethane-mattress-recycling

10. Holder, M. (2018, April 12) Covestro's manifesto for a sustainable, clean economy. *GreenBiz*. Retrieved from https://www.greenbiz.com/article/covestros-manifesto-sustainable-clean-economy

11. Laird, K. (2016, May 4) Mars goes for bioplastic candy bar wrappers. *Plastics Today*. Retrieved from https://www.plasticstoday.com/packaging/mars-goes-bio-plastic-candy-bar-wrappers/23736162124586

12. Sustainable Brands (2017, September 6) MARS Commits $1B to New Sustainability Plan, Launches Climate-Focused Campaign. *Sustainable Brands*. Retrieved from http://www.sustainablebrands.com/news_and_views/walking_talk/sustainable_brands/mars_commits_1b_new_sustainability_plan_launches_clim

13. Online Etymology Dictionary contributors (2018) Waste. *Online Etymology Dictionary*. https://www.etymonline.com/word/waste. Accessed 3 May 2018.

14. This case is an abridged version of RENAULT TRUCKS: REMANUFACTURING AS A STRATEGIC ACTIVITY (IMD-3-1447) Copyright © 2018 by IMD—International Institute for Management Development, Lausanne, Switzerland (www.imd.org). No part of this publication may be reproduced, stored in a retrieval system or transmitted in any form or by any means without the prior written permission of IMD.

15. The Volvo Group (2018) *Annual and Sustainability Report 2017*. Retrieved from https://www.volvogroup.com/en-en/events/2018/mar/annual-and-sustainability-report-2017.html

16. The Ellen MacArthur Foundation (2017, May 31) Groupe Renault renews commitment to the circular economy. *The Ellen MacArthur Foundation*. Retrieved from https://www.ellenmacarthurfoundation.org/news/groupe-renault-renew-their-commitment-to-the-circular-economy

17. Reed, S. (2018, March 4) Second-hand Shopping on the Rise, Signalling a Change in Millennial Spending Habits. *The Hollywood Reporter*. Retrieved from https://www.hollywoodreporter.com/news/secondhand-shopping-rise-signaling-a-change-millennial-spending-habits-1099203

18. Ethical Corporation (2016, May) *Patagonia Circular Economy Strategy: A Case Study*. Retrieved from http://1.ethicalcorp.com/LP=8770

19. GlobeScan SustainAbility Survey (2016) *The 2017 Sustainability Leaders: Celebrating 20 Years of Leadership*. Accessed 15 March 2018.

20. Patagonia (2018) Worn wear. https://www.patagonia.com/worn-wear.html. Accessed 3 May 2018.

21. This case is an abridged version of THE HAPPY SHRIMP FARM: SOCIAL RESPONSIBILITY & MULTIPLE STAKEHOLDERS (IMD-3-1903) Copyright © 2018 by IMD—International Institute for Management Development, Lausanne, Switzerland (www.imd.org). No part of this publica-

tion may be reproduced, stored in a retrieval system or transmitted in any form or by any means without the prior written permission of IMD.

22. All About Feed (2008, September 25) Happy Shrimp Farm to produce algae. *All About Feed.* Retrieved from https://www.allaboutfeed.net/Home/General/2008/9/Happy-Shrimp-Farm-to-produce-algae-AAF002277W/

23. This case is an abridged version of COCO-MAT: THE SPARTAN MATTRESS REVOLUTION (IMD-7-1802) Copyright © 2018 by IMD—International Institute for Management Development, Lausanne, Switzerland (www.imd.org). No part of this publication may be reproduced, stored in a retrieval system or transmitted in any form or by any means without the prior written permission of IMD.

24. PricewaterhouseCoopers (2015, January) *Deals 2014 in Greece.* Retrieved from https://www.pwc.com/gr/en/publications/assets/deals2014.pdf

25. DeMattia, N. (2015, November 12) The BMW i3: The car that changed BMW. Retrieved from https://www.bmwblog.com/2015/11/12/the-bmw-i3-the-car-that-changed-bmw/

26. Osterwalder, A. & Pigneur, Y. (2010) *Business Model Generation: A Handbook for visionaries, game changers and challengers,* Wiley press

11

Capturing the Sustainability Premium

Highlighting the importance of strategic partnerships for sustainability and the need to develop many alternative sustainable solutions (MASS), the previous chapter elaborated on the concept of a waste hierarchy, which proved useful in approaching portfolio transitions toward a circular economy. With a step-by-step process and a collection of company cases, circular strategies were examined for solution development.

In this chapter, we deepen the discussion on how to capture the sustainability premium, looking at potential innovation channels and how to change consumer behaviors. First, several innovative practices based on collaboration are discussed, starting with the example of the BMW Startup Garage. This example of how BMW became a *venture client* for startups, as opposed to an investor, can be seen as an extension of the BMW i3 team exercise presented earlier in the circular economy discussion, in Chap. 10. Next, different approaches to changing consumer perceptions and attitudes are explored, supported by examples from the food industry, such as the sustainability-driven turnaround of Coronilla, a Bolivia-based gluten-free pasta business. Finally, a few additional tools are added to the toolbox, mostly techniques to uncover customer requirements.

🗁 BMW Startup Garage: Venture Client Accelerator

After carefully pruning down the relevant sustainability challenges, an alternative route to sustainable innovation is forging partnerships through open innovation channels. Corporate accelerators and corporate venture capital

© The Author(s) 2019
B. Leleux, J. van der Kaaij, *Winning Sustainability Strategies*,
https://doi.org/10.1007/978-3-319-97445-3_11

have supported a wave of startup-driven innovations. While most innovation platforms do not explicitly incorporate sustainability challenges (such as water consumption, energy use, renewable materials and local community development), many do, and some are even prime promoters of the cause. An example of the latter is the *100+ sustainability accelerator* [1] created by global beer leader AB InBev to help it creatively tackle its sustainability challenges.

Other open innovation platforms are often used by large corporations to inspire startups to innovate in directions that are deemed strategic for the firms. A good example of this is the venture client model developed by the BMW Startup Garage (BSG). This open innovation platform was hatched to help BMW accelerate the identification and adoption of new technologies for the automotive industry, such as autonomous driving, improved car lights, intelligent communication, and the like. The BMW Group tasked BSG with scouting for and engaging startups that had technologies that could advance innovation at BMW. BSG would act as a bridge between the startup and the operational business units within BMW that could trial, co-develop and ultimately adopt the new technologies, in effect sourcing the startup's first customer and facilitating its acquisition of a full supplier accreditation. The underlying idea was to allow BMW to act as a late-stage incubator for the technologies, co-developing and testing prototypes within the various automotive departments. According to its founders, startup veteran Gregor Gimmy and seasoned BMW innovation expert Matthias Mayer, the model they promoted, which they called *venture clienting*, was about acting as a catalyst for the startup development process and accelerating adoption by BMW.

> Basically, we asked, 'What can we offer to the best startup on earth with the best technology, lots of venture capital cash, and a great pool of talents to come to us and not to someone else? The best thing we could offer is to be their first client, hence the name venture clienting. No VC or accelerator out there would say they can achieve that value proposition because they are not clients, they are investors. Ultimately, what makes a startup successful is a good client. That was really what kicked off the thought of becoming a Venture Client and working with startups at a much earlier stage than we normally do and getting them to succeed faster'. [2]

To attract the best applicants, BMW did not take control of any of the intellectual property and did not acquire equity stakes. Startups were not limited by exclusivity agreements and were not brought together in a central location. BSG was an ace in the hole for BMW innovation: the chance to attract top talent and technology from around the globe by leveraging the phenomenal power of the BMW brand as an early adopter. It also offered many startups the tantalizing appeal of the automotive industry, an estimated market of $10 trillion, 20 times larger than the $500 billion advertising business that Google, Facebook and others were competing for.

BMW Startup Garage operated in a pure, virtuous vectoring style, combining direction with speed and impact. It evaluated ideas put forward based on their fit with BMW's actual innovation needs. To pre-qualify, the applications had to fit into one of the five innovation areas most relevant to the BMW Group:

- Connected drive, with a focus on future car connectivity
- Efficient dynamics, looking at making engines operate more efficient
- Emotional experience, improving the experience for drivers
- Electric mobility, addressing issues around car batteries, driving range and electric engines
- Lightness, looking for new materials that make the car lighter and thus more fuel efficient

Although sustainability was not explicitly presented among BSG's objectives, at least three innovation areas directly supported sustainable mobility: efficient dynamics, electric mobility and lightness.

Selected startups participated in a four-month program with a single deliverable: a functional prototype with an application relevant to the BMW Group. Right from the beginning, internal clients were identified, and once a startup shifted into gear, they engaged it in a genuine innovation project, very similar to the process with which they would work with technology partners like Bosch or Continental [2]. Additionally, the startups received support building their network within the BMW Group and developing their business plans.

Back in 2015, BSG ran a startup competition to kick-start its activities and identify rapidly emerging technologies of interest. Dutch startup Leyden Jar won the competition with its proposal for a porous pure silicon anode that enabled up to 50% more energy density in lithium-ion batteries. The fit with BMW was almost perfect, since the company had committed to extend the range of electric vehicles in its catalog to at least 25 by 2025, with 12 of these fully electric cars.

Appropriately, the startup's company name of *Leyden Jar* was derived from an invention made independently a couple of centuries earlier by a German cleric and a Dutch scientist from Leiden (hence the name). A Leyden jar typically consists of a glass jar with a metal foil coating on the inner and outer surfaces, and a metal terminal projecting vertically through the jar lid to make contact with the inner foil. It was used to conduct early electricity experiments and was the first means of accumulating and storing electric charge in large quantities [3].

Another BMW Group company—daughter MINI—has also embraced the sustainability challenge and the idea of partnering for impact. In 2016 it joined forces with HAX, the world's first and largest hardware investment company, to create the Urban-X accelerator. With the worldwide population set to reach 9 billion by 2050 and a strong urbanization trend, cities face big challenges ahead. Starting in New York City, Urban-X backed 10 startups focused on intelligent cities, society scale challenges and urban hyper growth. By learning from experiences in accelerating hardware and software innovation and applying this knowledge to city-scale societal problems, innovations for future-proof cities could be unleashed. In the first year, 17 startups were backed and MINI learned valuable lessons along the way. This led to a switch in partners to Urban Us, whose sustainability goals were more closely aligned with the auto company. Every six months, up to 10 startups were selected and the partners together invested up to $100,000 per company. Besides funding, the 20-week Urban-X program provided access to both companies' networks and included mentoring for the startups in the quest to make cities more sustainable.

BMW's venture client accelerator is company-specific but open accelerators sponsored by multiple companies are quite conceivable as well. The fashion industry example below provides a wide constellation of change initiatives that all fall under the scope of the global Fashion for Good initiative with one common goal: accelerating sustainability in the fashion industry.

⌂ Accelerating Fast Fashion (or Slowing It Down): Open Platform

C&A Foundation, a spin-off of global fashion retailer C&A owned by the Brenninkmeijer family, aspired to transform the fashion industry by supporting the sector's transition to a circular economy. As part of its initiatives, C&A Foundation provided the initial grant for Fashion for Good, an Amsterdam-based innovation platform with the aim of fundamentally changing the apparel industry through innovation and new business models.

Our mission at Fashion for Good is to bring together the entire fashion ecosystem to reimagine the way fashion is designed, made, worn and reused.
 Katrin Ley, Managing Director, Fashion for Good [4]

Sector change can harness many different solutions. The way that Fashion for Good buttonholed the fashion ecosystem was by singling out several topics, such as materials, economy, energy, water and lives, in six complementary initiatives:

- **Early-Stage Innovation Accelerator** Together with Plug and Play—the world's largest accelerator program, with success stories including Dropbox and PayPal under its belt—Fashion for Good developed a 12-week startup accelerator to identify and accelerate startups that had the potential to fast-track the transition to a sustainable apparel industry. The startups, whose future-fit products and technologies included exciting concepts such as biodegradable glitter and seaweed-based fabric, were mentored by a host of impressive brands such as adidas, C&A, Galeries Lafayette, Kering, Target and Zalando that were looking for sustainable innovations and could become clients.
- **Late-Stage Innovation Program** Fashion for Good located innovations that already had proof of concept and helped them scale by, for instance, providing access to expertise, customers and capital.
- **Apparel Acceleration Fund** Fashion for Good collaborated with the Dutch Sustainable Trade Initiative (IDH), which had established a fund to facilitate access to finance for upscaling more sustainable production methods in fashion.
- **Good Fashion Guide** This open-source guide contained practical tips, a self-diagnostic tool and a step-by-step guide to production, based on lessons learned.
- **Circular Apparel Community** Fashion for Good rented a historic building in the heart of Amsterdam to bring like-minded organizations together such as the Sustainable Apparel Coalition, Zero Discharge of Hazardous Chemicals and Made-By.
- **The Five Goods** Three floors of the historic Amsterdam building were opened to the public to build a community around the ambition to make all fashion comply with the Five Goods: good materials, good economy, good energy, good water and good lives.

Collaboration was pivotal to the concept of the innovation platform. The initiative vigorously endeavored to connect a global coalition of brands, producers, retailers, non-profit organizations, funders and others and opened its doors to meetings between stakeholders of all kinds. In her speech at the launch of Fashion for Good, Leslie Johnston, executive director of the C&A Foundation, underscored the importance of value chain collaboration in the entire fashion ecosystem:

> This kind of transformation can only be done with others, so today we are calling for brands, manufacturers, funders and innovators to join us and work together to realize our shared vision! [5]

In the examples of BMW Startup Garage and Fashion for Good, two types of collaboration channels have been presented to illustrate the potential value of platform-based innovation initiatives. The major difference between the two approaches is that the automotive solution is driven by a single company that presents itself as a "venture client," while the fashion example is a broad partnering initiative with a comprehensive range of programs. In light of the variety of alternative innovation channels available to choose from, such as incubators, hackathons and accelerators, the next section seeks to aid decision making on which sustainable innovation channels to prefer.

Sustainability and Open Innovation Platforms

Companies worldwide have started to recognize the power of open innovation platforms and are using collaborative networks to fuel sustainability innovation [6]. And with 68% of the top 100 companies on the Forbes Global 500 list already engaging with startups, open innovation has become an accepted phenomenon [7].

During an investigation into the roles that different open innovation partners play in improving economic innovation performance and sustainability innovation performance, researchers found that in addition to partners such as universities and customers, increased collaboration with NGOs and intermediaries is gratifying for firms. Furthermore, in open innovation, economic innovation performance and sustainability innovation performance were found to correlate, indicating that the development of MASS does not negatively influence economic innovation performance [8]. Sustainability-driven innovations do not hamper economic innovations, they go hand in hand.

Where should companies place their bets with their sustainable innovation funds? Choosing the appropriate channels can be a challenge, so the bets are hedged. On average, Forbes Global 500 members working with startups are engaging with them through 1.6 different channels. The preferred channel is corporate venture capital (62.6% of cases), followed by startup competitions (29.0%) and accelerators or incubators (24.4%) [7]. Startup competitions and hackathon events, such as the GE and EURELECTRIC Ecomagination Challenge hackathon on decarbonizing energy and transportation in Europe, are less common. Support services such as *impact hubs* are regarded as useful but less suitable for effective corporate startup engagement.

Based on the Forbes Global 500 numbers, the most advanced industry in this respect is pharmaceuticals, with 94.1% of companies involved with start-ups. Of the 17 pharma companies featuring in the Forbes Global 500, 16 used one or more channels to tap into startup knowledge. Most of them engaged startups through corporate venture capital, with 13 out of the 17 owning a separate venture branch. Four companies, Eli Lilly, Roche Holding, GlaxoSmithKline and Novo Nordisk, even had different funds.

The most effective choice of channels depends on circumstances and the reason for starting the initiative. Generally, the objectives for embarking on an innovation initiative can be summarized in four categories: generate *innovations* for products and services, change the company *culture*, develop *new markets* and create a *platform* of partners to reinforce the competitive positioning. Each objective comes with its own recommended innovation channel. An overview of the potential channels and their most appropriate application is shown in Table 11.1.

Even if startups can benefit from different platforms and channels when developing sustainable innovations, they still face the huge challenge of successfully scaling their business, even if they are "green." A persistent green myth is that sustainable products will sell themselves, but unfortunately, they do not. Exemplified by a closer look at food consumption, the next paragraphs concentrate on addressing the additional marketing challenges that sustainability poses. How can organizations create and deliver the sustainability premium and finally capture its value while overcoming the hurdles of changing consumer patterns?

Table 11.1 Channel preferences for innovation platforms

Channel	Innovation	Culture	New markets	Platforms
Events	−	−/+	−	−/+
Support services	−	−/+	−	−/+
Startup programs	−	−/+	−/+	+
Accelerator/incubator	+	+	−/+	−/+
Spin-offs	+	−	−/+	−
Investments	+	−	+	+
Mergers and acquisitions	−/+	−/+	+	−/+

Source: INSEAD Business School, adapted

Opportunities from Changing Consumer Patterns

As described in Chap. 2 when introducing the concept of vectoring, on an aggregated level the business case for sustainability can be compiled from four distinct building blocks:

- Cost savings from eco-efficiencies, for instance, by reducing waste, water usage or energy consumption
- Revenue growth from sustainable innovations
- Enhanced reputation with stakeholders such as clients, employees and shareholders
- Lowering risk, for instance, by reducing cost of capital or dependence on scarce resources.

To create value and, more importantly, capture it, the drivers for the business case for sustainability need to be turned into real applications. As Table 11.2 shows, the company cases in this book present an insightful pattern for organizations looking to put together their business case for sustainability and deliver on it.

In some cases, designing and marketing sustainable products and services can be as straightforward as varying the range and reducing the price, as Intermarché—the third largest supermarket chain in France—did when it started selling imperfect fruits and vegetables in its stores at a 30% discount. In most situations, however, viable solutions are more elusive and more intricate to implement, especially when they also have to try to change existing consumption patterns.

In light of fundamental future changes in food demand and supply, the complexity of reaching the higher-hanging fruit is inescapable. According to the United Nations Food and Agriculture Organization's (FAO) food demand projections, it is estimated that the world needs to overcome a 70% "food gap" between the crop calories that were available in 2006 and the expected calorie demand in 2050 [9]. Relying merely on increased production yields to close the detected gap would exert unrealistic pressure on natural ecosystems through issues such as deforestation and lack of biodiversity. In brief, yield increases alone will be unlikely to close the food gap so other, consumption-based solutions are required, such as shifting the diets of populations that consume high amounts of calories, protein and animal-based foods (refer to Fig. 11.1).

Shifting diets that have developed over centuries is anything but straightforward. And the emerging dietary challenges are immense, as Fig. 11.2

Table 11.2 Applying the building blocks of the business case for sustainability to company cases

Value creation	Examples of value delivery	Company cases
Eco-efficiency	• Using less resources • Reusing resources	• Reusing residual energy—Happy Shrimp Farm • Remanufacturing—Renault/Volvo Trucks
Revenue growth from innovation	• Different business models • Provide access to new markets • Replace less sustainable products	• Repairing garments, not selling them—Patagonia • BMW Startup Garage; Fashion for Good • CO_2 replacing polyurethane in mattresses—Covestro
Enhanced reputation	• Badge value • Affiliation with others • Improve quality perception	• Certified fish—Marine Stewardship Council • Champions 12.3 coalition against food waste • Biological wines—Torres; sunglasses from ocean plastics—Sea2see
Lowering risk	• Complying with regulations • Avoiding upcoming externalities • Circumventing resource scarcity	• Privacy and security—Facebook • Supply chain labor conditions—Apple; renewable packaging—Mars, Unilever, Coca-Cola, Walmart • Recycled cobalt—Umicore

MSC is an ecolabel and fishery certification program aiming to contribute to the health of the world's oceans by recognizing and rewarding sustainable fishing practices, influencing the choices people make when buying seafood and working with our partners to transform the seafood market to a sustainable basis. Source: 20.msc.org

illustrates. The share of animal-based protein in people's diets relative to plant-based protein has been increasing rapidly. Between 1961 and 2009, the global average per person availability of animal-based protein grew by 59%, while that of plant-based protein grew by only 14%.

The food gap not only causes increased pressure on farming and agriculture but also impacts fisheries, since both food productions systems—sea and land—are closely interconnected. Fish plays an important role in global food security. It provides more than 3.1 billion people with at least 20% of their animal protein and is an important source of fatty acids and micronutrients [10]. However, the state of global fish stocks has become a big cause for concern. Of the scientifically assessed fish stocks, 31% are considered to be overfished. Demand for fish is currently much greater than can be supported by marine fish alone. Today, half of all fish in the world is farmed or comes from

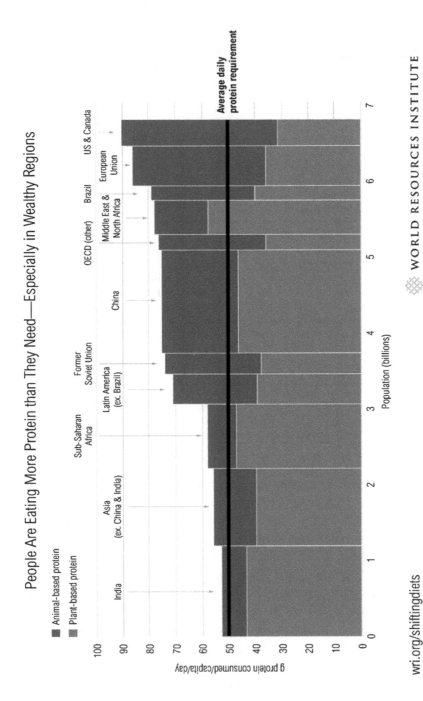

Fig. 11.1 Protein consumption exceeds average estimated daily requirements in all the world's regions and is highest in developed countries (Source: World Resources Institute)

The Shift Wheel: Changing Consumer Purchasing

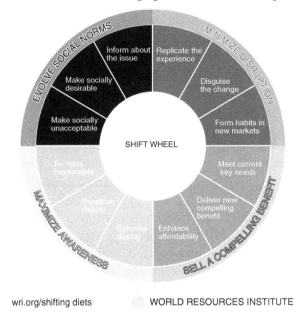

Fig. 11.2 The Shift Wheel (Source: World Resources Institute)

aquaculture such as the unsuccessful startup Happy Shrimp Farm referred to in Chap. 10. The fish farming part of the food industry, which has grown considerably over the last 40 years, requires both sea and land. Protein-rich soya is used in fish food, and fish meal and fish oil are in turn part of the feed diet for pigs and poultry.

Soya has long been known as an important source of vegetable protein. A more recent global "discovery" is quinoa, a pseudo-cereal botanically related to spinach. Once only known as a local grain crop primarily grown for its edible seeds, quinoa gradually made its way into global diets after it was found to be the only food of vegetable origin that provides all the essential amino acids and vitamins, equating its protein quality to that of milk. Moreover, its gluten-free grains are highly nutritious, surpassing in biological value, as well as nutritional and functional quality, cereals such as wheat, corn, rice and oats. Originating from the Andean region of northwestern South America, quinoa was domesticated 3000 to 4000 years ago for human consumption in the Lake Titicaca basin of Peru and Bolivia [11]. The UN declared 2013 to be the international year of quinoa, celebrating and further promoting the Andean "super food" for its important role in eradicating hunger, malnutrition and poverty [12].

📁 Coronilla: Super Food Innovation with a Social Purpose [13]

Coronilla and the Wille Family

Guillermo Wille, a Bolivian of German descent, founded Fideos Coronilla S.A. in 1972. After relocating down to Cochabamba, the fourth largest city in Bolivia, in the fertile Andes valley, the family had opened a pasta factory—which seemed an obvious decision, as Cochabamba was the nation's granary. From the start, the pasta plant was a family endeavor, and after a year it started producing wheat noodles. Business took off, and Coronilla soon achieved a 20% national market share. From an early age, Martha, one of Guillermo's daughters, showed a strong interest in the business and worked closely with her father while her siblings pursued their university education. In 1984, the second Wille son, Gerardo, returned from Germany with a degree in mechanical engineering. He entered the company as managing director with support from his father, who remained as president and technical advisor. Gerardo managed the technical aspects of the business while Martha handled its administration.

Economic Crisis in Bolivia

By 1987, Coronilla had tripled its production capacity to 100 tons (2000 quintals) per month. But the growth then plateaued, and gross margins on pasta products started to erode. Vertical integration through the purchase of a flour mill proved to be successful: it rebuilt Coronilla's profit margins and boosted turnover, resulting in a second growth phase. However, the renewed prosperity was short-lived. The Bolivian economy entered a period of severe crisis, with inflation skyrocketing. Government initiatives in the form of rigid price controls on food production and incentivized investments in the food industry leading to massive overcapacity did not help. For Coronilla, the financial problems were exacerbated by the heavy debt incurred by the purchase of the flour mill. The shaky financial situation eventually brought on a leadership crisis as well. In November 1997, Gerardo decided to leave the company. With little time for transition, Martha took the reins and started searching for a way to reverse Coronilla's fortunes.

The New "Super Food" Ingredient: Quinoa

Under Martha's leadership, Coronilla set up a small research and development initiative. Martha believed that pasta had no future; it was time to look for other lines of business and find a unique differentiator. Coronilla started conducting tests with native Bolivian cereals, fruit and root vegetables, producing samples of noodles made with yucca, plantain and even banana flour. Initially, both taste and consistency were sub-par; in many instances, the resulting pasta was even barely edible. After much digging, they discovered a hidden gem: quinoa, the only plant food in the world to contain all the essential vitamins, amino acids and trace elements, along with exceptionally high protein content. Yet at the time, few people had heard of quinoa. Martha discovered that quinoa, which had been grown in the Andes as far back as the Inca Empire, did not contain gluten. This aspect of quinoa represented a big bonus as the awareness of gluten intolerance grew. The culinary result was excellent: A pasta with the *al dente* feel of the traditional Italian product.

Resistance from All Sides

Coronilla's preliminary market research showed that gluten-free products represented a promising market. However, the switch to a new product line met with stiff resistance from the company's factory workers. Shareholders were also feeling increasingly impatient. The pasta trials had been underway for two years and the company's financials looked worse than ever. Coronilla was bleeding cash and falling commodity prices contributed to the problem. For staff, a series of drastic job cuts were indicative of the seriousness of the crisis. Martha's eldest son Diego came back home as his mother could no longer support his studies abroad after investing her own savings in the company. Diego enrolled in a local university while working informally for the company, together with his sister Ximena.

Martha's Turnaround Plan

At the 1997 annual shareholder meeting, Martha presented her turnaround plan to Coronilla's eight shareholders, who were all close family members. She needed their support for the turnaround, which required external financing. Martha was convinced that Coronilla's best chance for survival was to switch to gluten-free pasta and snacks for export. She explained that instead of competing on price (as the company had done in the first 25 years of its history), Coronilla would be competing on quality, product differentiation and brand value. Another key element of Martha's vision was her belief that the company should have a positive impact on society and the environment.

While the idea of ceding equity to outsiders was very painful, the shareholders finally supported Martha's plan. In 1997, however, no one was looking to invest in the gluten-free niche. Finally, Diego identified a local risk capital fund—Fondo de Capital Activo de Bolivia (FCAB)—which showed some interest. Although FCAB's valuation of Coronilla was disappointingly low, Coronilla's shareholders decided to pursue the financing agreement, and FCAB took a 45% equity stake in the company.

Pivoting with a Social Purpose

Martha quickly began to infuse Coronilla with a new purpose. After managing a business in a turbulent environment and national financial crisis, she had come to realize that the only thing that could make the job worthwhile was to imbue her work with a strong social purpose. Martha started making changes on all fronts, for instance, by starting to buy directly from impoverished farmers, which allowed them to take home almost 80% of the final sale price on quinoa (as opposed to the 7% to 14% they had received previously). For her, this was not a public relations exercise. Diego recalls:

> I heard all my mother's ideas, and to be absolutely honest, I thought she was crazy. It sounded wonderful. Her conviction was amazing; her vision was incredible. But, come on! We were broke, and she was thinking about corporate social responsibility, hiring handicapped people, employing minorities, buying our raw materials from the poorest communities at a higher price. That didn't make sense for me in those times. I thought it was a wonderful idea but that the company would crash before reaching its lofty objectives. It took me at least six years to start believing.

In 2005, the hard work started paying off: Martha's values-based leadership was honored with the Schwab Foundation Prize for Social Entrepreneurship. One year later, in 2006, the Wille family was presented with the unexpected opportunity to buy back the shares they had ceded when the outside risk capital fund was forced to make early divestments of many of its positions. Due to legal restrictions, Coronilla as a company could not recoup the investment fund's 45% equity stake directly. This problem was solved when Guillermo Wille Sr., then in his eighties, surprised the family by buying back the shares personally with his own savings. In a sense, this was an act of faith: Coronilla at that point was close to breakeven but still generating losses. Guillermo Wille Sr. nonetheless felt confident that the company's trajectory would continue upwards.

The Third Generation in the Starting Blocks

In 2015, Martha announced she intended to retire as CEO within two years, and it would be time for the third generation to take the helm of the family business. Daughter Ximena had told her brother Diego that she did not wish to take on the role of CEO. Diego, however, felt a strong attachment to Coronilla. Although he was only in his mid-thirties, he had been looking after the company's finances for almost 20 years and was enthusiastic about taking on the new challenge of leading the company.

Two elements boosted Diego's confidence in Coronilla's future. First, the family had recently professionalized its governance. A detailed "family protocol" had been approved, resolving that all-important decisions would be handled by its board of directors. This would encourage objective decision making since six out of the seven board members were non-family. Second, the company established a strong focus on social and environmental impact.

The gluten-free industry had grown rapidly in recent years, the quality of competitors' products was improving and an explosion in popularity[1] had caused an uptick in the grain's market price. And now that the genome for quinoa had been decoded, the logical next step would be for scientists to develop new strains of the plant. Within the next year it was quite possible that genetically modified quinoa, priced at one-third or one-quarter of the current price, might start appearing. What would Coronilla's claims to product differentiation be worth then?

A New CEO Setting the Compass

In April 2017, the family board officially designated Diego Pelaez as CEO. At the same moment, Coronilla was finally reaping the rewards of its radical change program. Top-line growth had increased steadily, and net profits had followed a similar upward course. Coronilla's profit margins had also improved and had been in the 15% to 20% range for more than five years. By 2016, Coronilla's return on equity (ROE) was reportedly 23% and its return on assets (ROA) had grown to 14.5%. But the next destination on the company journey was less certain. The recent soaring market demand for quinoa, the super food star ingredient in Coronilla's organic pastas and snacks, confirmed for Diego that Coronilla would need to renew itself once again. The competition had woken up, and Diego knew that some tough decisions would soon have to be made.

---

[1] In large part due to the United Nations declaring 2013 the International Year of Quinoa.

With this in mind, Diego identified three strategic issues that he would need to tackle. First, he thought about considering a brand development strategy. While the company sold 97% of its production under private label agreements, an experiment with an own brand for the Bolivian market had proved to be a success. But Diego hesitated to invest in launching the company's own international brand. Second, he worried about where Coronilla should build a new production facility, as the recently renovated plant in Cochabamba would hit its ceiling by 2018. Finally, Coronilla had drawn up a memorandum of understanding with its biggest client, a major buyer in Switzerland, for a Swiss-based pasta production joint venture. Transforming from a business that competed mainly on price to one that emphasized a positive impact on society and the environment and promoted quality, product differentiation and brand value had stood Coronilla in good stead over the last two decades. Diego needed to make sure that this continued in a market that was appealing to many new contenders.

Shifting Diets

To help change people's diets while addressing the complexities of global food production systems, the World Resources Institute developed a framework based on marketing tactics: the Shift Wheel. It was based on a range of already successful shifts in consumption such as the move from caged to free-range eggs and from higher- to lower-alcohol beer in the UK, and away from shark fins in China.

The Shift Wheel recommends four complementary strategies to change consumer diets:

- **Minimize Disruption** Changing food consumption behavior typically involves changing deep-rooted habits. This strategy seeks to reduce the disruption to consumers' habits caused by the proposed shift. It can include minimizing changes associated with the shift, such as taste, look, texture, smell, packaging and the product's location within a store.
- **Sell a Compelling Benefit** Benefit-based selling involves identifying and delivering product qualities such as improved health or affordability that will be sufficiently motivating to encourage consumers to change their behavior. Since plant-based proteins can be less expensive than animal-based ones, companies may have an opportunity to sell reformulated products with a greater share of plant-based ingredients at a lower price and/or an increased profit.

- **Maximize Awareness** The more consumers see or think of a product, the greater the chance they will consider purchasing it. Enhancing the availability and display of more sustainable food choices, and creating memorable advertising campaigns, increases the chances that consumers will purchase it.
- **Evolve Social Norms** What people eat is highly influenced by cultural, environmental and social norms. Informing and educating consumers, combined with efforts to make the preferred food more socially desirable or the other food less socially desirable, can influence or change the underlying social and cultural norms that underlie people's purchasing decisions.

Nudging for Nurture

Evolving social norms, one of the four basic strategies in the WRI's Shift Wheel, depends at least in part on the effective support of governments and stakeholders such as academia and NGOs. In this regard, *nudging* is a concept developed by Richard Thaler, a Nobel Prize-winning professor in behavioral economics at the University of Chicago. It promotes relatively subtle policy shifts that encourage people to make decisions that are in their broad self-interest and can also save governments money or encourage good behaviors. For instance, in 2015, Public Health England estimated e-cigarettes to be 60% more effective than other routes to quitting smoking. Ensuring widespread e-cigarette availability in the UK was a political decision based on nudging principles. It affected 9 million smokers, of whom 2.8 million smokers or ex-smokers went on to use e-cigarettes, making them the predominant way of quitting smoking in the UK. Similarly, a hospital in Australia found that it could save around US$50,000 per year if patients were on time for appointments. It experimented with the phrasing of an SMS reminder and the one that nudged people most effectively was "If you attend, the hospital will not lose the $125 associated with a patient not showing up." It reduced missed appointments by 19%.

While mostly touted for its influence on the way government decisions are implemented through "Nudge units [14]," other successful applications are also possible. When Dutch cardiologists considered how to change the increasingly unhealthy consumption patterns of youth in the Netherlands, they applied nudging techniques. *Spangas*, a television sitcom describing the lives of students at Spangalis College had been a hit for more than a decade. The show featured the perfect target audience, so script writers worked with cardiologists to introduce a number of relevant storylines into the sitcom. For instance, one of the parents suffered a heart attack induced by an unhealthy diet. After each *Spangas* episode finished, the scientists measured the hashtag-intensity of social media traffic on predefined topics among their target audience and found that their nudging efforts had worked, prompting further ideas for intervention. Likewise, in China, a recycling app showed smartphone owners the location of their nearest e-waste company. The app included rewards to nudge people into recycling more. After 2 pilots it was rolled out to 22 cities and on average around 6000 items were recycled per month.

☞ The Potential of Sustainable Innovation: Explore Your Customore

Explore Your Customore is a toolbox containing a set of inspirational cards with proven innovation methodologies to help firms understand customer requirements and encourage them to generate MASS (refer to Fig. 11.3). The toolbox is a free-to-use source of creativeness for teams working on customer-centered innovations and can be downloaded from www.vectoring. online.

The cards are subdivided into three categories that illustrate different phases in the innovation process:

Stakeholder mapping

HOW
Identifying the different stakeholders, their influence and their attitude toward the company, products or services.

WHY
Gaining insight in different stakeholder groups and the way they affect your product or service helps to create an effective positioning strategy.

Example:
A global chemical industry services company wanted to re-design and deploy their sustainability strategy. To pinpoint the most pressing issues for their key stakeholders, they did a mapping exercise, resulting in a tailor-made strategy for local communities that included their license to operate as well as their license to grow.

Finch ♀ Beak   Explore Your Customore

Fig. 11.3 Explore Your Customore cards, example stakeholder mapping

Table 11.3 Overview of the innovation process

Inspiration phase	Ideation phase	Implementation phase
Generating ideas	**Concepting of ideas**	**Prototyping**
Methods Multidisciplinary brainstorm sessions, harvesting ideas throughout the company	**Methods** Focus groups or interviews with customers and lead users	**Methods** Early stage business planning sessions focusing on proposition testing, business case and team composition
Result A large number of interesting ideas for sustainable innovations	**Result** Creating a deeper understanding of the customer, problems that need to be solved, and potential competitive advantages	**Result** A rough prototype and rollout plan
Pitfall Idea generation is never the problem; the real work lies in taking things further. Have a solid process in place before you start	**Pitfall** Not really listening to and understanding your customers' needs. This results in a mismatched proposition	**Pitfall** Lack of iteration. The implementation phase is designed to iteratively create a deeper understanding of the proposition before market introduction

The full set of Explore Your Customore cards can be downloaded from www. vectoring.online

- **Inspiration** The inspiration cards contain techniques that target the start of the innovation process. They help to focus on customer demands, generate new ideas and think beyond the obvious.
- **Ideation** The ideation cards include methods to further develop innovative ideas. In addition, they assist in gaining a clear understanding of the purpose and the customer value potential of the innovation idea.
- **Implementation** The implementation cards describe approaches for creating and validating the first prototypes of the innovation idea and suggest how to plan for a successful market introduction. Table 11.3 gives an overview of the three phases.

Tips, Traps and Takeaways

☝ Tips

- Consider the basic objective of working with startups when engaging with them. This to a large extent determines the channel of choice.
- When aspiring to achieve a change in company culture through working with startups, carefully design the programmed interactions with the business.

- Consider various ways of uncovering requirements, interests and trends such as stakeholder mapping, role-play and world café as described in the inspirational cards from Explore Your Customore.

💣 Traps

- Avoid getting stuck in one "default" channel of collaboration with startups. Consider the entire range of opportunities.
- Beware of overcomplication. Minimizing the required consumer learning and necessary value chain modifications increases the chances of a successful shift.

☝ Takeaways

Having discussed in previous chapters the importance of developing (strategic) partnerships to advance sustainable value chain developments, this chapter highlighted the potential of collaborating platforms with startups, next to value chain partners. From the platform examples provided by the BMW Startup Garage and the Fashion for Good initiative, startup companies emerged as relevant sources for sustainable innovation. Tapping into the experience with startups of Forbes 500 companies, the most important design criterion in the startup collaboration is the reason for the collaboration. The preferred channel for engaging with startups is largely determined by being clear about what the company is looking for: innovation, culture change, new markets or joint platforms?

For companies to find and capture the sustainability premium, the four elementary business case contributors—eco-efficiency, revenue growth from innovation, enhanced reputation and risk reduction—were explained and linked to the previously described company cases in the book such as Umicore, Torres and Apple.

Since the success of marketing sustainability solutions is often dependent on changes in consumer behavior, the Shift Wheel from the World Resources Institute was introduced. The wheel recommends four complementary strategies for changing consumer purchasing: promoting minimal disruption, selling a compelling benefit, increasing awareness and evolving social norms. Using global animal and vegetable protein intake as an example, the complexity of changes in consumption patterns was illustrated with the compelling story of the turnaround of Coronilla. This pasta-producing Bolivian company became a trailblazer in gluten-free food by innovating the raw material of traditional pasta by using quinoa, recently "discovered" as a super food. As an additional tool for behavioral change, the concept of consumer nudging was illustrated through a number of examples.

In the toolbox section of the chapter, the free-source Explore Your Customore self-help tool was introduced to better understand customer requirements and encourage firms to generate MASS in the search for innovations.

References

1. AB InBev (2018, March 21) AB InBev launches 2025 Sustainability Goals and 100+ Accelerator to advance local innovations for pressing global challenges [Press release]. Retrieved from http://www.ab-inbev.com/content/dam/universal-template/ab-inbev/News/press-releases/public/2018/03/20180321_EN.pdf
2. Berry, J. (2016, August 25) Why Did BMW's Startup Garage Invent the Venture Client Model? *The Innovation Enterprise.* Retrieved from https://channels.theinnovationenterprise.com/articles/why-bmw-s-startup-garage-invented-the-venture-client-model
3. Wikipedia contributors (2018, May 21) Leyden jar. *Wikipedia, The Free Encyclopedia.* Accessed May 21, 2018, from https://en.wikipedia.org/w/index.php?title=Leyden_jar&oldid=844106437
4. Hendriksz, V. (2018, January 9) Fashion for Good teams up with Zalando to advance sustainable innovation. *FashionUnited.* Retrieved from https://fashion-united.uk/news/business/fashion-for-good-teams-up-with-zalando-to-advance-sustainable-innovation/2018010927549
5. C&A Foundation (2017, March 30) C&A Foundation calls to reimagine fashion [Press release]. Retrieved from http://www.candafoundation.org/latest/press/2017/03/ca-foundation-calls-to-reimagine-fashion
6. Adamczyk, S., Bullinger, A.C., Moeslein, K.M. (2011) Commenting for new ideas: insights from an open innovation platform. *International Journal of Technology Intelligence and Planning,* Vol. 7, No. 3.
7. Bonzom, A. & Netessine, S. (2016, February) How do the World's Biggest Companies Deal with the Startup Revolution. *INSEAD Business School and 500Startups.* Retrieved from http://cdn2.hubspot.net/hubfs/698640/500CORPORATIONS_-_How_do_the_Worlds_Biggest_Companies_Deal_with_the_Startup_Revolution_-_Feb_2016.pdf
8. Rautera, R., Globocnik, D., Perl-Vorbach, E., et al. (2018, April 12) Open innovation and its effects on economic and sustainability innovation performance. *Journal of Innovation & Knowledge.*
9. Ranganathan, J., Vennard, D., Waite, R., et al. (2016) Shifting Diets for a Sustainable Food Future. Working Paper, Instalment 11 of Creating a Sustainable Food Future. *World Resources Institute.* Retrieved from https://www.wri.org/sites/default/files/Shifting_Diets_for_a_Sustainable_Food_Future_0.pdf

10. Quaas, M., Hoffmann, J., Kamin, K., et al. (2016, October) *Fishing for Proteins, How marine fisheries impact on global food security up to 2050. A global prognosis.* Hamburg, Germany: WWF Germany, International WWF Centre for Marine Conservation. Retrieved from https://c402277.ssl.cf1.rackcdn.com/publications/982/files/original/Report_food_and_fish_Final.pdf?1484256747
11. Wikipedia contributors (2018, May 22) Quinoa. *Wikipedia, The Free Encyclopedia.* Accessed May 22, 2018, from https://en.wikipedia.org/w/index.php?title=Quinoa&oldid=848757716
12. United Nations Food and Agriculture Organization (2013, February 20) Launch of the International Year of Quinoa [Press release]. Retrieved from http://www.fao.org/quinoa-2013/press-room/news/detail/en/.
13. This case is an abridged version of CORONILLA: CHANGE DILEMMA FOR THE WILLE FAMILY, GLUTEN FREE PASTA FROM BOLIVIA (IMD-3-1997) Copyright © 2018 by IMD—International Institute for Management Development, Lausanne, Switzerland (www.imd.org). No part of this publication may be reproduced, stored in a retrieval system or transmitted in any form or by any means without the prior written permission of IMD.
14. Halpern, D. & Sanders, M. (2016) Nudging by government: Progress, impact, & lessons learned. *Behavioral Science & Policy*, Vol. 2, No. 2, pp. 53–65. Retrieved from https://behavioralpolicy.org/wp-content/uploads/2017/06/Sanders-web.pdf

12

Stellar Performance from Sustainability Teams

After exploring the critical importance of partnering to achieve impact in sustainability as well as opportunities presented by the circular economy concept, we reviewed how to find and capture the sustainability premium. What remains to be examined is how to obtain superior engagement from teams focused on accelerating sustainability programs. By studying patterns observed in different industries, such as food, drinks, ingredients as well as haute cuisine, a four-pillar structure is presented to energize the teams in charge of sustainable innovation. First, pillars #1 and #2 are investigated, namely Direction and Diversity, by taking a peek inside the kitchen of Atera, the reputed Manhattan-based restaurant that underwent a complete cultural re-engineering while maintaining its two Michelin-star status. Then we examine pillars #3 and #4, Experimentation and Collaboration Culture, through examples from companies such as Tony's Chocolonely, Torres wines and Novozymes. The chapter concludes with an approach to help key account teams develop collaboration and engagement with their clients on sustainability.

The Innovation Legacy of ElBulli

Located in Cala Montjoi, a small costal town in Northern Catalunya, ElBulli featured at the top of the World's 50 Best Restaurants list a record five times before closing its doors in 2011 after 26 years in business. Despite its year-long waiting list and #1 rankings in the most acclaimed culinary rankings, the

© The Author(s) 2019
B. Leleux, J. van der Kaaij, *Winning Sustainability Strategies*,
https://doi.org/10.1007/978-3-319-97445-3_12

restaurant decided to close its doors, not because of poor results or organizational challenges but because owner and chef extraordinaire Ferran Adrià and his team felt they had achieved everything they had ever dreamt of. Short of ideas on how to outdo themselves, they reasoned it made more sense to shut down before disenchantment set in.

The ElBulli team stood out in the food aficionado world for its culinary innovation culture, in a league of its own. In 2011, as the food world was still reeling from the shocking news, Ferran Adrià announced the launch of the ElBulli Foundation, a new vehicle set up to try to capture and preserve the essence of ElBulli; Adrià and his team were going to endeavor to decipher the DNA of their own success and analyze how they reached this extraordinary level of achievement [1].

> ElBulli was the most creative restaurant in the world, but it was still a restaurant. Now there will be no limits.
> Ferran Adrià, explaining his new concept of ElBulli 1846 [2]

From the ashes of ElBulli, three new phoenixes arose: ElBulli 1846, ElBulli DNA and Bullipedia. ElBulli 1846 was an exhibition lab and museum designed around creativity and innovation for the restaurant and hospitality industry. Its name referred to the number of original recipes developed over ElBulli's 26 years in business, and it was projected in the expanded space of the original restaurant in Cala Montjoi, boasting a surface of approximately 4500 square meters, mostly underground to minimize the environmental impact. ElBulli DNA was aimed at documenting the experience from the past 26 years. One of the Foundation's ventures was to develop "Sapiens," a publication that documented the holistic innovation process used to develop ElBulli's dishes and concepts. Each and every one of the 1846 dishes ever developed by the ElBulli crew was carefully dissected and published as examples of innovation. A series of books on food and drinks was also scheduled for publication, the first volumes hitting the shelves in spring 2018. Bullipedia, the third leg of the project, was an online project aimed at decoding the genome of gastronomy and improving the performance of search engines related to the world of cooking, food and hospitality.

From the outset of ElBulli Foundation, chef Adrià stressed that his new venture would be "by all and for all" and that its knowledge would become public property. Inspirational as ever, he hoped to invigorate others to reach for ElBulli's level of innovation. Bullinianos such as superstar chef Ronny Emborg from Atera in New York and René Redzepi from restaurant Noma in Copenhagen heard the message and kept the legacy alive [3].

Liquid olives, a melon and passion-fruit caviar, a caramelized quail egg, a belly of tuna with blackcurrant and eucalyptus and many other dishes vindicated ElBulli as one of the leading exponents of gastronomy of its time. ElBulli did not become the world's most respected restaurant by accident. With a strong sense of direction, talented chefs-to-be from around the globe, continuous experimentation and a culture of collaboration, there was method in the apparent kitchen madness. And it is this method that we venture to examine, with the hope that the recipe can be translated for sustainability teams around the world trying to prime or solidify their creativity. The four pillars of the method are presented and explained hereafter.

Pillar #1: A Better Sense of Direction

The first pillar of the method to generate superior performance from sustainability teams should be quite familiar by now: start with a strong statement of direction. To illustrate the concept better in this specific context, we examine the story of another top restaurant in New York City, called Atera. Atera underwent a complete team culture change based on the Secure Base Leadership concept coined by IMD Professor George Kohlrieser in his book "Care to Dare." The book aimed to describe a powerful approach to liberate team members from fears that hinder performance. Rooted in instilling trust, Secure Base Leadership empowers teams and helps them tap into their full potential [4]. As will emerge from the examples below, a clear-cut sense of purpose and direction energizes the innovation process.

📂 Secure Base Leadership at Atera [5]

The story begins in February 2015. Jodi Richard, the owner of Atera NYC [6], was unsure what direction to take. Dozens of questions were swirling around in her head as she digested the news that Matthew Lightner, the executive chef of her two-Michelin-star restaurant in lower Manhattan, had just announced his resignation, the final straw in a long string of unfortunate events. The departure of the multi-starred chef left a huge vacuum in the restaurant's organization. But perhaps this disaster was the opportunity she was waiting for. She had been wanting to change course and implement a radically new leadership style, one she could not foster under Matthew's imposing stature. Maybe there was another way to run a star-studded restaurant and to engage employees.

Jodi Richard: An Entrepreneur with an Indomitable Willpower

Jodi was born in a small town just north of Pittsburgh, Pennsylvania. Despite nerve damage to her right shoulder and arm since birth, she had completed several marathons by the time she turned 50. Having earned a Master's in technical writing, Jodi started to flex her entrepreneurial muscles in a completely different arena as she opened the first physical therapy company for dogs on the east coast of the US. Now based in New York City, Jodi and her husband started taking wine-tasting classes and visiting high-end restaurants. A passion for good coffee was spurred when she found herself limited to one cup per day during her pregnancy. This inspired her to open a high-end coffee shop in available space in a property she owned for her business in downtown Manhattan. Jodi's first venture into the food industry was met with critical acclaim, encouraging her to consider using the remaining space in the building for a bar and a restaurant. This, however, turned out to be an unqualified failure. The menu was unappealing, and she and the chef disagreed on just about everything, including the freshness—or lack thereof—of the ingredients and the chef's inability to adapt the menu to seasonal products.

Reinvention with a New Star Chef

Jodi soon started looking for a new chef, and found the perfect candidate in Matthew Lightner, named one of the "Best New Chefs in America" by Food & Wine Magazine in 2010. They shared a similar vision for a high-end tasting menu restaurant featuring local and seasonal ingredients and modern cooking techniques. Within weeks, a deal was signed, and the new restaurant opened under the name Atera in March 2012. It immediately received glowing reviews from NYC food critics, and within six months, was awarded two Michelin stars, an extraordinary feat in the industry.

Yet the restaurant was not financially prosperous. Jodi was aware of the industry rule-of-thumb: it took at least two years to break even, with or without Michelin stars. By the fall of 2014 however, two and a half years after launch, Atera was still bleeding cash at the rate of US$25,000 per month. This started to weigh heavily on her relationship with Matthew. Something had to change to make the restaurant sustainable, that is, profitable.

Atera's Leadership Philosophy

During a dinner party in October 2014 at a restaurant outside Barcelona, Jodi met Ole Borregaard, an independent strategy and leadership consultant. Over a lengthy conversation, Jodi shared her leadership philosophy for the hospitality industry. She struggled to understand the dominant, fear-driven leadership style restaurants and their chefs were famous for. While the cuisine may have been inspiring, kitchens were often run like fiefdoms and early industrialization factories, with the head chef playing the role of labor-camp slave master. She explained to Ole that she truly believed that if leaders put trust in their employees, they would create the kind of open and honest work atmosphere that would allow employees to develop and grow and ultimately contribute more to the business.

Coincidentally, three months earlier Ole had attended a workshop with Dr. George Kohlrieser, a reputed Professor in leadership and organizational behavior at IMD in Switzerland. What Jodi referred to reminded Ole of a concept he discovered during his training called "Secure Base Leadership." Secure Base Leaders release their followers from the fears that hamper their performance by building trust, delivering the change, and inspiring the focus that underpins sustainable high performance. After reading two of George's books, (recommended by Ole), Jodi asked Ole to help her implement Secure Base Leadership in her organization.

Meanwhile, day-to-day business continued to deteriorate at the restaurant. To get things back on track, Jodi decided to bring in James to act as Atera's general manager. During a leadership workshop in January 2015, Jodi and James got to know each other better, sorted out potential issues and developed common goals for the future. This helped seal Atera's new work philosophy. Chef Matthew may have brought two Michelin stars, but it was time for a complete cultural re-engineering, and he was not going to be part of it.

Turbulent Times: Turnaround in the Kitchen

With the star chef gone, the whole kitchen in disarray and the restaurant unable to break even, several questions preoccupied Jodi. Should she just close the restaurant and rent out the space to somebody else? Should she change the restaurant concept completely, maybe to something simpler and more predictable? How would the staff feel about the chef's departure? Nothing would happen without the staff's support, so keeping the best of them was essential. Whoever the new chef would be, he would have to buy into this new philosophy as well.

An important component of this was Jodi's intention to make the new chef a part owner of Atera.

Change at Atera accelerated when Jodi hired Ronny Emborg, a celebrated Danish chef, as the new executive chef. Despite being only 32 years old, Ronny had already enjoyed a gastronomic career as the personal chef of Queen Margrethe II of Denmark and as a chef at three-star restaurants El Bulli and Mugaritz in Spain, and most recently at the Restaurant Marchal in the Hotel d'Angleterre in Copenhagen. Some food bloggers crucified Jodi's decision to hire Ronny as "a blow to American Cooking." For many, Atera's chef job was a prime opportunity for an American chef who cooked in a progressive style. Very few restaurants in the US offered progressive cuisine. It was openly questioned whether Atera would recover from this switch to an untested European chef, pointing out that most restaurants, especially those with Michelin stars and a cuisine closely linked to the chef's personality, did not survive such a change.

With Ronny on board, things came together rapidly. For Jodi, it was essential to have the restaurant's whole leadership team united behind goals they all believed in. During a four-day business meeting in Copenhagen, they came together to develop the values, vision and mission. This session also helped develop new financial forecasts and clear cost targets to ensure the business quickly became profitable. Despite some difficult discussions, key elements of the new Atera philosophy fell into place.

General manager James, however, seemed disengaged during the discussions in Copenhagen. Jodi could not understand his sudden resistance, as James had previously proven to be worthy of her trust, initiating many positive changes in the restaurant and among the service staff. As she interviewed more employees from the restaurant, she began to understand better the forces at play, and these could only lead to one outcome: she would have to let James go, too. This resulted in a new challenge: finding a general manager just weeks before the new restaurant was due to open.

New Leadership in the Cuisine

With the new budget agreed upon, it was time to execute the plan. After interviewing several candidates for the general manager position, Ronny and Jodi remembered Robert, a competent employee who had been offered promotions regularly in the past but who habitually turned them down. This time, he enthusiastically accepted. The restaurant management was now much more to his liking and he was delighted to be part of that team. A key position was thus filled with a much-respected internal person, reinforcing the team's cohesion. As bonding was an important part of Secure Base Leadership, Jodi tried to enhance this kind of experience in the restaurant as well. She found the right person immediately in Carl, Atera's tea curator, a genuine person who bonded easily and deeply with guests and staff. It did not take long to convince him to look after enhancing front-of-house team bonding and creating meaningful connections with guests to improve their dining experience.

Besides its unique leadership style, the restaurant would also be one of the first high-end restaurants to offer health insurance to all employees, including dishwashers and polishers. The new Atera would also be the second high-end restaurant in New York to include service in the tasting menu price so that guests did not need to worry about tipping. This allowed Jodi and Ronny more flexibility in the wages across front and back of house. With only two business partners involved, decisions were now made much faster, and Jodi could progressively step back. She trusted the new management and for the first time since she had opened the restaurant, she felt the positive energy and high drive every time she was on site. She also felt great about having a business partner who shared her goals.

Same Success: Very Different Way

Atera reopened on 12 May 2015. The restaurant positioned itself as "honoring the poetry of nature and creativity in pursuit of an immersive sensory dining experience," and offered a highly seasonal and continuously evolving tasting menu. After returning from a journey to Switzerland, Jodi was pleasantly surprised and touched at how the team handled the daily line-up meeting, which took place 45 minutes before guests arrived. They discussed the guests, dietary changes, allergies, anniversaries or any other special event that the guests may be celebrating. The meeting ended with the "gratitude game" where one staff member thanked another, who thanked another until every staff member had been thanked. The game brought out smiles and laughter and created a positive mindset to start the usually protracted evening. One employee said to Jodi: "Thank you for what you have done, I have to pinch myself every day when I arrive at work to make sure I am not dreaming."

The restaurant staff shined not only inside the restaurant but also outside. Guests could feel the difference the new philosophy made. Many customers raved about the warm, welcoming feeling of the restaurant. On the financial side, the numbers started to line up from the first week, turning "black" quickly. The first Saturday Atera opened, the new restaurant generated the highest income in its entire history—despite a lower menu price and the new "service included" system. In October 2015, Chef Ronny Emborg received his first two Michelin stars. For Jodi, it was the second time her restaurant had received two Michelin stars within six months of opening, a unique accomplishment in the industry.

Jodi's inspired approach to elevate creativeness in her team did not stop at Atera. At the end of 2015, she opened a "beers and bitters" bar with a menu designed by a different star chef, and she was already working with another chef and a group of investors to open a novel high-end concept restaurant following her rediscovered sense of direction.

Besides a strong sense of direction, for instance, by the application of Secure Base Leadership in the case of Atera, accelerating sustainable innovation also implies developing a large variety of solutions and capitalizing on the diversity of teams. As highlighted in previous chapters, developing more alternative sustainable solutions (MASS) is less likely to happen with homogenous teams that lack diversity of opinions and perspectives. In the next section, haute cuisine is revisited in Japan, where a kitchen strongly rooted in tradition demonstrated tremendous innovativeness by applying foreign techniques.

Pillar #2: Diversity in Solutions

Japan is known for its culinary aesthetics and emphasis of *umami*, the fifth taste, that is, quality (the other traditional four being sweet, sour, salty and bitter), named after the Japanese adjective umai (delicious). In recent years, the country has become a prominent haute cuisine destination, with Tokyo restaurants holding a total of 234 Michelin stars; more than any other city in the world [7]. Taking into account three-star restaurants alone, in 2017 Japan boasted 28 locations compared to 27 in France and 14 in the US (refer to Fig. 12.1) [8].

To most foreigners, Japanese food rings of sushi, tempura and teriyaki. But Japanese cuisine (和食, washoku) offers a wealth of gastronomical experiences with a long-standing tradition that earned it a UNESCO Intangible Cultural Heritage status in 2013 [9]. Tradition in this instance does not imply standstill; even though a strong wind of innovation is blowing on Japanese cuisine, the heritage is being protected.

After World War II, Japan became heavily reliant on imported food and was hit especially hard with shortages. The standard ration of rice—doled out in frugal quantities—became skeptically known as the "Five Color Rice": white rice, stale yellow rice, dried green beans, coarse red grains and brown

The Top Countries for Michelin 3-Star Restaurants
Countries by number of 3-star restaurants in November 2017

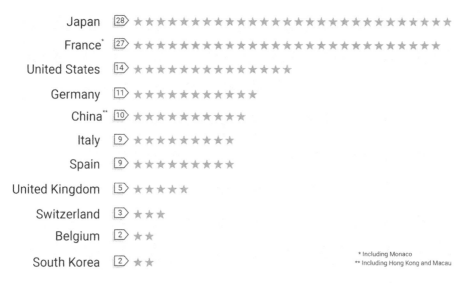

Fig. 12.1 Top ten countries with 3-Michelin-star restaurants (adapted) (Source: Michelin Guide via Trois Etolies)

insects, suggesting more diversity than was actually available [10]. Soon after, when the economic climate improved, the Japanese were suddenly presented with novel Western foods and a rainbow of ingredients. In response, cooks eagerly adapted them to fit their traditional ideas on finesse and harmony.

Resource scarcity has always been a concern in Japan, so sustainability has been part of the country's culture for centuries. Not surprisingly, it played a meaningful role in promoting innovation in Japanese cuisine. At Expo Milano 2015, the pavilion of the land of the rising sun adopted "Harmonious Diversity" as its central theme. The pavilion addressed four central sustainability issues—food shortages, uneven food distribution, challenges with agriculture due to climate change, and nutritional imbalances—and displayed the breadth of its traditional cuisine.

Yoshihiro Narisawa was celebrated as one of a handful of chefs in Japan pushing the boundaries of Japanese cuisine, creating new culinary experiences from the raw ingredients of traditional Japanese cooking [11]. Traveling throughout Europe to learn his trade in the legendary kitchens of Joël Robuchon, Frédy Girardet and Paul Bocuse, to name just a few, Narisawa mastered both the Japanese tradition and the refinements of European experimentation and cooking techniques. He combined both to add great diversity to his menus. Soon after opening, his restaurant "Les Créations de Narisawa" was awarded two Michelin stars in the star-spangled metropole of Tokyo. Now known as simply "Narisawa," the restaurant was recognized as best restaurant in Asia by San Pellegrino for three years in a row.

Chef Narisawa and his team emphasized in their preparations the two interrelated concepts of sustainability and gastronomy, based on the belief that both were vital to their central message of natural regeneration. The chef is unmistakably clear in his menus, which feature dishes with exotic names such as "Gift from the Soil," "Gift from the Sea" and "Gift from the Mountain." Over the years, the chef developed a signature style of cuisine labeled as "innovative satoyama." The word "satoyama" comes from "sato," meaning home or native place, and "yama," meaning mountain or woodland but also a sacred zone where one goes after death. "Satoyama" thus designates the "sacred home woodland [12]," the traditional rural landscape that once typified most of Japan. In such places, rice, vegetables, nuts, fruits and fish are still farmed in the traditional regenerative methods that have sustained locals for centuries. For instance, catfish from Japan's biggest freshwater lake, Lake Biwa, are encouraged to swim upstream and spawn in the rice fields to provide a future source of food. Oak trees were harvested every 18 years for their wood, on which prized shiitake mushrooms could be grown. Intercropping was not an afterthought but came naturally to satoyama inhabitants. As Sir David Attenborough narrated in the December 2000 documentary "Satoyama: Japan's Secret Garden":

> This is a land that has been touched by people, yet the people tread lightly upon it.

Building on this century-long tradition of regenerative ecosystems, chef Narisawa's innovative satoyama cuisine is based on the assortment of naturally available resources and the cooking techniques gained during his extended stay in Europe. Almost all ingredients used at the restaurant are locally sourced and the chef visits all producers personally. Restaurant guests fall under the spell of the seasons and absorb life itself since, in the view of chef Narisawa, no cook can perfect what nature has created.

Pillar #3: Experimentation

Chef Narisawa illustrates how introducing new techniques combined with novel ways of looking at available ingredients can bring about new traditions while preserving the regenerative nature of the traditional ways of cooking.

This section investigates the third pillar of superior performance in sustainability teams, namely experimentation. Again, the journey of discovery is grounded in examples, this time from Tony's Chocolonely and Torres wines, that highlight the role of experimentation.

Promoting a clear sense of direction and diversity in solutions contributes to team performance, but the third critical ingredient for superior performance in a volatile, uncertain, complex and ambiguous (VUCA) world is experimentation, that is, trials and errors. To illustrate the importance of this factor, another example from haute cuisine is introduced—the FoodLab initiated by René Redzepi and his crew at the famous Danish restaurant Noma. From its inception, the FoodLab's mission was to experiment wildly with ingredients. Ultimately, it enabled Noma to earn its stripes as a beacon of new cuisine, with seasonal menus exclusively based on Nordic ingredients. The soy sauce was produced from discarded cabbage leaves, some of the best edible ants in the region and the application of rediscovered (Japanese) fermentation techniques used to preserve fish. Voted the world's best restaurant by *Restaurant* magazine in 2010, 2011, 2012 and 2014, Noma became a hotbed of culinary experimentation [13].

The virtues of experimentation were discovered by other industries. At the beginning of Tony's Chocolonely, when reporter and founder-to-be Teun van de Keuken and his colleagues started to develop their chocolate bar, they looked for alternative ways to convey their message of slave-free chocolate to consumers. After addressing the obvious, like embellishing the brand logo with a cachet on slave-free chocolate, the team moved into less obvious ways to break the mold, in a literal but also metaphorical sense. For example, they defied an unwritten convention in the chocolate industry whereby chocolate bars are supposed to be rectangular, with evenly distributed pieces. Their bar would have a patchwork shape representing West Africa, the main source of cocoa beans, in particular the Gulf of Guinea, Ivory Coast and Ghana. Their attempt to represent even tiny countries such as Togo and Benin forced them to combine both so that a hazelnut would fit inside. The design signposted the inequalities in the cocoa sector:

> For us it doesn't make sense for chocolate bars to be divided into chunks of equal sizes when there is so much inequality in the chocolate industry! The unevenly sized chunks of our 6oz bars are a palatable way of reminding our choco-friends that the profits in the chocolate industry are unfairly divided.
> Henk Jan Belman, Chief Chocolate Officer Tony's Chocolonely

Much to the delight of CCO Henk Jan Beltman, the unequal division of the bars triggered customer complaints, as the split of the bar was unpredictable and therefore often deemed "unfair." When addressing large audiences, Henk Jan liked to share the story about a mother who was trying to give her two children half a bar of Tony's each in a hurry. When she tried to break the bar in half, the two pieces came out unequal and her kids fought each other hard over the biggest piece. Ingenious as ever, Henk Jan came up with a forthright solution to this real-life consumer experience: Why not give both kids an entire bar?

Experimentation at Tony's also meant continuously developing unusual flavors, such as the limited edition white raspberry with pop-candy, rhubarb-crumble, pretzel-toffee and stracciatella, to name a few. One of the more extreme experiments was Tony's Chocolonely Christmas bar, which had a chocolate Christmas tree with a hole so that it could be used as a decoration on the real Christmas tree (refer to Fig. 12.2). The tree part of the chocolate bar contained a surprise in the form of a drop of glühwein, a mulled wine originating from Austria.

At Bodegas Torres, experimentation was also one of the pillars of success. The company did not venture into adding chocolate to its wines, but it did find other radical ways to combine innovation with tradition in the most elegant and powerful manner. After the disastrous phylloxera bug hit the vineyards of Catalonia in 1887, many indigenous grape varieties were pretty much wiped out. This represented a huge loss of genetic capital for humanity, since each grape variety carried an original DNA. So, starting in 1984, Torres poured tremendous efforts into collecting and multiplying indigenous Catalan grape varieties. In a public appeal, the company asked consumers to send in any "unknown" grape varieties they still possessed. After careful selection,

Fig. 12.2 Tony's Chocolonely Christmas tree chocolate bar

some 45 historical grape varieties were rediscovered, most of which had been presumed lost to the phylloxera plague. Among these were two varieties known as Samsó and Garró, subsequently used in the creation of Torres's top-of-the-range wine, Grans Muralles. Louis Canellas, executive director at Torres for wine tourism and events, observed:

> Tradition and innovation at Torres should not contradict each other. If technology means a better wine; why not? Our vineyards are more natural today than 40 years ago.

Adapting to climate change was also the subject of experimentation at Torres, and the company developed new scenarios to adapt vines to the evolving climate reality. To measure the impact of global warming, research was conducted with different grape varieties such as tempranillo, verdejo and albarino in controlled greenhouses, for example, by raising the average temperature by 3°C and injecting three times more CO_2 than normal. Based on these greenhouse experiments, vintners were forced to change procedures and take counter measures, such as modifying their planting techniques. These changes included higher-density plantations and reduced thinning. The resulting denser vine canopies reduced evaporation. Because of the progressive increase in temperature, new regions were examined as potential locations for wine production. Torres bought land in the Pyrenees and started producing pinot noir and chardonnay wines from grapes grown at 1000 meters above sea level. Together with external partners, it developed renewable energy solutions and decreased the weight of wine bottles by approximately 20% to reduce the company's carbon footprint.

The first three pillars to energize teams that we examined in this chapter were Direction, Diversity and Experimentation. As concluded in detail in Chap. 9, collaboration with value chain partners is practically unavoidable in the acceleration of sustainable innovation, which leads to the fourth pillar: a culture of collaboration. The Deloitte Global Human Capital Trends Report pointed out in its 2018 version that increasingly teams from multiple companies collaborate successfully. Companies organized under a "network of teams" operating model were found to reach a higher level of collaboration, including with the company's external ecosystem [14]. Examples in the next section emphasize various ways to improve this growing sense of collaboration.

Pillar #4: A Culture of Collaboration

Experimentation occurs quite naturally in kitchens. Noma's chef and owner René Redzepi was all about experimenting with his FoodLab venture [15]. Experimentation extended beyond the industry boundaries, drawing on teamwork within the entire ecosystem. To develop its famous enzyme-based soy sauce from discarded cabbage leaves, Noma required not only experimentation but also knowledge and experience from outside the kitchen.

This need to externalize collaborations was also felt by Danish enzyme specialist Novozymes, which often relied on knowledge partners to adapt its enzyme solutions to specific customer applications. Partnering was pivotal to Novozymes' strategy, reflected in its statement of purpose: "Together we find biological answers for better lives in a growing world—Let's rethink tomorrow." The company ambitioned to replace chemicals with enzyme solutions, and this became a reality thanks in no small part to its "Partnering for Impact" strategy, which was completely centered around collaboration with external partners (discussed in Chap. 9). So how does partnering for impact work in practice? To understand better its premises and modus operandi, one needs look no further than to some transformative innovations that sprouted from the Novozymes nursery.

Palm oil and its derivatives are used in chocolate, baked goods, processed foods, cosmetics, pharmaceuticals, detergents and many other products. It is praised for its great cooking properties, even at high temperatures, and its lack of smell, making it a prized ingredient in many recipes. It is also considered an efficient crop compared to other sources of vegetable oil. It is no surprise then to see it account for 65% of all vegetable oil traded internationally. Global production of palm oil has increased tenfold since 1980, driven largely by population growth and rising incomes, and conservative estimates predict a further 50% growth by 2050 [16].

Unfortunately, palm oil production also has significant environmental implications for developing countries in Asia, Africa and Latin America. Vast stretches of land have been devoted to the crop in recent years, resulting in large areas of tropical forests with high-conservation value being cleared to make room for the extensive monoculture—destroying critical habitats of many endangered species, including rhinos, elephants and tigers. Palm oil production has clearly impacted the environment, and with demand for palm oil set to continue to grow and few substitutes in sight, plantations have quickly become obvious targets for yield improvement programs.

Oil extraction rates for palm fruits usually average 20%–24%, depending on variables such as fruit quality and seasonality. Over the years, the palm oil milling process has been optimized to minimize oil losses [17]. Studies on enzymes have shown their potential to improve the separation of oil from water, fiber and sludge in the raw pressed oil, optimizing extraction rates. Novozymes, as a pioneer in the enzymes world, developed Palmora®, a product that improved both the yield and the plant performance for palm oil producers [18], improving the environmental footprint of the end product.

Novozymes also relied on collaboration with external partners to develop another major innovation called Alterion®, a poultry probiotic that allows farmers to improve the gut health of their animals. According to the World Health Organization, antibiotic resistance is one of the biggest threats to global health, food security and development today [19]. In the past, broad-spectrum antibiotics were used extensively in animal production to improve productivity in livestock. But growing fears about drug-resistant bacteria in animals and humans has forced a reconsideration of the established policies, often leading to restricted usage. Through a partnership with Adisseo, a leading expert in feed additives, Novozymes formulated Alterion, a product that not only helps combat resistance to antibiotics but also increases feed conversion rates in the poultry digestive system.

> Our ambition is to offer safe and consistent alternatives to antibiotic growth promoters for the livestock production of the future. Building on the successful co-development and launch of Alterion, we are developing a joint pipeline of new products for swine and poultry.
> Camilla Bünner Kruse, Global Marketing and Partnership Manager [20]

The examples above illustrate how a culture of collaboration can improve the performance of sustainability teams, impacting not only external stakeholders but also internal team members. The crew of restaurant Noma in Copenhagen became so cohesive that each member was ready to stand up for any other member. When a Gambian colleague was prevented from attending the London ceremony for their first Best Restaurant in the World award because of visa problems, all his colleagues wore T-shirts with his face imprinted on them to the ceremony. To mark his support for team work and collaboration, chef Redzepi went even further. At a 2017 party in Copenhagen organized to mark the restaurant's last day at its waterfront location in Christianshavn, he announced that one of his dishwashers, who had worked in the restaurant kitchen since 2003, would receive shares in the business in "recognition of his hard work and enduring smile [21]." Two other employees were also made partners in the business in recognition of them being the "heart and soul" of Noma.

⚅ Key Account Teams and Sustainability: Bootcamps and Boosters

One way to enhance collaboration on sustainability within the ecosystem is by working through key account teams. The bootcamps and boosters approach provides an excellent opportunity to put into practice the four-pillar structure of a better sense of direction, diversity in solutions, experimentation and a culture of collaboration. Moreover, it represents a complementary and interesting way for commercial teams to leverage their company's sustainability programs for the benefit of key clients.

The first stage of the proposed approach is an internal bootcamp with a key account team, usually cross-functional. One example is a worldwide Unilever supplier that organized such a key account team bootcamp, involving representatives from sales, logistics, product development and communications alongside the sustainability team. During the one-day internal workshop, customers, competitors and other stakeholders were analyzed to discover the potential for collaboration on sustainability issues. To facilitate the discussions, a surefire model addressing the elements shown in Table 12.1 was used:

Once the team had completed the first stage, the second stage was initiated—a multi-stakeholder booster. Continuing with the example above, a half-day meeting between the client and the key account team was scheduled to share the bootcamp results and jointly develop potential solutions through a co-creation workshop. The agenda for the booster was relatively simple: first

Table 12.1 Key account management checklist

Focus	Questions
Description of the business model	How is Unilever's business constructed for our products? Who is the customer? Who are the users? How many of them are there?
Definition of the issues related to sustainability in the industry	Who are the other industry stakeholders and what are the relevant issues for them?
Ranking material sustainability issues according to stakeholder interest and the company impact	What is the business impact of these material issues? How do they relate to the Sustainable Development Goals?
Mapping the competitive environment in a value curve	What does the competitive environment on sustainability in the category looks like?
Setting ambitions and targets for future progress	What specific benchmarks and performance indicators are usable to demonstrate our product/service superiority?
Identification of opportunities	What solutions can we come up with in the areas of eco-efficiency, innovation and customer intimacy?

the grounds for the common sustainability efforts were scoped, then the key material issues performance was detailed, singling out relevant opportunities. Finally, a 100-day plan was jointly developed, and next steps were specified, assigning owners and timelines to monitor progress. These joint efforts contributed considerably to improving the sustainability performance of both companies, with the combination of bootcamp and booster leading to increased business and a more intimate collaboration.

Tips, Traps and Takeaways

♦ Tips

- As a team, do not limit the quest for solutions on sustainability to the existing boundaries of your industry. Look way beyond for inspiration!
- When looking for sustainable development within the value chain, create multi-functional cross-company teams diverse enough to effectively address the challenge.

♦ Traps

- Commercial teams sometimes fail to recognize the client's emerging requirements for sustainability. If not prompted, the possibilities of jointly addressing the sustainability issues might not reach the commercial agenda.

♦ Takeaways

In this chapter, the importance of teamwork was brought forward. Extrapolated from patterns observed in a range of sectors, a four-pillar approach was proposed to improve the performance of sustainability teams. In alignment with the concept of vectoring that underlies the whole book, pillar #1 relies on a better sense of direction, as exemplified by Atera's pivot to a Secure Base Leadership model. Pillar #2, diversity, is illustrated through the tale of chef Narisawa of Japan, who applied a palette of modern preparation techniques to the centuries-old principle of living in harmony with nature, leading to the development of an innovative, more sustainable way of cooking. A purposeful quest for diversity enabled the creation of solutions that combined tradition with the present reality of scarce resources. Pillar #3, experimentation, involves pushing the boundaries beyond the industry norms. In the case of Tony's Chocolonely, that involved, among other experiments, developing oddly shaped chocolate bars and rather unusual flavors. For Torres wineries, salvaging near-extinct regional grape varieties ensured a supply of original wines and blends for decades to come, as did its quest to find new terroirs that have become hospitable for vine growing as climate changes. Finally, pillar #4, a culture of collaboration, is illustrated by the exceptional achievements of two Danish pioneers, namely restaurant Noma in Copenhagen and enzyme masters at Novozymes. Teamwork is fundamental in the quest for performance in sustainability teams, as epitomized by Noma's Gambian dishwasher who saw his 14 years of service rewarded with co-ownership of the "most influential restaurant in the world [15]."

To reinforce the messages of the chapter but also roam new frontiers for performance improvements, the possibility of engaging key account teams in a co-creation process of sustainable development with key clients is outlined. To facilitate that process, a formal game plan involving two workshops, an internal bootcamp and a booster with the client and possibly other external stakeholders, was introduced with the purpose of improving the joint ecosystem performance.

References

1. Imedio, F. (2014, March 4) Ferran Adrià desvela las claves de la Fundación de El Bulli. *El Periodico*. Retrieved from https://www.elperiodico.com/es/gente/20140304/ferran-adria-desvela-claves-fundacion-bulli-3155149
2. Abend, L. (2017, August 17) The El Bulli Legacy, Six Years On. *Food & Wine*. Retrieved from https://www.foodandwine.com/travel/restaurants/el-bulli-restaurant-legacy-spain
3. ElBulli Foundation (2017) Bullianos A way of life. https://www.bullinianos.com. Accessed 27 March 2018.
4. Kohlrieser, G., Goldsworthy, S., Coombe, D. (2012, July) *Care to Dare: Unleashing Astonishing Potential Through Secure Base Leadership*. Wiley, Jossey-Bass.
5. This case is an abridged version of KEEPING THE MOMENTUM—ATERA NYC (A, B, C): TURBULENT TIMES IN THE KITCHEN (IMD-7-1786, 1787,1788) Copyright © 2018 by IMD—International Institute for Management Development, Lausanne, Switzerland (www.imd.org). No part of this publication may be reproduced, stored in a retrieval system or transmitted in any form or by any means without the prior written permission of IMD.
6. Atera (2018) Atera homepage. http://ateranyc.com/. Accessed 29 March 2018.
7. Burton, M. (2017, November 28) Michelin Announces 2018 Stars for Tokyo. *Eater*. Retrieved from https://www.eater.com/2017/11/28/16709504/tokyo-michelin-stars-guide-2018

8. McCarthy, N. (2017, November 23) The Top Countries for Michelin 3-Star Restaurants [Infographic]. *Forbes*. Retrieved from https://www.forbes.com/sites/ niallmccarthy/2017/11/23/the-top-countries-for-michelin-3-star-restaurants- infographic/#2b977f13704c

9. Nagata, K. (2015, May 3) Showcasing innovation, food culture. *Japan Times*. Retrieved from https://www.japantimes.co.jp/news/2015/05/03/national/show- casing-innovation-food-culture/#.WzzSDS2B3dQ

10. Eplett, L. (2016, March 3) How the Japanese Diet Became the Japanese Diet. *Scientific American*. Retrieved from https://blogs.scientificamerican.com/food- matters/how-the-japanese-diet-became-the-japanese-diet/

11. Storey, T. (2016, December 8) Yoshihiro Narisawa, Revolutionizing the World of Japanese Cuisine. *The Culture Trip*. Retrieved from https://theculturetrip.com/asia/ japan/articles/yoshihiro-narisawa-revolutionising-the-world-of-japanese-cuisine/

12. Sadamichi, K., Wallace, A. (2003) Satoyama: A Japanese Model of Sustainable Harmony. *Maine Organic Farmers and Gardeners Association*. Retrieved from http://www.mofga.org/Publications/The-Maine-Organic-Farmer-Gardener/ Summer-2003/Satoyama

13. Williams, G. (2017, February 22) Noma's taste of tomorrow: creating the future of food. *Wired UK*. Retrieved from http://www.wired.co.uk/article/inside-noma- copenhagen

14. Abbatiello, A., Agarwal, D., Bersin, J., et al. (2018) The rise of the social enter- prise, 2018 Deloitte Global Human Capital Trends. *Deloitte*. Retrieved from https://www2.deloitte.com/content/dam/Deloitte/be/Documents/human-capi- tal/0000_HC%20Trends_2018_BE.PDF

15. Tishgard, S. (2015, September 15) How Noma Became the Most Influential Restaurant in the World. *GrubStreet*. Retrieved from http://www.grubstreet. com/2015/09/history-of-noma.html

16. WWF (2014) *Responsible purchasing of palm oil: a guide for manufacturers and retailers*. Retrieved from http://awsassets.wwf.org.au/downloads/fs076_guide_ responsible_purchasing_of_palm_oil_28nov14.pdf

17. Rushworth, M. (2017) Enzyme assisted palm oil extraction with continuous ster- ilizer, WO2017182665A1. World Intellectual Property Organization.

18. Novozymes (2018) *The Novozymes Report 2017*. Retrieved from https:// report2017.novozymes.com

19. World Health Organization (2018, February 5) Antibiotic resistance. http:// www.who.int/news-room/fact-sheets/detail/antibiotic-resistance. Accessed 5 April 2018.

20. Novozymes (2018, May 17) Alterion gets European approval [Press release]. Retrieved from https://www.novozymes.com/en/news/news-archive/2018/05/ alterion-eu-approval

21. Connolly, K. (2017, March 1) Noma dishwasher becomes co-owner of world- famous Danish restaurant. *The Guardian*. Retrieved from https://www.theguard- ian.com/lifeandstyle/2017/mar/01/noma-dishwasher-becomes-co-owner- of-world-famous-danish-restaurant

13

Embedding Sustainability into the Business Core

So far, the journey has taken us from a clear statement of purpose to a concise set of relevant materialities, with further elaborations on the role of partnerships and circular economy models in accelerating innovation. In the previous chapter, we proposed four pillars (direction, diversity, experimentation and a collaboration culture) to increase the effectiveness of sustainability teams. The journey into effective sustainability implementation is now approaching its final destination, namely ensuring that the great strides made improving a firm's positive impact on society and the environment become sustainable. Discussing the sustainability of sustainability programs is the ultimate crowning moment of the journey, as it ensures sustainability's legacy for future generations of managers and stakeholders to enjoy. Conceptually, it is time to embed sustainability deeply into the business, so it can get safely and effectively transmitted and robust to outside forces.

In this chapter, we discuss how to make sustainability an integral part of the business and ensure its perennity. The vectoring approach promoted throughout the book to develop and execute sustainability strategies not only improves communication with stakeholders but also facilitates the effective and efficient reporting of sustainability performance. A limited set of relevant key performance indicators (KPIs) tightly connected to the company's core business helps focus sustainability activities and makes for more consistent communication.

As an alternative to describing the full change management process that is often required, we endeavor to uncover some of the principal preconditions for successful implementation, following a simple three-phase game plan:

© The Author(s) 2019
B. Leleux, J. van der Kaaij, *Winning Sustainability Strategies*,
https://doi.org/10.1007/978-3-319-97445-3_13

- Strategy compilation, that is, how to start with implementation
- Readiness assessment, that is, where to start the implementation
- KPI reporting, that is, measuring progress on a local level.

To present the distinct phases, real-life cases are introduced on companies such as Belgian chemical giant Solvay, with its original Sustainable Portfolio Management model, or Unilever Russia, which managed a zero-waste-to-landfill target in its Tula production cluster. The latter, rooted in the Unilever Sustainable Living Plan (USLP), is an outstanding example of local implementation under difficult circumstances.

To conclude, a holistic tool is introduced to facilitate the development of a high-level roadmap for the implementation planning of a company's sustainability strategy.

Compiling the Sustainability Strategy: How to Start?

In the first chapters of the book, we presented four sustainability program archetypes, each with its own distinct characteristics: traditional, communicative, opportunistic and transformational. The archetypes were identified by analyzing the risk-reward trade-off made by companies on sustainability. Did the companies maintain a balance between risk and opportunity, did they prioritize opportunity seizing over risk reduction or was their approach strictly based on risk reduction?

Before embarking on a journey to improve the sustainability performance of a company, capturing its starting position in the model presented in Fig. 13.1, draws a simple, but telling picture of the current situation. To estimate the company position, the performance on the main attributes of the four archetypes can be evaluated, such as where in the organization the sustainability department is located, what the main focus of the program is and what specific topics are of interest to investors (refer to Table 13.1).

Plotting the company's current position is definitely no replacement for an in-depth analysis as suggested in Chap. 4 on materialities and Chap. 6 on environmental, social and governance (ESG) ratings, but it provides a useful overview with which to start the implementation roadmap. It helps to visualize the destination of its sustainability journey, especially when combined with the executives' ambitions with respect to the improvement program.

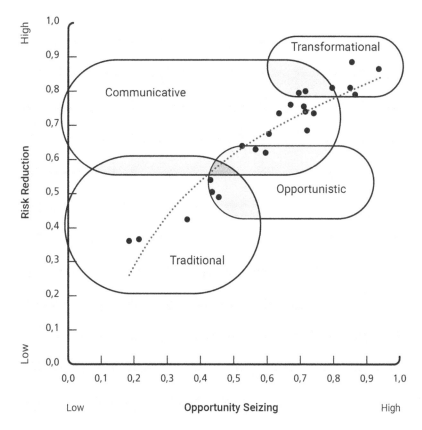

Fig. 13.1 Four sustainability program archetypes based on risk-reward mapping

When discussing McDonald's in an earlier chapter, we highlighted the importance of proceeding from *why* to *what* and finally *how* to obtain results. Soon after the arrival of its new CEO Steve Easterbrook, McDonald's announced its "Scale for Good" plan, which addressed *how* the company wanted to become relevant again. This approach not only landed McDonald's on *Fortune*'s Change the World List in 2016 but, more importantly, it also facilitated the implementation of sustainability in the giant restaurant chain.

As seen in Chap. 4 on materiality, the linkages between sustainability and risk disclosures are still feeble and in need of attention. The issues identified through the materiality analysis are often not connected with the enterprise risk assessment, putting into question the rationale for constructing materiality matrices. Research has pinpointed several reasons for this breakdown: limited understanding of sustainability risks, diverging reasons for sustainability versus risk disclosures as well as inconsistent time horizons. It should be very

Table 13.1 Overview of attributes to the four sustainability program archetypes

Attributes	Traditionalist	Communicative	Opportunistic	Transformational
Main focus	Regulations compliance	Communication	Decentralized Organization	Innovation Change
Most common reporting line	Corporate affairs	Corporate communication	Various, business unit level	Strategy, business development Line management
High occurrence sectors	Utilities, mining, oil and gas	Service industries, banks	Chemicals, pharmaceuticals	Food, fashion
Investors lens	Stranded assets Regulatory developments Resource dependency	Greenwashing Human capital development	Strategic coherence Resource dependency	Innovation pipeline Revenue growth Cost efficiency
Likely stakeholder scenario	Stakeholder management	Story-telling	Ad hoc Local	Co-creation

clear though that materiality and enterprise risk management ought to be combined to embed sustainability into the business strategy.

To map ESG materialities together with a company's risk assessment, a number of approaches can be used. To review these approaches, we look at Swiss Re Group, one of the largest global non-life reinsurance groups. When identifying its material sustainability issues, Swiss Re combines its own internal risk expertise with the knowledge obtained from stakeholder interactions and the criteria from various reporting and ESG rating systems. This three-way matching helps the company cover risk not only from a business perspective but also from a stakeholder point of view.

To identify emerging risks, Swiss Re has put into operation a process it calls SONAR (Systematic Observation of Notions Associated with Risk). Through an internal platform, employees report and discuss early signals of issues that might turn into risks for the company. Periodically, these signals, or risk notions, are clustered and assessed further by internal risk experts. Finally, in-depth investigations are carried out on selected topics and, where justified, the outcomes are integrated into the risk management process. SONAR is not limited to general topics; it also includes risks related to ESG, enabling Swiss Re to identify actual and potential risks at a very early stage [1].

Assessing the Business Readiness: Where to Start?

Once the sustainability strategy has been compiled and adequately documented, the next challenge is to identify where to start in addressing the issues identified and how to gain maximum momentum for change. To answer that challenge often means addressing a series of related questions, such as what parts of the business are easier to engage, what is the level of maturity of the different market segments and what are the specific complexities they face (refer to Table 13.2). To start formulating answers, it is useful to revisit the materiality complexities presented in Chap. 4.

It is not uncommon for various business units, divisions or product groups to be impacted differently by these complexities; hence, they may have different levels of maturity on sustainability issues and also varying market potential. A typical example of this would be a global beer brewer with factories in Europe working 100% on renewable energy, while its breweries in China are still running on coal.

Table 13.2 Most common business-induced complexities for selecting sustainability issues

Complexity	Description	Sectors	Threats
The Mixed-up Chameleon Complexity	Companies with material sustainability topics highly dependent on their value chain partners	Service industries such as consultancies and banks	Broad scope has a negative influence on the effectiveness
The Geography Complexity	Companies with material issues that differ markedly by region	Global manufacturing companies in, e.g. food or electronics	Non-simultaneous progress geographically carries reputational risk. Different regulations for individual regions
The Hodgepodge Complexity	Companies with highly diversified portfolios, without a clear core business driving materiality	Conglomerates with a broad portfolio of businesses facing different material topics, with little common ground	Little engagement from vision resulting in disappointing outcomes Decentralized sustainability efforts feeding potential inconsistencies

To identify the business units with the most potential for improvement requires conducting a portfolio sustainability assessment. In the past, companies' sustainability diagnoses were mostly focused on cost savings, compliance risks and top-line growth; today, companies are looking for a more refined view of the sustainability performance of their individual businesses. In collaboration with several of its members, the World Business Council for Sustainable Development (WBCSD) developed a framework to conduct such a portfolio sustainability assessment. The framework is not dissimilar to the GE-McKinsey matrix[1] developed in the early 1970s. It plots the business nit strength on sustainability against the maturity of its markets. This technique gradually makes its way into corporate strategy departments and the offices of ESG analysts, allowing both to re-evaluate the sustainability performance of their, sometimes extremely diverse, product portfolios.

---

[1] The GE-McKinsey matrix is a framework that offers a systematic approach for a multi-business corporation to prioritize its investments among its business units. Source: McKinsey.

📁 Sustainable Portfolio Management at Solvay

Solvay, a Belgian chemical company, provides a sophisticated example of portfolio assessment tool. Throughout its 150-year history, Solvay has adapted its business model to respond to societal trends and concerns. As it continues to transform, the company focuses on creating responsible, sustainable value. One of its five sustainability objectives is to generate at least 50% of its revenues with solutions addressing the challenges of sustainable development by 2025. The key to delivering on the promise is to evaluate the sustainability footprint of all its products. Based on the premises of the WBCSD framework, Solvay has developed a Sustainable Portfolio Management (SPM) tool to identify and analyze opportunities that could bring positive impact to its non-financial objectives (refer to Fig. 13.2). The SPM was designed to be a fact-based, robust compass for steering Solvay's portfolio toward more responsible business by factoring sustainability into the decision making.

The SPM is used to evaluate the company's products from a holistic perspective based on three sets of criteria: environmental footprint, social impact and the way in which they answer market demand and challenges. Solvay's applications or products are sorted on a two-dimensional matrix, also referred to as a "heatmap," either as stars, neutral or as challenges considering:

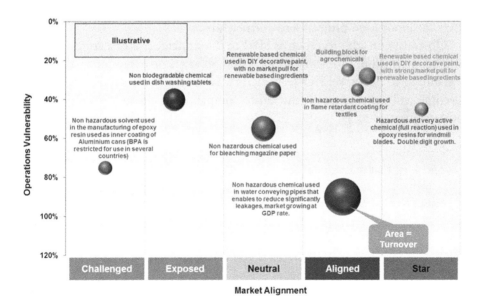

Fig. 13.2 Example of Solvay's sustainable portfolio management tool

1. The products' environmental manufacturing footprint and its correlated risks and opportunities plotted on the vertical axis of operational vulnerability based on a quantitative assessment (19 impact indicators).
2. The degree to which the products bring benefits or face challenges from a market perspective plotted on the horizontal axis of market alignment based on the results of a qualitative assessment (60 questions on social and environmental topics).

By identifying sustainability signals in a systematic way, decision makers are more accurately informed of the operating risks and opportunities; hence, they are in a better position to anticipate future developments. Over time, the tool has gained wide adoption at Solvay, supporting decisions and integrating sustainability across all key business processes: strategy, research and innovation, investment, marketing and sales and mergers and acquisitions.

A mere two years after its introduction, the sustainability performance of products accounting for 84% of the company's turnover was analyzed using the SPM. Forty-three percent of the products ranked as sustainable solutions, compared to only 18% in 2013. In the period 2015–2017, Solvay's products categorized as SPM solutions experienced an annual growth rate of +3%; those falling under the challenges category, that is, those facing sustainability concerns or roadblocks, declined by −2%. Moreover, SPM also created new opportunities as it enabled Solvay to engage with customers on sustainability topics aimed at differentiating and creating value, opening up new perspectives for innovation projects and partnerships.

Obviously, an addition such as SPM to the strategic lens of a company does not happen without top-level support and Solvay is no exception to that rule. According to Solvay's CEO Jean-Pierre Clamadieu, sustainability needed to become truly embedded in the entire company to help shape the company and its businesses:

> Sustainability is not some kind of add-on that comes on the side. It is really something that must guide the way we act daily to manage a Group like Solvay, at the highest level, but also on the operational level on the ground.
> Jean-Pierre Clamadieu, CEO Solvay [2]

Taking Value Chains as Starting Point

A sustainable portfolio assessment is a useful tool for prioritizing business units, divisions and product groups for sustainability implementation. But smaller or less diversified firms may see this as technical overkill, and they would be quite correct in that assessment. Very often, a simple value chain approach can provide the basic insights necessary for implementation.

When Brauunion, an Austrian brewer belonging to Heineken, researched consumer preferences, it discovered that buying sustainably brewed beer was important for 73% of its consumers. But when it started to comb through the results, it discovered that in fact the most important sustainability criteria were those related to a strong local connection between brewer and drinker. More specifically, the top four criteria were:

- Use of regional raw materials such as grain, water, hops, etc. (85%)
- Regional job creation and security (83%)
- Supporting the regional economy and farmers (80%)
- Avoiding long transport distances, carbon footprint (75%) [3].

These results supported the view that craft brewers were blessed with a more sustainable image than regular *old-school* brewers, because they are small, independent, and usually quite traditional in their methods, which explains in part how they gained large audiences. But craft brewers, because of their small scale, are also likely to be less efficient in their water and energy consumption, two of the largest material issues for the industry. In response, larger brewers have started to stress local sourcing, while at the same time highlighting their operational credentials.

Local craft brewers are not new; in fact, they have been very much a part of the social fabric in many European countries. In the late seventeenth century, brewers from major cities of the province of Brabant in the Netherlands managed to convince the Dutch parliament that beer-brewing in rural villages should be forbidden because of suspected tax evasion. Only after several appeals from rural breweries was this decision partially reversed. Commercial breweries were still not allowed within 1½ hours of a major city and the capacity of the rural brewers remained strictly limited to local consumption.

It is in this context that Dutch brewer Bavaria emerged as a local champion. The history of Bavaria, the largest independent beer brewer in Europe today, can in fact be traced back to 1680, covering 10 generations of brewers, of which seven carried the name Swinkels. In that year, the company featured for the first time on a tax invoice of the local municipality addressed to Dirck Franssen Vereijcken, the owner of "Brouwerij De Kerkdijk" (Brewery of Church Dike Road), a brewery located exactly where Bavaria's main brewery is still located today.

Bavaria, later rebranded as the Swinkels Family Brewers (SFB) because of several acquisitions, turned circularity into the keystone of its sustainability strategy, aiming to become a 50% circular business by 2020. As part of the company's ambitions, the SFB aspired to tackle water use and pollution beyond its operations. Years earlier, Bavaria had already initiated a local "Boer Bier Water" (Farmer Beer Water) initiative in the Netherlands aimed at ensuring the availability and sustainable management of water and sanitation for all by 2030. Bavaria collaborated with local farmers and other stakeholders to preserve soil and water resources. Recent milestones include the commissioning of new equipment in the sub-irrigation system, restoring purified wastewater through the Wilhelmina canal and the award of an Interreg Europe subsidy for a project on preventing agricultural drought.

Twelve years after starting, the project boasts a number of impressive achievements. In 2018 alone, the 40 participating farmers grew 60 hectares of brewer barley using about 100,000 cubic meters of purified wastewater. Another group of 10 farmers jointly worked on soil enhancements. Much of the projects success can be attributed to the geographical proximity of all the stakeholders. Most of them know each other and share the occasional beer together!

KPI Reporting

Building the KPI Dashboard: The Balanced Scorecard Example

With a better understanding of priority targets, that is, which part of the organization to address first in the sustainability implementation, it is then necessary to identify appropriate KPIs and reporting procedures for local implementation. As highlighted earlier, applying a vectoring approach to a company's sustainability strategy leads to more focused material sustainability issues, and a more manageable number of KPIs. Still, it is always important to prioritize and categorize those KPIs.

Non-financial reporting of sustainability KPIs requires solid frameworks, discipline and effective reporting tools, irrespective of the ultimate purpose of the information gathered (internal benchmarking, external ratings, annual reports, etc.). Sustainability KPIs, by definition, evaluate fundamental ecosystem issues. As such, they should not only cover the company's direct activities but also their impact on the value chain, for instance, if a company sources goods with a questionable sustainability profile.

Stakeholder theory posits that an organization's performance should be measured against the expectations of a broad range of stakeholders with vested interests in the impact of the organization's activities. Based on an original study called "Measuring Performance in the Organization of the Future [4]," the balanced scorecard concept by Kaplan and Norton earned its reputation as a performance management tool grounded in stakeholder theory. In their broader interpretation, balanced scorecards always included non-financial information, such as customer service levels and innovation effectiveness, a not-too-distant predecessor of what we aim for here, that is, the inclusion in the scorecard of all critical KPIs for measuring the company's role in society.

To illustrate the challenge, let us use the case of a decentralized business-to-business service provider, with over 70 locations around the globe and a well-defined, customer-centric business strategy. With a workforce of almost 10,000 employees, the company boasted annual revenues of over €1 billion and was regarded as a leader in its industry. Checking its various operational websites, the company reported visibly on 23 non-financial KPIs, all aligned with the Global Reporting Initiative (GRI).[2] Internally, the collected KPIs were not converted into a formal, usable dashboard and sustainability was clearly deemed a low strategic priority.

Unsurprisingly, once the KPIs were finally mapped on a balanced scorecard, the picture that emerged was quite disturbing (refer to Fig. 13.3). Only one of the sustainability KPIs addressed the client-side of the business, and only two monitored the learning and growth of the organization. Not exactly fitting for a customer-centric service provider. How did it end up that way? Well, with little attention paid to the overall challenge, sustainability slowly slipped into a health and safety issue, best left to the operational side of the organization. As the commercial staff was insufficiently trained on the company's sustainability efforts, emerging client signals begging for sustainability improvements fell on deaf ears.

Intervention was needed to restore a proper sense of direction and reengineer a dashboard better aligned with the company's strategy. After refreshing the company's materiality matrix, the number of KPIs on the sustainability dashboard was pruned to 18, more evenly distributed over the four axes of the balanced scorecard. The new list of KPIs presented more valuable insights into the financial relevance of the company's sustainability efforts. As a bonus of the refresher exercise, the non-financial reporting became more aligned with the company's strategic objectives and, therefore, more directly addressed the

---

[2] The Global Reporting Initiative is an international independent standards organization that helps businesses, governments and other organizations understand and communicate their impact on issues such as climate change, human rights and corruption. Source: Wikipedia.

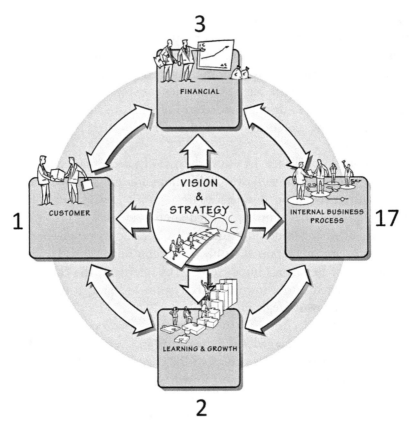

Fig. 13.3 Analysis of the number of KPIs per balanced score card quadrant

needs of all stakeholders, as originally intended by the scorecard methodology devised by Kaplan and Norton.

📁 Unilever Russia: Executing Sustainable Living [5]

The Unilever group of companies was founded in 1930 by a merger of the Dutch margarine producer Margarine Uni and the British soap maker Lever Brothers. Unilever developed into a global leader in the production of fast-moving consumer goods, with over 172,000 employees worldwide and a turnover in 2017 of €53.7 billion. The company operated in four broad categories, namely personal care (Dove, Brut, Lifebuoy, Axe, etc.), home care (Cif, Persil, Omo, etc.), food (Ben & Jerry's, Magnum, Hellmann's, etc.) and refreshments (Lipton, Pure Leaf, etc.).

Unilever entered Russia in 1992, and by 2016, it was using four large production clusters situated in the Tula Region, St. Petersburg, Ekaterinburg and Omsk. It employed about 7000 people in the country and was proud to list its Tula food concentrate plant as one of the most advanced facilities in the world for the production of instant food.

New Paradigm and New Goals: Unilever Sustainable Living Plan

In 2016, Unilever was ranked number one in the Dow Jones Sustainability Index (DJSI), and it stood out as a leader in sustainable development among household and personal product[3] companies [6]. In 2010, the company published the Unilever Sustainable Living Plan (USLP), which aimed to double the company's business by 2020, while reducing its environmental impact. The following goals were also set to be achieved by 2020:

- Help one billion people around the world improve their health and well-being
- Halve the environmental impact of its products at all stages
- Obtain 100% of its agricultural raw materials from renewable sources.

These goals were supported by nine pillars, each with one or more commitments and targets. Exhibit 13.1 contains an overview of these goals and pillars, and a sample of the associated targets. A critical part of the USLP was the reduction of the environmental impact of production waste, and the issue of shipping waste to landfill was especially pressing in Russia. According to various estimates, only 3–4% of the production waste was recycled in Russia at the time, and the rest was simply sent to landfill. Unilever's concept of "zero waste to landfill" (ZWTL) implied that all non-hazardous waste would be eliminated at its source or recycled at the plant, with nothing sent to landfill or incinerated without extracting energy.

In the first version of the USLP, the target was to eliminate the shipment of non-hazardous waste to landfills by 2020. However, by November 2013, many of Unilever's plants around the world had already achieved that goal, which made the company optimistic enough to update the tar-

---

[3] Unilever was previously categorized in the food products segment but was later reclassified as household and personal products.

get date to the end of 2014. Top management supported the new target date and assigned it to all production divisions in early 2014, without any concessions for regional specifics. Meeting the target was simply made a requirement for continuing the operation of production sites. As a result, Unilever's Tula management team put this target at the top of its priority list.

In February 2014, Konstantin Voytikov, director of the Tula site, returned from a meeting with top management in Moscow with disparaging news. At the meeting, the Unilever chief supply chain officer Pier Luigi Sigismondi restated the global objective of ZWTL. And if the point had not been made clear enough, he announced that non-compliant facilities would be shut down—no ifs, ands or buts about it. The challenge was humongous for Voytikov, as most of Tula's non-hazardous waste was still landfilled. He was given ten months to achieve what no other company in Russia had ever done before.

Initial Plans: Recycle and Incinerate

The first step, minimizing the waste volume, had already been taken, but about 7000 tons were still landfilled each year. About half of that was flotation foam from the ice-cream plant in Tula, a residue of the waste water treatment. Initial assessments showed the goal to be technically achievable, but the costs would be huge, and they would shatter Voytikov's cost targets for 2014.

With a tight schedule and budget, Voytikov rushed to put together a cross-functional working group. All members of the team, including Voytikov, had a clear goal of zero waste to landfill by the end of 2014. The KPI was directly tied to annual evaluations, remunerations and future career opportunities.

The team created various options and evaluated them one by one. A first proposal was for the site to build its own waste recycling facilities and incinerate the final residue, a costly endeavor. After a number of iterations, the working group converged on two options: (1) building an anaerobic digester for the organic waste, and (2) incinerating the waste to generate electric power. Voytikov took these options to Moscow, hoping to get some additional budget allocated. The response was rather stern: the head office was willing to provide some budget support but any increase in operating expenses would have to be covered by savings and efficiency increases at the plant.

This forced the team back to square one, and the consideration of even more creative approaches to solving the challenge.

The 5R Philosophy: A New Perspective on Production Waste Management

The Tula team studied the solutions of the teams that had successfully introduced the ZWTL plan in other countries. One of the approaches—the 5R approach—seemed to have been particularly effective. It consisted of sorting the waste into groups according to the way in which it could be managed:

- **Reject**—from the production process entirely
- **Reduce**—by modernizing the production process or better sorting
- **Reuse**—in production
- **Recycle**—and use again
- **Recover**—incinerate to generate energy and other inputs.

In two weeks, the 5R approach was implemented on all production lines. All waste was properly classified, with the appropriate treatment and resulting operating and capital expenses calculated. The results were quite interesting: they showed that sorting alone would lead to a reduction of the waste to levels that could be dealt with, either through further use or processing. There was no need for anaerobic digesters or fancy incinerators anymore.

The full implementation plan ultimately required (1) searching for technical solutions to reduce the amount of waste generated, (2) modifying processes at the plants, (3) searching for contractors that specialized in the disposal of production waste, and (4) informing staff and changing the corporate culture.

Implementing the Measures

The implementation required modifying daily procedures and impacted practically every employee. Procedures were put in place to carefully weigh all waste. Stricter sorting was implemented directly at the production line to minimize the need to sort post-production. To minimize human labor, technological solutions were developed, such as a press to separate liquid waste from solid waste. Finally, the range of waste that could be recycled was significantly expanded.

By April 2014, a technological solution had been found for the flotation foam sedimentation problem, which decreased its volume by 73% and doubled the output of solids. Meanwhile, the procurement team was searching for suppliers and estimating potential costs; the engineering team for its part was looking for solutions to reduce the amount of waste. Finding contractors that could comply simultaneously with the laws of the Russian Federation and Unilever's requirements proved to be one of the most difficult tasks.

The methods selected were found to be six to eight times more expensive than simply shipping waste to landfill, but a subsequent analysis proved that these costs did not lead to losses—the company even began to make a profit by selling recycled waste. Finally, it implemented measures aimed at increasing employees' awareness and getting them involved because it became clear that without their participation it would be impossible to complete such an unusual project under Russian conditions.

Project Results and New Challenges

All the measures taken enabled the plant to eliminate the waste shipped to landfill by October 2014. The volume of waste in all categories decreased significantly, thus practically eliminating the adverse environmental impact. The capital expense for installing the press unit was modest, and the treatment facilities were modernized from the budget for expansion, as one Tula plant relocated to the new production cluster.

The Unilever Tula cluster became the second production site, after St. Petersburg, to reach the set goal. This achievement was a turning point for the company in Russia and, in early 2015, this stage was officially completed. However, the USLP also included another series of tasks to be resolved in the future. Those goals were clearly stated as well: reduce CO_2 emissions to zero by 2030, reduce water consumption and further reduce production waste quantities.

Voytikov and his team had already developed a master plan to reach these goals, assuming the initial deadlines would not be changed again to something more ambitious. The lessons from the ZWTL project were clear; it is not the amount of investment or even the technological solutions applied that drive success; instead, it is well-organized processes and the total involvement of the employees and top management.

☞ Developing a Roadmap: Plotting the Future

Plotting the Future is a planning tool focused on actions to achieve defined sustainability goals. The purpose of the tool is to develop a concrete roadmap on how to get from the current situation to the desired objectives. In a 3.5-

hour workshop, a team of four to eight persons develops an action plan to achieve the set goals. If required, several teams can work in parallel, for instance, to cover the objectives of different business units.

The Plotting the Future tool is based on *back-casting*, a technique that starts by projecting a future objective on a time horizon and then plans backwards toward the present. The team assignment starts with jointly developing this future objective. Next, the team is tasked with prioritizing the milestones, which are presented in the form of future statement cards. These cards cover a broad array of topics and are supposed to represent focal points for the project. For instance, future statement cards might state milestones such as, "We created a green team to work on climate change," "We conducted a life cycle analysis of all our packaging" or "Our entire organization was made aware of the strategic decisions and upcoming changes." Examples of future statement cards from a wine industry workshop are downloadable from www.vectoring. online and can be adapted to specific needs and prepared upfront. During the workshop, participants can also create additional milestones to complement the pre-prepared ones; hence, it is advisable to bring a few blank cards to produce additional future statement cards on the go. Once all potential milestones are generated, the next task is of course to prune the list and prioritize these milestones. A maximum of 15 statements should be selected and placed on the time horizon.

When all selected future statements have been organized on the time chart, the action plan can be developed. Based upon the selected statements, a detailed plan needs to be developed that contains features such as the actions to take, the resources required, who will be responsible, which stakeholders need to be involved and the schedule of the actions.

At the end of this process, a complete roadmap is delivered, enabling the team(s) to get started on the implementation. To improve the roadmap further, it is often a good idea to also develop an explicit 100-day plan that includes actions, timing and resources.

Tips, Traps and Takeaways

👍Tips

* Compose a one-page summary of the sustainability strategy for use by senior management. The summary should include top-level targets, SDG framing and clear linkages to the core business.

- Effective implementation requires selecting the most appropriate starting point. What part of the business is best suited to the intervention?
- Dust off the old balanced scorecard and equip it with the (proposed) sustainability KPIs. This will allow you to assess whether these KPIs provide a sufficiently complete view from a stakeholder perspective.

☄ Traps

- Beware of KPI overload; managers have limited bandwidth and hence can only effectively track and influence a limited number of factors. Be very selective on the materiality issues that are reported and the number of associated KPIs.
- Sustainability is a dynamic concept. New issues will keep popping up that will have to be addressed by the sustainability strategy. Remember Swiss Re's SONAR: Systematic Observation of Notions Associated with Risk.

✍ Takeaways

This chapter focused on how to effectively embed sustainability into the core of the business, as a means of ensuring its own sustainability. Some of the principal preconditions for successful implementation were uncovered by following a simple three-phase game plan:

1. Strategy compilation, that is, how to start the implementation,
2. Readiness assessment, that is, where to start the implementation,
3. KPI reporting, that is, measuring progress on a local level.

Practical examples from Solvay, Swinkels Family Brewery and other companies were presented to illustrate the three phases. Balanced scorecards, that is, management dashboards with sustainability KPIs, were shown to be very convenient tools for measuring a company's key material issues but also for representing the various stakeholders' opinions.

The example of Unilever in Russia served as a comprehensive example of implementation. The waste management program at the Tula production cluster showed the relevance and potency of the vectoring approach to sustainability strategy definition and implementation under difficult circumstances; the Unilever Sustainable Living Plan forced the site management to achieve zero waste to landfill with practically no dedicated budget.

Finally, the Plotting the Future instrument was introduced as a convenient planning tool focused on action to increase the odds of achieving the defined sustainability goals or vision.

Exhibit 13.1 Goals, Pillars and Example Targets of the Unilever Sustainable Living Plan

Improving Health and Well-Being for More Than One Billion People

Pillar	Commitment	Target date	Unit of measure	Results 2015	2016	2017
Health and hygiene	By 2020, we will help more than a billion people to improve their health and hygiene. This will help reduce the incidence of life-threatening diseases like diarrhea	2020	The number of people reached on a cumulative basis by an intervention through our programs on handwashing, self-esteem, oral health, sanitation and safe drinking water	482	538	601
Nutrition	By 2020, we will double the proportion of our portfolio that meets the highest nutritional standards, based on globally recognized dietary guidelines. This will help hundreds of millions of people achieve a healthier diet	2020	Percentage of sales volume of Unilever's food and refreshment products meeting the criteria for highest nutritional standards, based on globally recognized dietary guidelines	34	35	39

Reducing Our Environmental Impact by Half

Pillar	Commitment	Target date	Unit of measure	Results		
				2015	2016	2017
Greenhouse gases	Halve the greenhouse gas impact of our products across the life cycle by 2030	2030	Percentage change in the greenhouse gas impact of our products across the life cycle per consumer use between the 2010 baseline and the current period	7	8	9
Water	Halve the water associated with the consumer use of our products by 2020	2020	Percentage change in Unilever's water impact (water added to the products and water associated with the consumer use of our products) per consumer use between the period measured from 2010 baseline and the current period	−1	−7	−2
Waste	Halve the waste associated with the disposal of our products by 2020	2020	Percentage change in Unilever's waste impact (packaging that is not recycled or recovered, and leftover product) per consumer use between the period measured from 2010 baseline and the current period	−26	−28	−29
Sustainable sourcing	By 2020 we will source 100% of our agricultural raw materials sustainably: 10% by 2010; 30% by 2012; 50% by 2015; 100% by 2020	2020	Percentage of agricultural raw materials sourced sustainably	60	51	56

Enhancing Livelihoods for Millions

Pillar	Commitment	Target date	Unit of measure	Results		
				2015	2016	2017
Fairness in the workplace	We will source 100% of our procurement spend through suppliers who commit to promote fundamental human rights as specified in our Responsible Sourcing Policy	2020	Percentage of procurement spend through suppliers meeting mandatory requirements of our Responsible Sourcing Policy	54	67	55
Opportunities for women	By 2020, we will empower 5 million women by advancing opportunities for women in our operations; promoting safety; providing up-skilling; and expanding opportunities in our value chain	2020	Women to access initiatives aimed at promoting their safety, developing their skills and expanding their opportunities	806,000	920,000	1,259,000
Inclusive business	We will engage with at least 500,000 smallholder farmers in our supply network to help them improve their agricultural practices, enabling them to become more competitive	2020	Smallholder farmers in our supply network we have enabled to access initiatives aimed at improving their agricultural practices	600,000	650,000	716,000

References

1. Swiss Re (2018) *Our SONAR framework*. Retrieved from http://reports.swissre.com/corporate-responsibility-report/2017/cr-report/risk-intelligence/emerging-risks/our-sonar-framework.html
2. Bande, M. (2017, October 4) Companies vs Climate Change, The Compass to more Robust Business, company presentation
3. Straka, G.M. (2018, June 8) Good, better, greener, Brau Union Österreich. Presentation at the Brewers of Europe Forum, 7–8 June 2019
4. Norton, D.P. (1991) *Measuring Performance in the Organization of the Future*. Lexington, MA: Nolan Norton & Company.
5. This case is an abridged version of the case UNILEVER PRODUCTION CLUSTER IN TULA: ZERO NONHAZARDOUS WASTE TO LANDFILL IN TEN MONTHS, by Andrey Shapenko, Moscow School of Management SKOLKOVO, Russia, May 2016. Copyright © 2016 by SKOLKOVO, Moscow, Russia. Used with permission.
6. Unilever (2016, September 8) Unilever named as an industry leader in Dow Jones Sustainability Index [Press release]. Retrieved from https://www.unilever.com/news/Press-releases/2016/unilever-named-as-an-industry-leader-in-djsi.html

14

Epilogue

In one of the first case studies of this book, we introduced the purpose-driven business of Tony's Chocolonely, an original, small-scale Dutch effort to combat the forced labor, deforestation and poverty often clouding the cocoa supply chain. In subsequent chapters, we developed the argument that a clear sense of direction, a narrow list of relevant materialities and a strong focus on execution (an approach referred to in this book as vectoring) were key success factors in developing an effective, impactful sustainability strategy. We conclude the journey of *Winning Sustainability Strategies: Finding Purpose, Driving Innovation and Executing Change* with another powerful example from the cocoa industry, one that provides a perfect ending to the virtuous circle started in the first chapter. Barry Callebaut and its "Forever Chocolate" program provides an inspirational narrative of a multinational company pursuing a vectoring approach to its sustainability efforts and qualifying as a game changer for the complete sector (refer to Fig. 14.1).

CSR Unplugged: Vectoring in the Cocoa Industry

Barry Callebaut is recognized as the world's leading supplier of high-quality chocolate and cocoa products, with over 11,000 employees worldwide and sales in 140+ countries. Headquartered in Switzerland, the company is the result of the merger in 1996 between Belgian chocolate maker Callebaut and French chocolate producer Cacao Barry, which traces its roots as far back as 1842. Although listed on the SIX Swiss Exchange since 1998, the company

© The Author(s) 2019
B. Leleux, J. van der Kaaij, *Winning Sustainability Strategies*,
https://doi.org/10.1007/978-3-319-97445-3_14

F O R E♥E R
C H O C O L A T E
Our plan to make sustainable
chocolate the norm

Fig. 14.1 Barry Callebaut pictorial for its Forever Chocolate sustainability program (Source: Company information)

remains at heart very much a family business, encouraging entrepreneurship, innovation and responsibility.

By launching its Forever Chocolate program in November 2016, Barry Callebaut proclaimed that sustainable chocolate would become the norm. The program was very ambitious, going way beyond another extensive updating of the company's materiality analysis. It pioneered a complete shift from a corporate social responsibility (CSR) program focused on the well-being of the cocoa suppliers to a true business-centered sustainability approach, including measurable impact targets. Forever Chocolate guided the company toward the integration of sustainability into the core of its business, while disengaging the existing, but peripheral, CSR activities.

CEO Antoine de Saint-Affrique, who joined Barry Callebaut in October 2015 after 15 years at Unilever, brought first-hand experience as one of the co-architects of Unilever's now famous Sustainable Living Plan. His vision for Barry Callebaut was simple: sustainability not only has to make moral sense but also business sense to be truly sustainable. The company's sustainability program had to focus on material issues and serve as a beacon for the industry, resetting the pace of change for the whole cocoa industry and profoundly changing the game.

> As a result of our Forever Chocolate program, we have unplugged traditional CSR: Sustainability must be at the heart of our business model rather than at the periphery and we want to inspire a movement for the entire cocoa and chocolate industry to make sustainable chocolate the norm.
> Antoine de Saint-Affrique, CEO Barry Callebaut

De Saint-Affrique's strategy did not seek to address more sustainability issues than before, or even the existing ones better. In line with the vectoring precepts, Barry Callebaut sought to prevent diluting their sustainability efforts by concentrating on just a few, carefully selected material sustainability issues and committing fully to executing them. Pivotal to the Barry Callebaut approach was the focus on improving the well-being of the cocoa farmers at the bottom of the cocoa value chain. Solving the poverty issue there would go a long way toward solving child labor and deforestation issues too. The Forever Chocolate program contained only four materialities and each was tightly linked to an ambitious and measurable 2025 impact target:

1. We will eradicate child labor from our supply chain.
2. We will lift more than 500,000 cocoa farmers out of poverty.
3. We will become carbon and forest positive.
4. We will have 100% sustainable ingredients in all of our products.

Focus on Impact

To reach these targets, the company's sustainability team was embedded within the business rather than organized as a separate corporate department, that is, each team member also had a non-sustainability business role. For execution, Barry Callebaut had to rely extensively on local partners as the objectives could only be achieved through a multi-stakeholder ecosystem approach. In collaboration with scientists from Wageningen University & Research from the Netherlands, the company developed a theory of change (illustrated in Fig. 14.2) targeted at creating stable and diverse income streams for smallholder cocoa farmers. Barry Callebaut assessed the practical validity of that model in pilot projects in Indonesia and Côte d'Ivoire, with Ghana, Brazil and Cameroon to follow.

> Child labor still exists in the cocoa supply chain, despite all of the work that has been done by numerous partners throughout the industry consistently fighting its occurrence. That's the hard truth. We admit we have to learn a lot about this complex and challenging problem, which is why we are reaching out to experts in the field in order to test and implement the most effective solutions to eradicate child labor from our supply chain.
>   Nicko Debenham, Vice President, Head of Sustainability, Barry Callebaut

The key hypothesis behind the whole effort was that by first addressing farmer poverty, child labor and deforestation would also be positively impacted. Low productivity on cocoa farms from poor agricultural practices, nutrient depleted soil and aging cocoa trees meant that many farmers languished in a permanent state of poverty. Unable to invest, they were locked in a state of low productivity and low income, increasing the likelihood of child

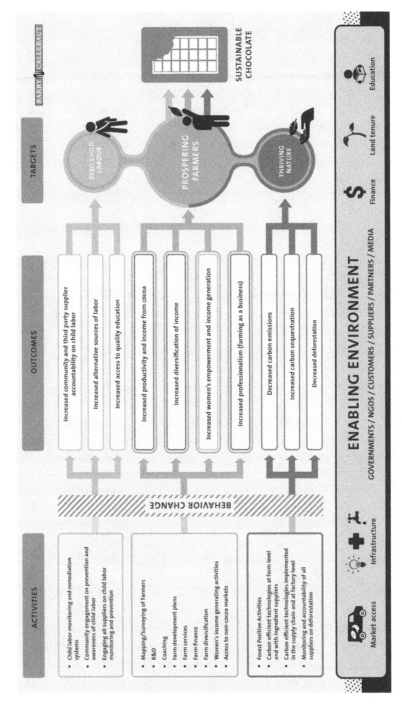

Fig. 14.2 Barry Callebaut's Theory of Change (Source: Company information)

labor. The creation of individual, multi-year farm development plans helped determine the most suitable crops that would best be able to help diversify the farmers' income.

Barry Callebaut was strengthened in its efforts by the signing of the Cocoa and Forests Initiative presented in Bonn at the COP23 UN Climate Change Conference in 2017 [1]. Twelve of the world's leading cocoa and chocolate companies agreed to a statement of collective intent committing themselves to work in partnership to end deforestation and forest degradation in the global cocoa supply chain, with an initial focus on the Ivory Coast and Ghana. These two countries, which collectively account for nearly two-thirds of the world's supply of cocoa, have suffered immensely from deforestation of their tropical rainforests. Over the last ten-year period, approximately 2.1 million hectares of forest area were cleared in the Ivory Coast and 820,000 hectares in Ghana. With one-quarter of this deforestation attributed to cocoa production, companies and governments pledged at the COP23 to eliminate illegal cocoa production in national parks, combined with stronger enforcement of national forest policies and the development of alternative livelihoods for affected farmers. Concurrently, as part of the efforts to improve the livelihoods of cocoa farmers, Barry Callebaut's Cocoa Horizons Foundation was launched to promote sustainable, entrepreneurial farming, improve productivity, bring the much-needed traceability of cocoa to the supply chain and support communities in general.

Education and Partnering

One pivotal element of elevating farmers out of poverty was the provision of an infrastructure for education. By 2014, Barry Callebaut took full ownership of the Biolands Group, one of Africa's largest exporters of certified organic cocoa working directly with farmers. Barry Callebaut had been purchasing all of Biolands' top-grade cocoa since 2000. Another main client was Kim's Chocolates, a Belgian supplier of high-end chocolates. As one of Belgium's largest manufacturers, Kim's purchased around 10,000 tons of cocoa products per year, and marketed the end products under its own brands, such as Cachet and KC Chocolatier but also produced for others, such as Tony's Chocolonely.

Tanzanian-based Biolands partnered with Kim's Chocolates in more than just the supply of *bio-beans*. After visiting the plantations in 2010, Kim's Chocolates founder and CEO Fons Maex decided to also intervene directly in the education of the farmers' communities. New classrooms were built, and books were brought in to support training. What initially started as a €5000 contribution to buy 2000 books turned into an ambitious initiative to renovate 650 classrooms, finish construction on another 600 and build yet another 700 before 2023. Funded in large part by Barry Callebaut's Quality Partner Program, the project grew into a full-scale effort with a budget in excess of €800,000. Faced with the double challenge of a lack of funds and overpriced building materials, Maex took it upon himself to turn this project into a real business. While engaging around 140 villages to participate, Maex never relented on the pursuit of the business model:

> The villagers themselves are responsible for the provisioning of the construction work that needs to be done. We will support them with technical expertise, good building materials and finance, but they need to do the work. That also brings commitment. [2]

The project's ambition did not stop at classrooms. A solar panel project was developed to co-finance the purchase of another 430,000 school books and four cocoa tree nurseries were developed to help improve the quality and yield of the cocoa fields. Employing only women, the four nurseries provided 350,000 new trees over the first three years and helped start 30 demonstration pilots, each of which were to educate 20 farmers. Intercropping was promoted to further improve the stability of income as was the replacement of old, less productive trees by new ones.

Early results indicated that the Forever Chocolate program was delivering on its promises. In 2016–2017, 17.36% of all cocoa beans were sourced through sustainability programs, an increase of 13% compared to the previous year. Over that same period, Barry Callebaut trained over 157,000 farmers in good agricultural practices [3] to improve productivity. To provide access to financing for smallholder farmers, the company also set up a risk-sharing facility with IDH[1] and the International Finance Corporation, the private sector arm of the World Bank, to provide loans to farmers, which enabled them to invest in productivity packages.

Besides working upstream with suppliers, Barry Callebaut partnered with key global customers. In addition to the strategic partnership with Tony's Chocolonely to produce chocolate from fully traceable cocoa, the company collaborated with clients such as Australia Target, K-Mart and Edward Marc to source sustainable cocoa and other ingredients, such as cane sugar, that passed the same stringent tests on sustainability. Confectionery market leader Mars, a company sourcing just over 50% cocoa from certified suppliers in 2016, signed agreements with Barry Callebaut and others to reach an objective of 100% certified cocoa by 2020.

---

[1] IDH is an organization aimed at the design, co-funding and prototyping of new economically viable approaches to realize green and inclusive growth at scale in commodity sectors and sourcing areas.

The Value of Strong ESG Performance

With banks developing a more positive attitude toward sustainability, a convincing environmental, social and governance (ESG) performance scorecard is becoming a prized possession. At Barry Callebaut, this became unmistakably clear when the ESG performance of the company jumped from 67/100 to 72/100 in the Sustainalytics [4] ESG ratings, making it one of the best ESG performers in the industry. In 2017, the company was able to extend its revolving credit facility from €600 million to €750 million to strengthen the groups' liquidity profile. The Forever Chocolate program was a key facilitator for accessing that new credit facility as the syndicate of 13 banks that provided it agreed to couple the interest rate on the facility with the company's ESG performance, as rated by Sustainalytics.

> Barry Callebaut is clearly a frontrunner on ESG matters and is leading the sustainability transition of its industry. We are proud to implement the first sustainable improvement loan based on Sustainalytics rating with a leader in the cocoa sector. At ING, we are convinced that sustainable finance will be a new standard to our industry and will continue to find innovative ways to support and stimulate our clients on their sustainability journey.
> Léon Wijnands, Global Head ING Sustainability

Linking the interest rate to the company's sustainability performance made perfect business sense for both Barry Callebaut and the banking syndicate as the capital markets in general were becoming more sensitive to environmental and social issues. It was the first time ever in Switzerland, famous for its chocolate as much as for its banking, that such a credit facility was negotiated and approved, turning Barry Callebaut into one of the pioneers in the green loan arena.

These Aren't Pyjamas! This Is a Warm-Up Suit

During the investigation phase of a book, encouragement comes in all sorts and sizes. When looking for the appropriate framing of the patterns of sustainability leaders uncovered by the research, inspiration came from a cartoon. In the computer-animated comedy film "Despicable Me,"[2] the villain

---

[2] Despicable Me is a 2010 American 3D computer-animated comedy film from Universal Pictures and Illumination Entertainment that was released in 2010. In the film a super-villain seeks a loan from the Bank of Evil to steal the moon.

Victor changes his name into Vector because he is intending to commit crimes with both direction and magnitude. This sparked us to dub the suggested concept that forms the backbone of our book as vectoring. When challenged by his father on his new, corresponding outfit, our villain Vector cries out that "These aren't pyjamas! This is a warm-up suit." In parallel, our book is not intended as a set of pyjamas to comfortably fall asleep in, it is envisioned as a well-founded warm-up for things to come.

With global challenges on the rise as illustrated by the world's nine warmest years on record all having occurred since 2005 [5], organizations are increasingly confronted with the prerequisite of making their business more sustainable. The journey of *Winning Sustainability Strategies: Finding Purpose, Driving Innovation and Executing Change* has presented vectoring as an effective concept to address both the opportunities and risks that are associated with that immense challenge. By combining direction and speed in a series of (downloadable) tools, examples and case studies, the book aims to provide inspiration and guidance for those companies that are about to accelerate their sustainability programs.

With a well thought-through and focused combination of strategy and execution, doing well by doing good is no longer a mirage; it is an achievable business objective. Now it is up to you to make it happen.

References

1. IDH Sustainable Trade Initiative (2017) *Collective Statement of Intent: The Cocoa and Forests Initiative*. Retrieved from https://www.idhsustainabletrade.com/uploaded/2017/03/StatementOfIntent_Eng.pdf
2. Maex, F. (2018, May 25), interview with Jan van der Kaaij
3. Barry Callebaut (2018) *Sustainability Section Annual Report 2016/17*. Retrieved from http://annual-report-2016-17.barry-callebaut.com
4. ING Bank (2018) Tasting good—and doing good. https://view.ingwb.com/tasting-good-and-doing-good. Accessed 9 May 2018.
5. World Meteorological Organization (2018) *WMO Statement on the State of the Global Climate in 2017*. Retrieved from https://library.wmo.int/opac/doc_num.php?explnum_id=4453

Index[1]

---

[1] Note: Page numbers followed by 'n' refer to notes.

CPSIA information can be obtained
at www.ICGtesting.com
Printed in the USA
LVHW081738021218
598992LV00001B/1/P